Improvisation i

Improvisation in Drama

Second Edition

ANTHONY FROST and RALPH YARROW

palgrave
macmillan

First edition published 1990
Second edition published 2007 by
PALGRAVE MACMILLAN
Houndmills, Basingstoke, Hampshire RG21 6XS and
175 Fifth Avenue, New York, N.Y. 10010
Companies and representatives throughout the world

PALGRAVE MACMILLAN is the global academic imprint of the Palgrave Macmillan division of St. Martin's Press, LLC and of Palgrave Macmillan Ltd. Macmillan® is a registered trademark in the United States, United Kingdom and other countries. Palgrave is a registered trademark in the European Union and other countries.

ISBN-13: 978-1-4039-8686-3   hardback
ISBN-10: 1-4039-8686-X   hardback
ISBN-13: 978-1-4039-3670-7   paperback
ISBN-10: 1-4039-3670-6   paperback

This book is printed on paper suitable for recycling and made from fully managed and sustained forest sources. Logging, pulping and manufacturing processes are expected to conform to the environmental regulations of the country of origin.

A catalogue record for this book is available from the British Library.

A catalog record for this book is available from the Library of Congress.

10   9   8   7   6   5   4   3   2   1
16   15   14   13   12   11   10   09   08   07

Printed and bound in China

For those who go on inventing: à vous de jouer

and
in memoriam Kathleen and William Frost
for Amanda, Cathy and Alex Frost

Contents

Acknowledgements

We owe a considerable debt of gratitude to performers we have talked to and worked with, especially Jacques Lecoq, Roddy Maude-Roxby (Theatre Machine), James MacDonald and Malcolm Tulip (I Gelati), Simon McBurney and Clive Mendus (Théâtre de Complicité), Rena Mirecka (Teatr Laboratorium), Shôn Dale-Jones (Hoipolloi); and to friends and colleagues who have read and commented on the book at different stages, in particular Julian Hilton, Frances Babbage, David Bradby, Franc Chamberlain and Todd Wronski. Thanks also to several generations of UEA drama students; and to those from whom we have learned or continue to learn in other contexts: Clive Barker, Nicholas Brooke, Douglas Brown, Max Flisher, Tony Gash, Tony Hall, David Hirst, Val Taylor and Amanda Frost.

Introduction

Improvisation is a particular mode of performance activity in which key characteristics of 'performance' can be precisely located. It issues as *performances* (the production of work which is made 'on the spot', or is explicitly open to amendment during performance) and as the culturing in the body of skills and attributes of *performativity* – training for making performance, development of individual and group resources, of the aptitude for renegotiating being and doing in the world.

The first (1990) edition of this book charts a history and a theory of improvisation in theatre work alongside a taxonomy of its practice. It identifies improvisation as a productive and performative mode of behaviour, and is concerned to site it particularly within the spectrum of *theatre* practice, identifying how, where and when it operates as a mark of style in production and a mode of training for performers. Since then, much of this territory has been retraversed in terms of performance theory, and a whole raft of publications have appeared, focusing on performance trainers and makers and on the contexts in which they work; many of these books contain explicit examples of exercises and games targeting specific performative purposes.

So it is important in this revised edition to signal how far these developments confirm or revise the perspectives we originally set out. It is still important to trace the origins of impro and its influence in the history of drama and performance-making, both as a social and political phenomenon and as a marker of the position it now occupies in performance training, which is even more pronounced than we indicated previously. It is useful to check the key criteria we identified against the kinds of model currently in use, and to ask why they are relevant to the aims of contemporary practitioners. And if impro has become not only more widespread but also more 'accepted', it is also important to ask whether its processes have within them the resources to resist the crystallisation of habit and fashion. The final part outlines a poetics or theoretical framework placing improvisation in the context of the exploration and extension of human capacities; and further proposes a politics of impro work, in the sense that it engages bodies, validates individuals and provides means of intervening in the forms and structures of the social as well as the artistic and psychological world.

The first edition established the presence of improvisation across a spectrum of the 'histories' of theatre and performance, in many periods, modes and cultural spaces; but, in line again with much recent thinking, a new edition gives us the opportunity to underline the transhistorical and multicultural through the work of practitioners from a greater range of cultures, which is also signalled in the scope of the bibliography. At the same time, we have tried to use the new examples to focus questions about the old ones, which means that much of the detail of the original has been condensed or recontextualised in order to highlight these perspectives. For example, kinds of impro work used in performance training intersect with the understanding of performance practice as a mode of psychosocial and political intervention. If impro games and exercises are recycled in a host of educational and even entrepreneurial contexts, they have, in perhaps their most significant reincarnation since the days of Copeau and Keith Johnstone, emerged as the core of Boal's 'Theatre of the Oppressed' and are practised in Brazilian *favelas* as well as in the UK with homeless people (Cardboard Citizens) and the disabled (Lawnmowers). The psychopolitics of these applications seem to confirm that impro work is 'on the edge' in a number of ways which continue to ask key questions about values and behaviours in society.

The three main questions the book still asks are: What? Why? How? – which often include Where? and When?

What are the kinds of practice which can be described as improvisation (categorisation)? Where and when do they occur (history, distribution)? Why are they significant and why do people want to do them (poetics)? How do they engage with the spectrum of performance production and training, in particular for the theatre, and with the business of 'making work' (theory and context)? What can you do and how should you do it (practice)? Where will you find other detailed guides to this kind of work (reference)?

Part II categorises the main stages of impro work as used in performance training in much the same ways as in the first edition, from ice-breaking through work on individual creativity, to working together and developing a group performance outcome. Although practitioners use different terminologies, the kinds of work are largely similar, and we have tried to suggest a useful way of organising them in sequence. We have somewhat extended the range of examples but retained the same taxonomy, because we think it is still viable and useful as a way of identifying aims and suggesting appropriate exercises. Practical work is also described in Part I and indicated in the notes; the bibliography specifically identifies books containing practical exercises. We have worked through most of the exercises we describe or refer to, with drama and scriptwriting students, with practitioners in this country and in India, the USA and Africa, with groups working to devise or create conventional performances and with those whose aim is to develop group skills, work with particular social groups or engage with political realities. We started out from an experience of the work of Barker, Lecoq and Keith Johnstone, and have gone on to explore ways in which their methods have been recontextualised and recombined by Boal, Callery, Chris Johnston and others. The parameters of this journey thus reflect the historical development and extended reach of improvisation during the period between the first and second editions.

We have also retained the original title. The book focuses, as it originally did, on examples from theatre and drama work, which is of course performance; and the performative nature of much creative activity, if indeed not of pretty nearly any activity at all, has been emphasised by intervening publications. It has always been clear to us that the performative, and hence momentary and transitory, as well as transactive and transformatory, is located above all in improvisatory work, and that this constitutes a central indicator of its significance. But we are not writing in any detail about performance art, or music, or site-specific work; so it seems more appropriate to continue to signal the boundaries within which we are working.

Definitions and attitudes

> There are people who prefer to say 'Yes', and there are people who prefer to say 'No'. Those who say 'Yes' are rewarded by the adventures they have, and those who say 'No' are rewarded by the safety they attain. There are far more 'No' sayers around than 'Yes' sayers, but you can train one type to behave like the other.
>
> Keith Johnstone, *Impro* (1981)

Improvisation: the skill of using bodies, space, all human resources, to generate a coherent physical expression of an idea, a situation, a character (even, perhaps, a text); to do this spontaneously, in response to the immediate stimuli of one's environment, and to do it *à l'improviste*: as though taken by surprise, without preconceptions.

All performance uses the body of the actor, giving space and form to an idea, situation, character, text or event in the moment of creation. It does not matter if the work has been rehearsed for a month, with every move, every nuance of speech learned and practised. In the act of performance the actor becomes an improviser. The audience laughs, and she times the next line differently. She hears the lines of her fellow performers as if for the first time, each time, and responds to them, for the first time. She keeps within the learned framework of the play; she does not make up new lines, or alter the play's outcome in any drastic way. Yet, the actor improvises; and the relationship between formal 'acting' and 'improvising' is so intricate that we might say that each *includes* the other. Improvisation is a part of the nature of acting, certainly. But, more importantly, acting is only one part of the creative process of improvising.

Improvisation is immediate and organic articulation, including the verbal; not just response, but a paradigm for the way humans reflect (or create) what happens. Where improvisation is most effective, most spontaneous, least 'blocked' by taboo, habit or shyness, it comes close to a condition of integration with the environment or context. And consequently (simultaneously) expresses that context in the most appropriate shape, making it recognisable to others, 'realising' it as act.

Some teachers of juggling begin by giving the pupil three balls and getting the student to throw them up in the air. The tendency is to clutch reflexively, to tighten up, to panic and to try desperately to catch the balls. The teacher will smile, shake his or her head, and make the beginner throw the balls again, this time making no effort to catch. The hardest thing to learn is not 'how to juggle', but how to let the balls drop (see Gelb 1981: 103ff.).

It is the same with improvisation. The hardest thing to learn is that failure doesn't matter. It doesn't have to be brilliant every time – it can't be. What happens is what happens; is what you have created; is what you have to work with. What matters is to listen, to watch, to add to what is happening rather than subtract from it – and to avoid the reflex of trying to make it into something you think it *ought* to be, rather than letting it become what it *can* be.

What happens in a 'theatre' or other 'performance space' is important in the context of the world 'outside'. They exist in a dialectical relationship with each other, rather than in separate compartments. Just as theatre may not merely mirror society, but acts as a force within it which changes its shape, so too improvisation of various kinds has often changed the shape and direction of theatre. Habit is the great enemy of evolution, as rehearsal (repetition) may be the enemy of innovation. Is the kind of thing that happens in improvisation similar to the processes by which, for instance, a biological structure evolves to new levels of order? It might well be, for improvisation is about order, and about adaptation, and about truthfully responding to changing circumstances, and about generating meaning out of contextual accidents.

Early history: shamans, clowns and actors

Improvisation, both within and without drama, is not a new phenomenon. We point to some moments in its history in order to signal the forms it takes and the kinds of effects it incites.

One channel is located in the shadowy figure of the *shaman*: performer, doctor and priest, story-teller and clown. Repository and creator of his people's mythology and cosmology, he is the 'bringer of tales' from that other world. He is a healer, a 'clever-man', a conjuror, in part a charlatan; but also the shape-changer, the agent and site of transformation. He can contact and *make visible* the 'double', the other side of our nature, the spiritual or inner self. It is this shamanistic function of manifesting those forces which are believed to operate on the dark side of human consciousness to which Artaud refers to in *The Theatre and its Double* as 'active metaphysics' (Artaud 1938: 33). Whatever means (s)he uses, the shaman says 'yes' to something more than everyday personality and reality, (s)he marks and embodies a threshold state, a capacity for accepting otherness as a source of empowerment.

But the comic genius is not confined to ritual or to trance. The clown:

> represents a vision of the world that both intellectual and so-called primitive cultures have valued highly, a sense of the comic meaningful to children and adults alike, and a dynamic form of acting based on startling technique and inspired improvisation. (Towsen 1976: 4–5)

Clowning often begins within a sacred or religious context, burlesquing sacred ritual *within* the ritual. Often, too, the clown represents the regressive element, acting out childish or adolescent fantasies of sexuality and scatology which adulthood represses. But the clown soon escapes from the confines of the sacred.[1] His true origin is in the play instinct itself, and the pleasure he provides is too valuable to be restricted to a holy day.

The theatre clown is universal. He appears, for example, in the Sanskrit drama of India, as the apparently slow-witted servant Vidusaka (whose name means 'one given to abuse'). John Towsen makes the important point that the clown's ability to improvise has allowed him to become (for example, in modern Asian drama) a privileged political satirist, outside the confines of the censor (Towsen 1976: 37). That political role has been there throughout the history of clowning: its chief exponent in recent Western drama is, perhaps, Dario Fo.

Clowns were known among the ancient Greeks, too, where they were called, among other things, *planoi* (Nicoll 1931: 253). One history of the actor begins (according to Aristotle, who well understood that the improviser antedates the tragedian; see Aristotle 1965: 34) in the *polis* of Megara, which had a developed tradition of secular drama, known as the Dorian *Mime*. Companies of masked actors popular among the Dorian Greeks specialised in tiny farces on everyday subjects. They were known, most significantly, as *autokabdaloi*, which means 'buffoons' and 'improvisers' (Beare 1950: 149). Their performances probably included obscenities, acrobatics, juggling. At the heart of the performance lay both the burlesqueing – the relativising – of sacred myth, and the celebration of the human body.

The parodic impulse coexists with the religious; the profane is intermingled with the sacred. Two thousand years later in Western Europe, the little devils who run amok through the spectators at the Mystery plays, with gunpowder squibs 'in their hands, ears and arses',[2] represent an enduring sense of fun and love of spectacle: the spirit of carnival.

The mime *humanises* the drama. In counterbalance to the demonic he offers the *corporeal*. He is, after all, a physical being; nothing godlike about him! He has a body which likes to stuff its face with food, to shit, to fuck. He is constantly reminding us of our humanity. His costume grotesquely extends his body: a big nose, belly, phallus (Bakhtin 1965: 317).[3] His jokes are crude, even gross. He can reduce Herakles the demi-god to a mere glutton, Dionysos to a drunkard, the sacramental to the excremental.

The mime took many forms in many countries. From the Saxon *scop* and Middle English *gleeman* (and sexy 'glee-maiden' sometimes), to the German *minnesinger*, the French *jongleur* and *trouvère*, the Russian *skomorokhi*, and the Italian *giullare* their talents ranged from juggling, rope-walking and animal training to minstrelsy and acting. What links them is the way all clowns work with their audiences. The clown has to make contact swiftly. He has to keep our attention in the noise and bustle of a street. That dictates the size and scale of his gestures. Watching good street entertainers is the first step towards understanding the power of *commedia*.

Commedia dell'arte means (approximately) the comedy 'of the professional actors' (the *comici dell'arte*); in contrast to the *commedia erudita* (or the *commedia sostenuta*), the 'erudite', written plays created by the courtly amateurs of the theatre in sixteenth- and seventeenth-century Italy.

Sometimes the companies were highly renowned and could afford permanent bases; at the other extreme, the poorer players were attached to, for example, the Venetian *mountebanks*, using their clowning skills to draw crowds in the streets to whom a quack doctor (again a shamanistic echo) could peddle his nostrums. Each mountebank employed a *zanni*, a zany clown to pull in and please the crowd by his clever improvisations. The clown would pretend to mock his master, providing a parallel to the master–slave comedies of the ancient world, and a bridge to the farcical master–servant relationship of Pantalone (or Dottore) and Zanni (Arlecchino, or Brighella) in the Italian comedy.

Perrucci's description of *commedia all'improvviso*, in his *Dell'arte rappresentativa, premeditata, e dall'improvviso* (1699) (Perrucci 1969: 258), provides a very salutary qualification of what professionally improvised drama is really like. Professionals, even professional improvisers, leave very little to chance. *Commedia* is improvisational, but it is rehearsed and practised improvisation. The actors wear stock masks, each performer as familiar with his mask as with his own skin. It is *commedia a soggetto*, on a subject, or on a scenario (*canovaccio*), known and prepared in advance. As well as the agreed *soggetti*, the performers could fall back on fairly standardised routines called *lazzi*, pieces of rehearsed comic business, accompanied by *battute* (standardised repartee) and *concetti* (premeditated rhetorical passages). The *lazzi* and *concetti* would be mastered by all the members of a troupe as part of their training, regardless of which mask they commonly wore.

The *commedia all'improvviso* dominated the European stage for three hundred years, spawning local imitations in many countries, and influencing many major playwrights; among them Shakespeare, Molière, Marivaux, Gozzi and Goldoni. Nor are its techniques forgotten. They are still with us in, for example, the work of actors from the Lecoq school, and in the plays and more especially the live performances of Dario Fo. Improvisation does not vanish – improvisation is at the heart of all theatre – but the tradition of improvised play-making disappears with the development of the enclosed, plush and decorous theatre space during the eighteenth century. The rise of the function of the director, too, contributes to the disappearance of the tradition. No longer just the stage or company manager, or one of the actors; no longer just the organiser of rehearsals, the *concertatore*, but an *auteur* in his own right; the director's vision of the performance has often promoted a style of work in which improvised creativity *on stage* is not valued, and taught rather than communally worked out or improvised moves, gestures, deliveries become the order of the day.

In the last decades of the twentieth century many approaches and practices containing strong elements of what we in this book describe as the *improvisatory* begin to influence performance practice, particularly in the 'West', in significant ways. Drama training and production is now scarcely understandable without reference to many of the people we discuss in this book: Keith Johnstone, Jacques Lecoq, Clive Barker and Michael Chekhov are paramount, but many directors and trainers have garnered attitudes and practices which draw on their work and on that of their forebears like Copeau, or on kinds of mind/body preparation found in Indian or Japanese actor training.

Nick Moseley reports that 'it is generally agreed within the drama school world that there is a need for more practical books which outline and explain the processes of actor training and rehearsal' (Moseley 2005: 3). Nevertheless, there is now a fairly wide selection of books which approach these areas from the angle of improvisation, games and exercises (see Bibliography). Moseley's own *Acting and Reacting* is concerned to promote 'performance as a social and transactional process' (4), which for him is a way of targeting an immediacy and authenticity more rooted in real events occurring between actors than reliance on the more internal focus of some of Stanislavsky or Strasberg's work. In many ways this is the focus too of both Chris Johnston's *House of Games* (1998, reprinted 2005) and

Dymphna Callery's *Through the Body* (2001), which draw on the earlier work of Keith Johnstone, Clive Barker, Augusto Boal and Jacques Lecoq among others. This represents a substantial body of work and is a token – as both Callery and Johnston observe – of specific and conscious trends in actor training and performance style in Western theatre over recent decades.

Whereas Johnston's book is targeted towards community and participative theatre practice and therefore chiefly presents strategies for working with groups, Callery is concerned with processes and methodologies for developing individual performative resources. However, both books include a section on devising, in a similar position (towards the end) of their sequence of exercises and tactics. To that extent they both follow the broad trajectory – from freeing up the individual for performance through working together and on to collaborative production – that we trace out in this book. It is significant that books which respond to contemporary felt needs in theatre practice (both authors are practising drama teachers) should signal this path and pass through many of the same stages: working with bodies and working with groups are themselves indicative of the extent to which 'theatre' no longer means only the presentation of a 'finished' product in a purpose-built venue, but has become co-extensive as process with understandings of performance and performativity as negotiable sites of political and psychological construction.

As far as the organization of games and exercises in these books is concerned, Johnston has sections on Initial Focus (Attention, Energy, Imagination and Communication) and Building Group and Teamwork (Supportiveness, Spontaneity, Adaptation and Empowerment); Callery works through Awareness, Articulation, Energy and Neutrality towards Presence, Complicité, Play, Audience, Rhythm, Sound and E-motion. Virtually everyone who has produced this kind of work deals with these aspects, sometimes under slightly different terminologies and with slightly different aims; but there is a general consistency about the ground covered and the kinds of methodologies suggested. The workshop aims suggested by Johnston (recreation, learning, experimentation, debate, confidence-building, research into social conflict, devising a play) are in no sense incompatible with Callery's aim 'to develop understanding of acting as a combination of imagination and technique' (Callery 2001: 4), or indeed the 'actor's need to . . . be "in the moment" and to react truly instinctively to the other people on stage' identified on the back cover of Moseley's book. The destined operational contexts are different, but the conception of operational strategies and requirements is remarkably similar. Where Callery for instance echoes Johnston in targeting The Playful Body, The Sentient Body and The Physical Text, Moseley deals with The World of Play, Transactional Improvisation, Learning to Trust your Body and Approaches to Text.

Moseley cites David Mamet's scepticism about the internalized focus of much post-Stanislavskian work, suggesting that dominant twentieth-century acting 'mythology' conditions actors to hide from genuine spontaneity in order to construct a fictional stability to counteract the vulnerability of a 'precarious profession'; however he qualifies Mamet's rejection of actor training as too sweeping, and argues for a 'space between' Mamet and Stanislavsky (Moseley 2005: 20), which is charted by a combination of Meisner and Transactional Improvisation. For him, training needs to 'give actors a *craft* and a *process*, while at the same time allowing them to retain total spontaneity' (p. 21): 'transactional improvisation helps actors to understand their interactions with others and to break out of habitual patterns, while the Meisner-based repetition work trains them to respond to each other without self-censorship'. There are strong echoes of Keith Johnstone here, in the sense that the latter charges conventional ratiocentric models of education with constructing barriers to spontaneity; Moseley's requirements that actors should 'become emotionally open by being physically open' (p. 24), recognise the need to let go of 'defence mechanisms' (p. 25) and 'get into the habit of making big offers' (p. 30) are summarised in the Johnstonian recommendation to adopt a 'yes' attitude (p. 26) to training: do it first and ask questions afterwards, largely in order to play the risk which, according to him, social conditioning tends to minimize. Consequently it is possible to read into Moseley's emphasis on individual openness the seeds of a *politics* of interaction, (p. 33, 171), which moves from the need to encounter one's own otherness towards the ability to develop play-skills within a group. Moseley's book, like Callery's and Johnston's, is clearly and directly written, and testifies to the experience of working with actors in training in the context of the contemporary worlds and the theatre practice which it requires; it is perhaps more trenchant in places, but persuasively constructs an argument for methodologies which seek to foreground the immediacy of the events which occur for actors as they work. Its clearly articulated premises thus provide a valuable extension to the slightly narrower focus of the other two books discussed here; taken together, they indicate the relevance of many of the central tenets of improvisatory work – presence, play, availability and so on – to contemporary training and practice.

Part I

Who? Major Practitioners of Improvisation

Introduction

Part I offers a survey of major practitioners across time and space, suggesting key areas in the history and range of performance which have been significantly influenced by the principles and processes of improvisation. The material is organised in several ways. The first sections look at the work of 'early' (late nineteenth and early twentieth century) practitioners in the European and American context in order to establish routes into Academy and Drama School Training; 'traditional' and 'alternative' imply different kinds of performance outcome and hence different working methods – roughly, those in the tradition of Stanislavsky, and those derived from Johnstone or Lecoq, tending towards different models of identity and role in performance. Geographical and cultural factors (UK, USA, Europe, Africa, the Middle East) produce distinct uses and forms of the improvisatory in different contexts and spaces; and applications 'beyond theatre' extend the use of the 'games' model towards psychological and political encounter. All of these lines of investigation work on the one hand towards the definition of the theatrical frame as representational matrix, and on the other to its exploitation as generic productivity for performers and 'participants'. In not a few cases, these roles and functions overlap. They may also represent or engender different models of the self and its place in society.

Chapter 1

Improvisation in Traditional Drama

The principle of improvisation

Improvisation is not just a style or an acting technique; it is a dynamic *principle* operating in many different spheres; an independent and transformative way of being, knowing and doing.

The twentieth century witnessed an explosion of experiments which have embraced the principle of 'improvisation'. Music, for example, was transformed by the various forms of jazz: technical proficiency allied to improvisation to create a practically inexhaustible synthesis. In modern dance, Isadora Duncan and Martha Graham, in different ways, opened up a wealth of new, plastic possibilities for the expressive body. The former immediately and spontaneously danced the truth of what she felt. The latter broke down the rigid formulae of classical ballet and replaced them with a language that responded to the world around as well as within the dancer. The 1960s political philosophy of situationism in Europe and happenings in the US celebrated the spontaneous and site-specific, most importantly perhaps the conjunction of site, moment, performer and spectator: the place, time and bodies of new event-structures. Many of these forms have been reconfigured in the performance work of the early twenty-first century, although it is not always clear that the aims and principles, let alone the political perspective, are identical.

However, it is true that all theatrical performance ideally strives for a rigorous authenticity: what Stanislavsky called 'artistic truth', perhaps? The lines of development we discuss in this section lead in three principal directions, but each ultimately demands the same degree of commitment, and is concerned – though from different angles – with an exploration of 'self' and 'reality' for performers and/or audience.

Improvisation is used in three major contexts. It feeds firstly into what we might call traditional theatre training, as a preparation for performance and a way of tuning up the performers. We can place this in the (Stanislavskian) tradition of 'character' preparation, or, to put it another way, as a method of schooling the actor to project the 'reality' of the character; a process which involves the development of imaginative skills so that the body can experience and express appropriate emotional states: discovering in oneself the self or being of 'another' and presenting it.

We discuss the use of improvisation in actor training below; this line of work initially tends – though not exclusively or rigidly – towards the naturalistic, the documentary, the socio-political, with a relatively clearly defined concept of 'character' as the focus of deterministic forces: what D. H. Lawrence called the 'old stable ego of personality' clings to this and inhabits the structure and content of the 'well-made play'. Perhaps the most extreme development occurs in the improvisation-for-performance work of Mike Leigh, where a scripted text arises from improvisation fleshed out by 'sociological' research.

The second tradition (or perhaps anti-tradition) rests on a more radical acknowledgement of the fragmentation of nineteenth-century notions of a consistent personality. The comic and satiric vein, often allied to improvisation, challenges assumptions about stable social personality and 'bourgeois' respectability; taken to extremes, it undercuts political, religious and philosophical myths about the coherence of individual identity and its consonance within a system of stratified order and significance. The work of Jarry, Artaud and Beckett, for instance, extends and foregrounds this destabilisation; it also requires a more radically physical and improvisatory approach to acting, and it is not surprising that alongside this eventually scripted and accepted form of theatre, work on and with improvisation should have continued to develop almost as a form in and for itself. Improvisation of this kind both serves as an exploratory form of theatre and – here we move into the third, 'para-theatrical' context – also locates the issue of self and reality in spheres other than the narrowly theatrical.

The more radical modes of improvisation both accept the consequences of the disintegration of the existential self and attempt to use them positively. Grotowski's actors learn to 'disarm', to arrive at a condition without the protective masks of the familiar or the comfortable escapes of dramatic cliché. The work focuses not on the reality of the character but on that of the *performer*; where it emerges as public theatre, it is the inventiveness and authenticity of the performers in their relationship with the spectators which is fore-grounded, as opposed to the presentation of a narrative. Here impro-visation and performance are seen as part of a developmental process which can thus extend beyond theatre into, for example, psychother-apy, education and politics.

John Martin (*The Intercultural Performance Handbook*) indicates that improvisation is used as pre-rehearsal, rehearsal and perfor-mance, and offers examples of four ways of working with it: solo, in pairs, variations and for groups. He indicates that in addition to Western actor training, it is found in Boalian Forum Theatre (responding to spectator interventions), Japanese *Noh* (gauging the state of the audience), South Indian *Kathakali* (play with audience by popular characters) and West African performance, where dances are 'never the same' (pp. 102–3). Exercises are organized according to the kinds of energy level they seek to generate and the ways in which they change the nature of the performer's relationship to space. Martin trained at the Lecoq school and has worked extensively with performers from many traditions.[1]

Martin's proposed divisions can be seen to relate both to what we discuss in Part I about training and trainers and to the way Part II (the 'how' section) is organized. The use of improvisation as a strategy of training is a process of developing the performer's resources, which as it is formalised or repeated develops into a methodology; impro-visation as a way of creating or amending performance alters its nature and effect, inflecting its status and meaning. Pre-rehearsal involves the preparation of bodies and groups for *disponibilité* and play, and the exploration of the relationship between the body of the performer and the space of performance. Improvisation in and as rehearsal continues these moves with reference to the performance-text (the ensemble of signs and codes which constitute the perfor-mance); it develops the contexts and 'back-stories' of characters and situations through exercises like 'hot-seating' or affective memory work; and it works on strategies to energise relationships and inten-tions, by attempting to find ways to 'raise the stakes' and intensify the degree of attention to what is happening between performers and in the space. Improvisation in and as performance can be the most risky venture possible – for a clown courting failure, for a participant in a scenario whose parameters are known but whose detail, order and meaning is liable to be changed by any performer; or a subtle variation registering the receptive condition of the audience or the specific dynamics of the moment by a highly skilled performer; or uncensored or deliberately invoked interventions from spectator-participants to which performers respond supportively. In what follows we discuss both forms of training (process) and uses in performance (application or product), which often feature in parallel in the work of trainers and theatre-makers, or follow directly on from each other.

Precursors: Stanislavsky, Meyerhold and Chekov

We might assume that Constantin Stanislavsky (1863–1938) was the originator of the modern use of improvisation, at least as a rehearsal and training device. Many of the scenes described in his books, *An Actor Prepares*, *Building a Character* and *Creating a Role*, in which the director 'Tortsov' guides his young protégés through the processes of self-discovery, are improvisatory in nature. But these books are the product of Stanislavsky's later years, after a heart attack had forced him to give up acting. They do not necessarily relate to his own theatrical practice, particularly in the early days of the Moscow Art Theatre (MAT).

Stanislavsky did use a form of 'proto-improvisation', a kind of imaginative projection of oneself into a role, and began to suggest to his actors (*a*) that they might do this together, as a group, away from the pressures of actual rehearsals; and (*b*) that they do it continually, *outside the theatre*, while practising simple physical activities. The concentration required led them towards group outings, boating or mushroom picking, away from the bustle of 'normal' town life, so that the actors could slowly become immersed in their characters.

Although knowledge of Stanislavsky's practice has until recently been limited by lack of access to his writings in the original Russian, he seems in fact to have made use more consistently than hitherto recognized of exercises aimed at physical, emotional and intellectual integration in order to produce a multi-layered spontaneous 'truth'. Some of these exercises resemble the kinds of energy work used extensively by Michael Chekhov (Carnicke 2000, 22); improvisation was particularly important in working on structure, rhythm, atmosphere and social context in Stanislavsky's last (posthumously performed) production, *Tartuffe* (1939).

It took a long time for Stanislavsky to come to the central conclusions of his early work: that a director should be interested in the actor's process rather than trying to dictate a result; that an actor should blend himself with the character he plays; that when playing a villain one should look for his good side; that it was not important that one played 'well' or 'ill' – what mattered was to play truthfully. But Stanislavsky was also, at this time, overimpressed by the externals of naturalism; by a scenic naturalism which gave the illusion that genuine emotions were being played out within it, and also by the autocratic example of Ludwig Chronegk's practice with the Duke of Saxe-Meiningen's company. Only later in his work, after the famous vacation in Finland in 1906, would he consciously transfer the emphasis to the inner life of the character: in effect, the creation of the Stanislavsky 'System'.

It was not until 1911, when Stanislavsky founded the First Studio of the MAT, that improvisation became in any way central to the practical work (and even later before it became part of the theory). According to Paul Gray, improvisation was first introduced by Stanislavsky's trusted friend and associate Leopold Antonovich Sulerzhitsky, whom Stanislavsky had put in charge of the Studio's developmental work (Gray 1964: 25). Improvisation immediately became the rage among the younger generation of actors and actresses who made up the First Studio, and was equally powerfully resisted by the older generation. For Olga Knipper, Ivan Moskvin – even for Nemirovich-Danchenko himself – there seemed nothing practically useful in the Studio's work at first. But for Yevgeni Vakhtangov,[2] Mikhail Chekhov, Maria Ouspenskaya and Richard Boleslavsky, Sulerzhitsky's technique was a liberation.

It was really only in the last phase of his work, when he had ceased to act and when the translator Elizabeth Reynolds Hapgood had prevailed upon him to write down his way of working, that Stanislavsky himself began to consider seriously the techniques of improvisation, making the students work on scenes entirely without a text.

As David Magarshack points out, Stanislavsky had never really applied this purely theoretical idea to prove its efficacy in practice. It would be his successors who would elevate this experimental way of working into a central tenet of the 'Method'. Stanislavsky's work has led directly to that of modern America (both the 'Method', and the

'New York School' of improvisation discussed below) and to the plays of Mike Leigh, in which the *sine qua non* of performance is the truthful depiction of naturalistic character. His influence on the theatre of the twentieth century is still immense, but the naturalistic theatre's development of applied improvisation is due to his successors and emulators rather than to Stanislavsky directly.

Bella Merlin's two books (*Beyond Stanislavky* and *Konstantin Stanislavsky*) contain a full and more detailed discussion of, for example, the 'The Method of Physical Actions and Active Analysis' (Merlin, 2001) and a short and very accessible account of Stanislavsky's life and work, with detailed discussions of *An Actor Prepares* (Merlin, 2003). The latter also focuses discussion on three Stanislavskian methods: early 'round-the-table' analysis ('table work', which she stresses is active and fun rather than dry and scholastic) and the 'System' (pp. 117–25); an introduction to the 'Method of Physical Actions' (pp. 126–42); and an introduction to 'Active Analysis' (pp. 143–54). There's a useful glossary (pp. 157–62) which discusses key terms such as 'grasp' and 'communion' as well as the more obvious System terminology, and relates them directly to the main text, and to Stanislavsky's own writings (see also Part II below).[3]

If it can be argued that both Lee Strasberg and Stella Adler, though in different ways, pursue Stanislavsky's aim to enrich the actor's inhabiting of the present through their work on emotion, Sanford Meisner is particularly concerned to centre all exchange between performers in a developed sensitivity and openness to what is happening to them in the moment. Exercises which appear to consist of the banal repetition of surface observations are guided in such a way as to lead to acknowledgement and articulation of subtle shifts of attitude, and also aim to engender a spirit of play between actors. What is improvisatory here – and has links with aspects of Copeau's, Johnstone's and Grotowski's work – is the way in which 'text' becomes a porous field of interplay and revelation, where actors begin to develop the kind of antennae which can pick up their own 'pre-expressive' shifts which are so essential, for instance, to the red-nosed clown, but also to sensitive acting in all kinds of performance. Moseley (2005: 9–10) frames Meisner's work well and presents a good selection of his exercises.

The modern 'alternative' examination of improvisation 'begins' with Vsevolod Meyerhold (1874–1940), one of the MAT's leading actors during the early, autocratic stage, who left Moscow in 1902.

Stanislavsky invited him back to join the MAT Studio Theatre project in 1905. Meyerhold's disagreement with the MAT's 'realistic' concept of theatre soon became apparent. A conflict between him and Stanislavsky ensued; the Studio Theatre was closed before it had opened. For Stanislavsky, especially as his work developed, the actor was the focus of theatre. For Meyerhold, the focus was the director's art. The division between them was a formal one, and should not obscure the great respect each had for the other.

In 1910 Meyerhold opened the 'Interlude House' at the former Skazka Theatre at 33 Galernaya Street, St Petersburg, to explore aspects of popular and street theatre and, especially, *commedia dell'arte*. Because he was working at the conservative Imperial Alexandrinsky Theatre at the time, he was asked by the management to conduct his experimental work under a pseudonym. At the suggestion of the composer and poet, Mikhail Kuzmin, he took the name of 'Doctor Dappertutto', a character from E. T. A. Hoffmann's *Adventure on New Year's Eve*. Doctor Dappertutto was a real-life manifestation of the mask, a ubiquitous *doppelgänger* who assumed responsibility for all Meyerhold's experiments in the eccentric and the supernatural for the rest of his time at the Imperial theatres (Braun 1969: 115, 119–28).[4]

Although the Interlude House was short-lived, the Dappertutto experiments continued for many years. Meyerhold's fascination with *commedia dell'arte* had a number of levels. Where Stanislavsky's theatre explored the 'inner truth' of character, Meyerhold glimpsed the equally profound 'exterior truth' of the mask. He was also fascinated by the figure of the *cabotin* (which he regarded in a very much more positive light than Copeau later did). The figure of the itinerant, poor, professional actor, descended from the classical *mimus*, via the Russian *skomorokhi* (Russian equivalent of the *jongleur*) and *balaganschik* ('fairground booth-player') no less than the Italian *comici dell'arte*, attracted him powerfully.

His awareness of *commedia dell'arte* was conditioned by his acquaintance with a number of European sources: the drawings of Callot, with their grotesque and malicious, sexual and scatological figures; the *fiabe* of Carlo Gozzi, with their deliberate room for actors' improvisations, their poetic, magical delicacy; the plays of Goldoni, with their developing interest in psychological realism and their literary grace; and, finally, the works of the Romantic Hoffmann, with their masked and transformed mysticism, their fascination with reality and its double.

Beyond his initial intellectual, literary and aesthetic interest, Meyerhold was engaged with the actor's physical skills: the extraordinary plasticity of the street entertainer would ultimately become the basis of the scientific bio-mechanics with which his name is associated, and which led to an investment in the *actor's* independent creativity. He returned to the idea of the *commedia dell'arte* scenario, set in advance by the *concertatore*, or laid out by a master dramatist like Goldoni or Gozzi.

Michael (Mikhail) Chekhov (1891–1955) was the nephew of the playwright Anton Chekhov. He worked at MAT from 1912 to 1918, and later in Berlin, Paris, Dartington, New York, Connecticut and Los Angeles. Franc Chamberlain describes Chekhov as 'an outstanding actor and author of one of the best actor training manuals ever published in the European tradition' (Chamberlain 2000: 79). His approach is now incorporated into the curriculum of many training establishments.

Over 100 of Chekhov's exercises have been published. Much of Chekhov's focus is on developing inner resources, and the exercises aim to:

- link inner and outer, psychological and material (via work on energy and focus)
- create and inhabit imaginative space
- locate and inhabit imaginary bodies and centres
- explore psychological gesture, archetype
- develop imagination and concentration
- activate higher ego
- explore atmospheres and qualities
- develop a sense of form, beauty and wholeness.

The general context of his work is towards the evocation of 'atmosphere, actors' creativity, physicalisation of inner experience' (Chamberlain 2000: 80). It is important for the actor to 'become an active participant in the process of imagination' (p. 86).

Rudolf Steiner's Theosophy and associated practices were useful to Chekhov in overcoming a personal crisis and leading to 'liberation from his self-indulgent and self-destructive tendencies'; from this Chekhov acquired a distance from the everyday self which he was able to incorporate into acting strategies, moving away from the Stanislavskian emphasis on personal emotion towards activation of a Steineresque 'higher ego' (the 'artist in us') (Chamberlain 2000: 81), which has attributes such as detachment, compassion and humour. Chekhov also stressed the importance of the condition of 'two consciousnesses' – 'real acting was when we could act and be filled with feelings, and yet be able to make jokes with our partners' (Chekhov 1985: 102). This suggests parallels with Copeau's and Lecoq's work on 'neutrality', discussed below; but also with non-Western actor training rooted in particular understandings of mind/body integration and models of consciousness. Chekhov himself also used aspects of eurythmy (Steiner/Dalcroze), and worked with Vakhtangov to synthesise the approaches of Stanislavsky and Meyerhold.

Franc Chamberlain writes: 'the basic principles of his technique will allow as many variations and creations as there are creative individualities' (pp. 113ff.). So exercises can be adapted; they should also be explored at length in order to allow new outcomes to emerge. Chekhov requires this openness and 'wanted an attitude of warmth, friendliness, freedom and ease in the workspace. Giving and receiving, underpinned by a sense of joy, is at the heart of the work' (p. 115). Chekhov's 'Four Brothers' is a set of exercises designed to stimulate these kinds of experience.

These criteria exemplify important improvisatory principles and form a link between the psychological and inner-directed end of the Stanislavsky spectrum and the kinds of spatial and element work partly derived from dance and *mime blanche*, but also figuring extensively in Lecoq's sport-derived methodology.

The first person, however, to investigate improvisation as *the* means to explore the nature of acting, the first man to grasp the full significance of this way of working, was Jacques Copeau. In Limon, in 1916, he wrote:

> It is an art which I don't know, and I am going to look into its history. But I see, I feel, I understand that this art must be restored, reborn, revised; that it alone will bring a living theatre – the theatre of players.   (Kirkland 1975: 58)

France

Jacques Copeau and Suzanne Bing

Albert Camus said: 'In the history of the French theatre there are two periods: before and after Copeau' (cited in Saint-Denis 1982: 32).

This judgement might be extended to the history of improvisation: Copeau (1879–1949) truly began the modern tradition. John Rudlin enumerates the many debts which the modern theatre owes to Copeau's teaching and practice:

> In no particular order: drama games; improvisation; animal mimicry; ensemble playing; writers-in-residence; *commedia dell'arte* revival; mime; mask-work; repertoire rather than repertory; community theatre; theatre as communion.   (Rudlin 1986: xiv)

And not to Copeau alone. His assistant (lover, mother of Copeau's son the writer Bernard Bing, partner in all but name) the actress Suzanne Bing (1885–1967) has been unfairly neglected, due largely perhaps to her own diffidence and deference to Copeau's memory. Much of the credit for discovery and invention in this new mode should rightly be hers.[5]

Copeau was not the first to use improvisation as a rehearsal and training technique: Stanislavsky, we have seen, used it at the Moscow Art Theatre Studio; Taïrov had employed it at the Kamerny, too. But Copeau, at Le Vieux-Colombier and in his teaching, was the first really to base a system of exploratory work upon it, and the impact of his decision is still reverberating.

Jacques Copeau (born 1879) was a drama critic before he became a full-time practitioner. He was part of the reaction against the realism of Antoine's Théâtre Libre (though he knew and admired Antoine and regarded Stanislavsky as a source of creative inspiration), against the false rhetorical style of the Comédie Française, and against the crassness of boulevard theatre. He read and in many ways admired Craig and Appia, but disagreed with their proposed alternatives. Instead, in 1913, he published his own 'manifesto' – his *Essai de Rénovation Dramatique* – and founded his own theatre in the rue du Vieux-Colombier in Paris. Bing was a young actress, recently divorced from the avant-garde composer Edgard Varèse by whom she had a daughter, who took Copeau's call for renovation of the stage literally and joined his new company that year.

She (like Copeau) became interested in the ideas of Émil Jaques-Dalcroze, which included music improvisation and its expression through the body, and had experimented with them teaching children with Copeau in Geneva before rediscovering them again via Margaret Naumburg in New York, where the Vieux-Colombier spent two important seasons during the First World War as part of the propaganda war effort.

Margaret Naumburg (1890–1983), then the wife of the novelist Waldo Frank, had been quietly instrumental in introducing the ideas of Dalcroze and Alexander technique to America. She was a passionate and devoted educationist, trained with Maria Montessori, whose ideas she refined. She wrote an article popularizing Dalcroze's ideas in America, and (when the Great War put his business at risk) personally invited Alexander to New York, where she introduced him to her former teacher, the Pragmatist philosopher and progressive education advocate John Dewey. Waldo Frank had written an account of the Vieux-Colombier (Frank 1918), and he and Margaret entertained the actors during their stay. Bing (then nursing a baby) was offered a teaching job at Margaret's Walden Infant School. Here she observed and practised Margaret's use of games.

Bing's resultant physical theatre training exercises – masks and animal games in particular, which derived in part from Naumburg's work – would be crucial to Copeau's project to eliminate '*cabotinage*' (the actor's reliance on a repertoire of stale tricks; 'ham' acting). She taught them first to the French actors at Morristown. They would contribute directly to the formation of '*les Copiaus*' – Copeau's experimental troupe in Burgundy – and, later, la Compagnie des Quinze under Michel Saint-Denis. It was Bing's personal tuition which directly led to the developmental mime of Etienne Decroux and through him to the extraordinarily influential teaching of Jacques Lecoq. If Copeau is the father of physical theatre, then Suzanne Bing is its mother.[6]

In the beginning, Copeau did not so much have a vision of a future theatre, as a certainty that such a theatre would be possible – if only the right conditions were fulfilled. His manifesto ended with the now famous plea, '*Pour l'oeuvre nouvelle qu'on nous laisse un tréteau nu!*' (For the new work, just leave us bare boards!) (Copeau 1913: 72), and almost his first act, practical and symbolic, was to empty the stage of the old music-hall building. He ended the 'tyranny of the technician', leaving the stage open and free for the actor to perform and (just as importantly) to rehearse on. By 1921, he had stripped away the proscenium arch and replaced it with an open, multi-levelled end-stage.[7] Yet, with a minimum of technical means, Copeau's actors achieved a remarkable degree of realism when they wanted to – even astounding Antoine with Charles Vildrac's *Le Pacquebot S.S. Tenacity* (1920), in which a few tables, chairs and bottles were enough to create the ambience of a seamen's café in a harbour.

As a director, Copeau was renowned both for his fidelity to text, and for his ability to train and develop actors. He employed an 'organic' approach, aiming to discern what the written text demanded of the actor. He came to improvisation in an interesting way. Copeau believed in ensemble acting. He believed deeply in truth on the stage. But he also believed in liberating the physical and vocal creativity of the actor. Acting in Paris in 1920 was still dominated by two highly contrasted schools: broadly, the classical (exemplified by the Comédie Française) and the naturalistic (Antoine's Théâtre Libre). The 'classicists' over-elaborated the text, using it as a vehicle for displays of virtuosity. The 'naturalists' stripped away the beauty of the text, 'deflating' it (in Saint-Denis's terms) and losing touch with the actor's essential theatricality.

So this great lover of the text resolved, for a time, to take away the text from his actors – to withhold it from them – in order to force them to rediscover the essentials of the craft of acting. He had no real idea, at first, of how to achieve his aims. It is possible that he was as 'thrown' by the withdrawal of the script as his students. But he had intuition and remarkable teaching skills (complemented by those of Suzanne Bing, his best actress), and he was a great risk-taker. He knew where the work should start, that was enough:

> Therefore in his teaching Copeau temporarily withdrew the use of texts and made the study of the expressiveness of the body – Improvisation – his point of departure. He led all the work in an empiric fashion, guided by experience, observation and experiment. With the support of his collaborators in various fields, he invented exercises with many progressions and developments. (Saint-Denis 1982: 32)

Copeau and Bing developed a hierarchy running from immobility and silence through movement to sound and finally to words and text (Felner 1985, 38). This underpinned much of his work, particularly with mask, which Copeau regarded as of great importance:

> The departure point of expressivity: the state of rest, of calm, of relaxation, of silence, or of simplicity . . . this affects spoken interpretation as well as playing an action . . . An actor must know how to be silent, to listen, to respond, to stay still, to begin an action,

to develop it, and to return to silence and immobility. (Copeau 1955: 47–53)

This is the first expression of the central concept of *neutrality* to which we shall return in Parts II and III. This work on neutrality included what Bing called 'pre-formation of the expressive idea', a phrase which suggests strong parallels with the later work of Eugenio Barba on 'pre-expressivity'.

The scenic innovations represent one aspect of Copeau's genius. The other was his ability to teach actors. Many of his early collaborators later went on to become teachers of drama in their own right, especially Suzanne Bing, Charles Dullin, Louis Jouvet and, of course, Michel Saint-Denis. Their influence upon drama, in France and beyond, is incalculable. Suzanne Bing taught drama games, animal mimicry, mask-work and mime (she taught Etienne Decroux, who later taught Marcel Marceau). Dullin founded L'Atelier, where Decroux also taught. Among their pupils were Jean-Louis Barrault and, briefly, Antonin Artaud. Both Jean Dasté and Barrault contributed to the teaching of Jacques Lecoq. Jouvet, Copeau's greatest actor in the early days, founded a company at the Théâtre des Champs-Elysées and later became a professor at the Paris Conservatoire, as well as a resident director of the Comédie Française. Michel Saint-Denis was responsible for founding no fewer than five major drama schools, two in London, the others in Strasbourg, New York and Montreal: Jerzy Grotowski referred to Saint-Denis as his 'spiritual father'.

Already in 1913, Copeau had dreamed of a new type of theatre school alongside the Vieux-Colombier theatre. He felt that actors were 'the enemy of the theatre'. More precisely, the enemy was *cabotinage* – we might translate it as 'ham' but it also implies a kind of clinging to habits of thought and action. The *cabotin* is fundamentally uncomfortable on the stage: he looks for things to do, for 'business' to hide behind (Rudlin 1986: 45).[8]

Jacques Lecoq – a spiritual descendant of Copeau – taught clowning at his Paris school. The centre of this work is learning how to be at home on the stage – even when the clown has nothing to fall back on except himself, his audience and what can be created between them in the moment of performance. Sending the clown out to amuse an audience, armed with absolutely nothing (no 'gags', no jokes, no script, perhaps not even speech) is a way of 'de-cabotinising' the student actor.

By 1916, Copeau had sketched out the prospectus of his ideal training establishment, and the school itself opened its doors in 1921. The prospectus is worth describing.

1 *Rhythmic gymnastics*, based on the eurhythmics of Jaques-Dalcroze. (Later Copeau revised his opinion of this type of work.)
2 *Gymnastic technique.* Breathing exercises, sport, fencing, athletics. The aim was total possession by the actor of his physical resources. Copeau based much of this work on Georges Hébert's *L'Education Physique de l'entrainement complet par la méthode naturelle* – a series of books that revolutionised the French system of physical education. Copeau used Hébert's methods as ways of developing the *play instinct* through physical ability and instinctive action (see also, on Lecoq, p. 87 below).
3 *Acrobatics and feats of dexterity.* To give the actor suppleness as well as strength. Ideally taught by a clown, and of great use in comedy and farce work. (Copeau was impressed by circus clowns; he invited the Fratellini Brothers to teach at the school.)
4 *Dance.*
5 *Singing.*
6 *Musical training.* The actors were to be taught at least the basic skills of playing various instruments.
7 *General instruction.* For two hours a day, the children of the school (for Copeau believed that the future would lie with those brought up under this method rather than those retrained in it) would have academic studies. The adults would develop their cultural awareness through seminars and by conversation with artists and writers.
8 *Games.* Copeau and Suzanne Bing were perhaps the first drama teachers to recognise the value of *games* work (discussed further in Part II). They recognised that children learn through play, and that the responses of play are natural and authentic. Copeau speaks here not of a system but of an 'experiential education'. He writes: 'Somewhere along the line of improvised play, playful improvisation, improvised drama, real drama, new and fresh, will appear before us. And these children, whose teachers we think we are, will, without doubt, be ours one day.'
9 *Reading out loud.* Copeau was a brilliant reader. He felt it was vital to inculcate in his students the ability to respond to a text

immediately and fully; to be able to vocalise a text at sight
required quickness and flexibility of mind as well as voice.

10   *Recital of poetry.*
11   *Study of the repertoire* (which, of course, meant mainly the
     French classical repertoire).
12   *Improvisation* (see below).

To this list Copeau added mask and mime work and (after a discussion with Craig) study of the technical crafts of the theatre. The
Vieux-Colombier School operated from 1921 to 1924. Much of what
is envisaged in this prospectus could not immediately be realised, but
there was enough success eventually to move Copeau to close the
theatre in order to concentrate on the laboratory work of training.

The prospectus of the second year, as taught by Copeau and Bing
(and with movement directed by one Lt. Georges Hébert himself)
lays out the whole programme – not just for the Vieux Colombier
actors, but in embryo the entirety of subsequent improvisation and
impro-based training.

> Dramatic training . . . cultivation of spontaneity and invention in
> the adolescent. Storytelling, games to sharpen the mind, improvi-
> sation, impromptu dialogue, mimicry, mask work . . .   (Rudlin
> and Paul 1990: 43)

On improvisation, Copeau wrote in the same 1916 prospectus:

> Improvisation is an art that has to be learned . . . The art of impro-
> vising is not just a gift. It is acquired and perfected by study . . .
> And that is why, not just content to have recourse to improvisation
> as an exercise towards the renovation of classical comedy, we will
> push the experiment further and try to give re-birth to a genre: the
> New Improvised Comedy, with modern characters and modern
> subjects.   (Rudlin 1986: 44)

What Copeau envisaged in *la comédie nouvelle* was a twentieth-
century revitalisation of the energy of *commedia dell'arte*. He understood that simply to re-create *commedia* was of no use: the masks,
situations, *lazzi* of the Italian comedy belonged inextricably to their
own time. Academic reconstruction was of use only as an aid to the
generation of a New Improvised Comedy (as Rudlin translates it) –
a new form for the present.

Copeau conceived of a company entirely devoted to such work. Each actor would develop and play one specific role, just as the performers of *commedia* had. At first, Copeau himself would be the well-spring of the work, providing scenarios and training. But, gradually, the new characters – the new masks – would become independent of him:

> Choose from the company the six or eight actors most appropriate to such an enterprise, the ones with the most go in them, the most self-confident, and the best assorted ensemble – who would henceforth dedicate themselves almost entirely to improvisation. A genuine brotherhood: the *farceurs* of the Vieux-Colombier. Each actor would light upon a single character from this new *commedia*. He would make it his own property. He would feed it. Fatten it from the substance of his own being, identify with it, think of it at all times, live with it, giving things to it, not only from his own personality, external mannerisms and physical peculiarities, but also from his own ways of feeling, of thinking, his temperament, his outlook, his experience, letting it profit from his reading, as well as growing and changing with him.   (cited in Rudlin 1986: 96)[9]

The attempts to put this dream of a twentieth-century *commedia* into practice were, unfortunately, beset by apparently insuperable difficulties.[10] Where could he find such a troupe, willing to make the act of dedication he envisaged? What sort of character types would so vividly encapsulate the preoccupations of the twentieth century as Arlecchino, Pantalone and Pulcinella had those of the sixteenth? What should the scenarios be about? Copeau didn't know – but he was willing to find out.

There were willing actors, too, among them Jean Dasté, Aman Maistre, Suzanne Bing, Jean Villard, Léon Chancerel, Auguste Boverio, Copeau's children Pascal and Marie-Hélène and his nephew Michel Saint-Denis. In 1924 Copeau relinquished the Vieux-Colombier and withdrew with a dedicated group of actors (affectionately nicknamed *les Copiaus*, or 'Little Copeaus', by the locals) to Pernand-Vergelesses, a village near Beaune in Burgundy. There, for the next five years, he based his work in an old *cuverie*, or store for wine vats.

The work was developmental, ranging from the austere discipline of *Noh* drama, singing, dance, mime and acrobatics, to comic improvisation, *commedia* work and, later, character improvisations with and without masks. Shows were devised for the region (for example, a play based on the labour of the vineyard worker, performed before 2,000 such workers in the village of Nuits Saint-Georges after the wine harvest).

> Our comic improvisations were instantly accepted by this audience. Because there was never any barrier between players and audiences, the spectators sensed how much they influenced the actors, how they could affect their performances, indeed, how at times they could lift the actors to a rare degree of exhilaration. (Rudlin 1986: 26)

Throughout his work, from 1916 onwards, Copeau had been making notes towards the creation of *la comédie nouvelle*. Now it was possible to attempt it with the Copiaus. They worked in 1925 on classical *commedia*: Jean Dasté (Copeau's son-in-law) played Arlequin; Copeau himself played Pantalon; Jean Villard worked on Pedrolino and Léon Chancerel on the Doctor. The group did evolve new, personalised characters, too. Chancerel developed the Mask of 'Sebastien Congré' ('archivist, timid paleographer, molly-coddled and ridiculous'). Jean Dasté created 'César' ('an old "quacker" with a keen nose for business'). Suzanne Bing created 'Célestine'. Boverio invented 'Lord Quick' (a 'thoughtless, fat old man, who delighted in recalling his entire past life, both literary and worldly'). Michel Saint-Denis created the Masks of 'Jean Bourgignon' and 'Oscar Knie': he made the latter mask himself, by hand, and found it to be 'a violent character who made great demands on him and became a parasite on his own personality' and who both hated and was inseparable from 'César' (Rudlin 1986: 102–3; Rudlin and Paul 1990: 232).

The Burgundy period with *les Copiaus* came to an end in 1929. The ensemble had reached a point where, in Copeau's opinion, it needed to return to the mainstream of French theatre – though without him.

> We could act, dance, sing, improvise in all kinds of ways, and, when necessary, write our own dialogue . . . [We had] become an ensemble with a fertile imagination and the technical means to represent in our work many aspects and facets of the world. What we were lacking was, no doubt, a few more actors and, above all, a writer. (Saint-Denis 1982: 26–7)

Copeau's closure of the Vieux-Colombier was itself a kind of 'instinctive' rather than rational act, in order to 'start . . . over again, [to] learn what we did not know, experiment with what we vaguely felt' (Rudlin and Paul 1990: 168–70).[11] The work at Pernand-Vergelesses served to bring the actors 'back to a naïve state . . . their natural position before a world of possibilities where nothing is corrupted by habits of imitation, nor perverted by an acquired virtuosity' (ibid.).

Copeau encouraged the group to return to Paris. Michel Saint-Denis reformed *les Copiaus* into the Compagnie des Quinze and the work moved on to a different level. Devoted to physical expression still, the Compagnie des Quinze nonetheless wanted to work with a writer. Basing themselves again at the rebuilt Vieux-Colombier, they continued to improvise,[12] but now in collaboration with the young André Obey. Together, they continued to evolve theatrical languages (including *grummelotage*, a mixture of real words, mime and silent improvisation derived from the study of *commedia* and popular theatre). It was a creative tension between text and improvisation, with the constant danger that one would overwhelm the other. Plays such as *Noah*, *Le Viol de Lucrèce* and *Don Juan*, however, showed that the collaboration could succeed brilliantly.

From 1931 to 1934 the Compagnie des Quinze took Europe by storm. In Paris, though, the Vieux-Colombier was still regarded as an 'art house', distrusted by the traditionalists and (perhaps) not radical enough for the modernists. The company tried to repeat Copeau's experiments by retreating again to the country – this time to Aix-en-Provence. Within six months the company had disbanded, defeated by financial pressures and the strain of communal living.

But Copeau's vision of *le tréteau nu* had been realised. The experiments of the years 1920–34 had demonstrated that a way back to the simple power of the medieval trestle-stage was possible, that community drama based on improvisation could succeed where the sophisticated classics had failed, and had proved beyond doubt that improvisation itself could form the basis of a system of training that could reinvigorate and revitalise the whole craft of acting.

Some of the principal elements of Copeau's theory and practice can be summarised as follows:

1   Much of Copeau's work was directed not immediately towards performance, but towards *readiness for performance*, as an underlying educational and developmental goal for himself and his actors.

2   The company learned (with lots of ups and downs) about working for each other, functioning – even living – as a group (with, ideally, no emphasis on 'stars').

3   Copeau himself learned as he went along; his directing included large elements of responsiveness, intuition and adaptation. The principles of change and, involvement in a process were more important than the need to conclude or arrive at a finished product.

4   Improvisation operated within the context of games, mime and mask work, *commedia* and so on, and could develop along with any of these towards new forms of theatre. Copeau started by using text-related improvisations but later developed a freer and more eclectic use of text in the search for *comédie nouvelle*.

5   Copeau's subsequent concern with theatre-as-communion can be seen retrospectively to illuminate much of his career, from sincere and passionate critic of sterility, via the function of *patron* of a group enterprise culminating in community-rooted performance, to identification of theatre as a shared creative act with para-theatrical significance for individual and society.

It is no exaggeration to say that practically every major initiative in modern theatre can trace its lineage back to Copeau in some degree. His influence is subtle and often very tenuous, but it persists. He worked at some time with virtually every major figure in the French theatre of his day, and his students and collaborators have spread that influence to succeeding generations. The Theatre Guild and the Group Theatre in America acknowledged his influence. Most of the major British actors of the late 1930s onwards worked with Saint-Denis. And, most important, Copeau and Bing's initiatives still permeate (often without conscious realisation) drama training at all levels (see 'Genealogy of Modern French Mime', in Felner 1985: 49).

Improvisation and 'traditional' theatre training

The decision of the Compagnie des Quinze to work with a writer seems in retrospect an almost symbolic act, representing a shift of emphasis – a movement from improvised back towards scripted drama. The collaboration of Saint-Denis's troupe with André Obey seems to symbolise a particular reaccommodation of the script-based play.

Of course, neither Copeau nor Saint-Denis had any desire to abandon the written play permanently. What was important about Copeau's experimentation was the creation of a new type of *performer*, out of which a new type of drama might one day emerge. It was a way of renovating the classical drama from within, rather than an abandonment of it. As Rudlin puts it: 'Actors of *parts* are sustained by a dramatic illusion of which they are part; performers of *plays* by a nothing-to-hide, open contact with the spectator' (Rudlin 1986: 60).

The relationship with Obey was a step towards that new openness, a true collaboration of creative performers with a sensitive and gifted playwright rather than a resubmission of the actors to the text. The collaboration showed that there was, indeed, a new way to create plays.

But the return to the Vieux-Colombier with Obey marks the reincorporation of improvisation into traditional forms of play-making. Improvisation becomes just one of the many means of theatre, valuable certainly as a process which develops the actor, and which the actor and writer may use explicitly to develop the final play, but no longer the primary method of creativity.

And that is what, basically, improvisation has remained for 'mainstream' theatre, under the pressures of time, the constraints of economic resources and the fear of failure. In the UK, neither the National Theatre (which has offered workshops on improvisation) nor the Royal Shakespeare Company, nor any of the major subsidised repertory theatres has ever mounted a fully improvised show. (Plays created by improvisatory means are a different matter).[13]

One cause may lie in the *training* of actors and directors, who have been taught to regard improvisation only for its developmental value in actor training, and for its occasional usefulness in the rehearsal situation. Virtually all modern drama schools, in varying degrees, use improvisation (just as they might use games, mask work, mime and so on) in the training of actors. In this they follow, consciously or unconsciously, the precepts of Michel Saint-Denis. After the collapse of the Compagnie des Quinze, he was responsible for the development of no fewer than five major drama schools. He set up the London Theatre Studio in Islington (1935–9), his experiences at the LTS and later in teaching or planning for the Old Vic Theatre School (1947–52), L'Ecole Supérieure d'Art Dramatique, Strasbourg (1952–7), the National Theatre School of Canada (1960), and the Julliard School Drama Division, New York (from 1968) all laid down what we might call the 'invisible curriculum' of most drama schools in Europe and America with regard to improvisation.

Saint-Denis's principle for training was to 'stimulate the initiative and invention of the future interpreter by making him pass through the experiences of the actor-creator' (Saint-Denis 1982: 81–2). The search would be for the performer who could more successfully interpret a text than evolve one; and many of the students were, indeed, professional actors, already fixed in their habits of work and thought.

Accordingly, the training programme was primarily based on improvisation work. But now Saint-Denis added 'a carefully selected group of Stanislavsky's exercises: those which would not lead our actors to an excessively subjective concentration which might prove detrimental in acting a classical role' (p. 48).

His own *ideal* four-year curriculum – which he describes in *Training for the Theatre* (pp. 88–99) – is very clear on the relationship of improvised work to formal rehearsal of plays. The first year is largely improvisatory, with no public performances. This is the 'Discovery Year'. Mask work, observation, transformation and solo and group non-verbal improvisation are stressed. But in the last term of the second ('Transformation Year') we find that the Improvisation work is to cease to give more time to the Interpretational work – specifically a Chekhov play. In the third ('Interpretation') year, Improvisation work is suspended altogether (except for two weeks in the middle term on preparatory exercises in the Restoration style). He splits his curriculum throughout into two groupings: 'Technique' and 'Imagination'. Both Improvisation and Interpretation come under 'Imagination'. By the middle of the course, then, the imagination is entirely given over to interpretative rather than purely creative work. Improvisation has become the servant of interpretation. In the final ('Performing') year there is 'no improvisation work, unless something special is needed for the rehearsal projects for the repertory season or unless there is opportunity to offer a unique master class' (p. 98).

The drama school curriculum is clearly designed to 'produce' actors and, in their final year, present them to potential employers in a series of public 'coming out ceremonies'. Improvisation in this context is one of the tools by which 'an actor prepares' for the job.

The two main uses of improvisation in traditional drama (including drama training), then, are (*a*) to do with the exploration of a character's inner nature and the accommodation of that nature to the actor's own; and (*b*) the further exploration of character within situations which extend beyond those contained within the play.

The director may set up an improvised situation in order to let the actors discover what they themselves, as human beings, might do or feel in such circumstances. The actors gain insight into the circumstances with which the characters in the play have to contend, and their responses become more authentic as a result. The actors can draw upon their own vicarious experiences at difficult moments in the performance.

Or it may be that an actor will use 'improvs' to explore his assumed character in situations outside those explored in the play. An actor may ask, 'What is my character like when he is alone? when he is with his friends? his boss?' Out of this kind of work the actor may build up a wealth of small, circumstantial details – how his or her character walks, talks, drinks, handles props. In rehearsal this work is developed and crystallized through the use of the well-known 'hot-seating' technique, where a character is interrogated by other cast members and has to stay in role whilst replying. In performance these details will inform his or her playing and lend it credibility. It will be nearer the truth since it depends upon experiential discovery via the body of the actor rather than upon imposed externals.

In developing the 'reality of character', Stanislavsky was concerned with 'inner truth': the performer needs to develop emotional and physical resources which clearly are his or her own, even though they are used to invite empathy with (or in Brecht's view, to signal) some specific or typical behaviour patterns which constitute a fictitious character to be 'read' by the spectators. Saint-Denis paraphrases it thus: 'It is only from within himself [i.e. the actor], and through physical actions inspired by or drawn from his own inner resources, that the character can be realised' (1982: 82).

This realisation has to be coherent, not a matter of bits and pieces stuck on (a collage of a style of walking, a tone of voice, an accent); even Brecht, who was not concerned with all-round characterisation, demanded a complete *Gestus*. Saint-Denis sees it emerging from an alternation between this 'subjective' work on oneself and a more 'objective' understanding, via the text, of the role. Balance between 'reality of self' and 'reality of role' is an important basis *either* for mainstream acting or for more exploratory and ultimately extra-theatrical work. The essentials of improvisation can underpin both strands, and it is only the difference of focus which separates them.

Ultimately, theatre is a way of 'knowing ourselves' better, and improvisation energises that process, whatever channel it may take. In the USA, the main line of development of character work passes through Lee Strasberg, whose work we shall examine in detail below. In the UK, there is, however, one area in which improvisation and what we are here calling the 'traditional' theatre have formed a new and experimental liaison. In the field of play-creation a new synthesis has recently taken place. It brings together the concern for detailed and truthful characterisation as the basis of acting, the idea of the actor as part-creator of the work, the methods of improvisation and the traditional crafts of the playwright. The focus of this synthesis is the playwright and director, Mike Leigh.

Britain

Mike Leigh

Mike Leigh, the son of a doctor, was born in Salford in 1943 (Clements 1983: 7) and grew up 'as a middle-class kid in a working-class area', which gave him an ambivalent but deeply perceptive view of class relationships. He was also, as his latest play *Two Thousand Years* makes clear, born into a Jewish family, which stimulated questioning about identity. 'All my films and plays have in one way or another dealt with identity ... Who is the real you, and who the persona defined by other people's expectations or preconceptions?' (Leigh 2006: v–vii). The negotiation of identity and role within ethnic, religious, national, historical, linguistic or regional contexts is thus fundamental to his interrogation of what makes up a 'character'.

Leigh's training at RADA included virtually no improvisation work. Improvisation was simply not a part of actor training at that time, even though innovative theatre directors such as Joan Littlewood and film directors such as John Cassavetes were using it quite commonly.

> Two aspects of [Leigh's RADA] training did make an impression ... He became fascinated by some exercises with the director James Roose-Evans, who employed a method derived from a visit to Lee Strasberg's Actors Studio in New York. This was to do with expressing the inexpressible through the movement, and touching, of hands (Leigh has subsequently used this technique to allow

actors to progress beyond the parameters of naturalistic improvisations). And he was touched, too, by one particular improvisation conducted by Peter Barkworth in which two talented students – Sheila Gish and Ian McShane – were separately briefed with incompatible information and then thrown together . (Coveney 1996: 61)

With hindsight, one can see the indirect influence of Strasberg and, even more importantly, the principle of separation: the isolating of the actors before allowing their fully developed *characters* to meet on stage or screen.

Leaving RADA in 1962, Leigh worked as an assistant stage manager and bit-part actor in films before enrolling in the pre-diploma course at Camberwell Art School. Sitting one day in the life-drawing class:

> I suddenly realised what it had been that we hadn't experienced as actors. In the life drawing class there were a dozen or fifteen kids and everyone was making a serious and original investigation into a real experience. Nobody was doing a second-hand rendering of something. I began to think that acting could be creative in the same way that any artist is. (Clements 1983: 10)

Leigh went on to study Theatre Design at the Central School of Arts and Crafts. He also studied for a period at the London Film School. After training, he worked as an actor, director and designer. He directed the first production of his friend David Halliwell's play *Little Malcolm and his Struggle against the Eunuchs*. The production was difficult, and the company that Leigh and Halliwell had set up, Dramagraph, sank without trace, leaving Leigh with doubts about his directing abilities. It also left him with a desire to write his own plays.

Leigh was impressed by Beckett's ability to make his audience share his characters' time, to concentrate on the moment of performance itself, and by Peter Hall's work at the Royal Shakespeare Company, which allowed Brechtian values to creep into the English theatre. Hall also brought Saint-Denis and Peter Brook into the RSC, and Leigh saw much of the work being produced by them. Most interesting for us is Leigh's response to Peter Brook's 1964 RSC production of Weiss's *Marat-Sade*, in which the actors were asked to base their characterisations upon actual case-histories of mental patients. When some of the rehearsals were broadcast on BBC Television's *Omnibus* arts programme, Leigh thought, 'If they can do all that, why don't they take it a stage further and make up a play?' (Clements 1983: 11).

So Leigh himself began to make up plays with young amateurs. The first of these, *The Box Play*, taught him a number of valuable lessons. Although the play was highly successful – it was fun to see and to perform, and its subject matter (a family of six living in a cage-like box in the middle of the stage) worked well as 'cartoon' – Leigh wasn't satisfied with it. He regarded it as 'force-bred' – the inexperienced actors had to be coached throughout the improvisations. He created parts for everyone who came to the rehearsals, and he describes the methods as being fairly arbitrary ('you're the dog; you're the dad; you're the mum – improvise'). Leigh felt that the work in this play and in subsequent workshops was too shallow.

His second play, *My Parents have Gone to Carlisle* (1966), established some of the basic principles which have guided his work ever since. The improvisations were kept private (to avoid the actors trying to 'perform' before they were ready). The play started from an event (a teenage party) to which the players could relate personally. The actors were encouraged to build up biographical details about their characters, and improvisation extended beyond the immediate situation of the play to look at those characters in other contexts. He drew the final play out of the 'real events' of the improvisations.

There remained the problem of the play's final organisation. The improvisations were realistic and truthful, but not very communicative. The natural tendency of such sensitive exploratory work without an audience is to be 'introspective and inaudible'. There is nothing wrong in this: the work is for the *actors'* benefit. But the transition from private to public had to be made, and Leigh felt the need to impose his own sense of order. He shaped the final play out of the actors' work, but in order to do so he often had to work against the 'naturalism' of the rehearsals.

In 1967, Leigh joined the RSC as an assistant director. This allowed him to work with professional actors on *NENAA*. Here he realised that:

> if an improvised play was really to be a totally organic entity, genuinely evolved from characters and relationships, then I had been wrong in starting rehearsals . . . by stating plot or theme and then 'filling it in' . . . I saw that we must start off with a collection

of totally unrelated characters (each one the specific creation of its actor) and then go through a process in which I must cause them to meet each other and build a network of real relationships; the play would have to be drawn from the results. (cited in Clements 1983: 15)

In some ways this type of work can be related to Copeau's experiments in the 1920s (though it merely echoes them unconsciously). The idea of a play evolving out of characters created by the actors is not so far from the ideals of *la comédie nouvelle*; though instead of *masks*, which the actors would develop throughout their lives, we have naturalistic *characters* evolved for the duration of a play's work period.

Leigh began rehearsals for *NENAA* by providing a series of receptacles, objects such as 'boxes, suitcases, egg-cups, a bucket, a coffin', and getting the actors to build characters suggested by one of the objects. This is analogous to mask work, responding to an object which gives the actor a starting point for improvisation. But, in Leigh's 'pre-rehearsals', where the actors work singly (and privately) with the director, the object (as in Stanislavsky's work) is to create the 'inner lives' as well as the external physical mannerisms of the characters. The job was then to structure situations in which the characters thus created could meet and interact. Finally, an overall situation had to evolve which would contain the action that developed between the characters. Between 1965 and 1969 Leigh created nine plays based on improvisational work. Until then (says Paul Clements in his book on Leigh, *The Improvised Play*) he still believed he would become a solitary playwright. It took him a long time fully to understand that working via improvisation was a way of being a dramatist.

Mike Leigh *is* a playwright; all the more so, perhaps, in that his plays are wrought rather than written. He is a writer of plays in the other sense too; though his plays are written *on* and *with* his actors. The early choices are all his. He asks his actors to make lists of potential characters, but they may never know what has attracted him, what possibilities he has glimpsed for future developments, or why he has chosen one character for them to work on rather than another. The process of keeping the actors apart from one another until the characters have been formed is directly analogous to the mental compartmentalisation of the more traditional writer of scripts. One level of the play is very privately developed and, while the actors are never puppets, they never really have access to that level of the composition. When they are brought together and begin to interact, many of the fundamental choices will already have been made. The possibilities will have been narrowed down. The future pattern will not be predictable but its shapes will have been conditioned by Leigh.

The plays themselves are 'traditional' in two senses: first, in that Leigh has said he is not interested in 'happenings' and they are therefore not improvised in performance (although one knows that the depth of characterisation is such that, if anything accidental were to happen during performance, the actors would be able to accept and incorporate it *in character*); second, in that the result is always a tightly crafted and (usually, apparently) naturalistic drama.

In Leigh's best-known early works (the play and film *Bleak Moments* (1970–1), the film *High Hopes* (1989), and his published plays *Abigail's Party* (1977), and *Goose Pimples* (1981) this is quite obvious – as the 'finished' and 'published' versions of the original performances make clear. The publication of the playscripts of these works, which were 'evolved from scratch entirely by rehearsal through improvisation' (Leigh 1983: 7), reaffirms Leigh's status as a 'traditional' playwright. The plays can be (and are) performed by actors other than their original creators without recourse to further improvisation.

At the time of Leigh's breakthrough success with *Abigail's Party* at Hampstead, the critic Sheridan Morley discussed Leigh's early career in more detail. By the time of *Abigail*, he points out, Leigh had already been responsible for over thirty plays in the previous ten years, many of them devised and improvised. The method had been established carefully, and by working with many actors in many types of theatre. Leigh himself was keen to stress that *Abigail's Party* had a socially critical *raison d'être*, and his conception of improvisation in the making of these works is rigorous and demanding in the extreme:

> [A]s soon as you start talking about improvisation people expect anarchy: in fact our objectives . . . the things we wanted to say about these people and their social habits and surroundings, remained rock solid from the very first: only the surface text is flexible. (Morley 1977)

Mike Leigh's influence has spread: actors and actresses he has worked with have gone on to direct in their own right (Les Blair was in *The Box Play* right at the beginning; Mike Bradwell, the founder of Hull Truck, played Norman in *Bleak Moments*; Sheila Kelley was in *Babies Grow Old, Nuts in May, Ecstasy* and *Home Sweet Home*). Sara Pia Anderson and Phil Young are other deviser-directors who have essayed play creation in the improvised style after Leigh.

Paul Clements, however, makes the very telling point that it was not until after Phil Young's *Crystal Clear* in 1982 (televised by the BBC in 1988) that any major drama critic explicitly acknowledged that:

> improvised plays are just as much plays as any other kind . . .
> Indeed the tendency with improvised plays appears to be towards
> a much higher degree of accuracy in characterisation than with the
> average pre-conceived authorial script.   (Clements 1983: 57)

And the general critical tendency is still to regard the improvised play as somehow too 'loose', too 'unfinished', perhaps as not 'a real play' at all.

Leigh's works are certainly 'real plays'. They are created experientially. They are based upon observation. They are authentic, carefully crafted and detailed examinations of character and social environment. They are drawn from life – 'serious and original investigations into real experiences', the crucial discovery of the Camberwell art classes applied to the theatre – but they are also shaped and purposive events, poetic and symbolic statements about the ways in which human beings live and relate and fail. Leigh and those who have collaborated with or learned from him have shown that improvisation need no longer be just a rehearsal device of the drama schools. With Leigh's plays, improvisation has become the source and means of dramatic creation itself.[14]

USA

New York Giants

The development of improvisational drama in America is complex, and falls quite outside the pattern described so far, which is primarily European. *Applied* improvisation derives ultimately from Europe, but has become so thoroughly naturalised as to be distinctively American. There is also a native tradition distinct from anything we have met so far in this study.

Because there is a geographical as well as metaphorical distinction to be made, we can categorise the former, naturalised tradition as the 'New York' school, while the latter, native impro is associated with the 'second city', Chicago.

We noted that there was considerable traffic between Europe and New York in the early part of the century, one example being the meeting of Copeau and Bing with Waldo Frank and Margaret Naumburg. The interchange was fruitful, and Copeau's methods later attracted young Americans (among them actress Cornelia Otis Skinner and director Harold Clurman) to train with *les Copiaus* in France.

Michel Saint-Denis (through his influence on the drama school curriculum, especially at the New York Julliard School) added a great deal to American actor training, as he did to that of Europe. But the use of improvisation in American acting pre-dates Saint-Denis, stems more directly from the Russian rather than the French tradition, and is inextricably bound up with the development of American written drama. As Clurman put it: 'Copeau's attitude was creative . . . but we believed we were on the road to learning a sounder technique for the actor . . . the so-called Stanislavsky "system" ' (Clurman 1975: 17).

Richard Boleslavsky (born Boleslaw Srzednicki in Poland, 1889, and educated in Russia) had trained at the Moscow Art Theatre since 1906. Like Michael Chekhov, he had been a leading member of the First Studio under Sulerzhitsky, remaining a member of Stanislavsky's company until 1920. Boleslavsky fled, first to Warsaw, and thence in 1922 to New York, where he worked as a director for an *émigré* revue company.

In 1923, following the celebrated tour of the MAT to America, there was enough interest in Stanislavskian acting techniques for Boleslavsky to be asked to run a Laboratory Theatre based on Russian rehearsal techniques. He was joined by Maria Ouspenskaya, one of the MAT's actresses who had chosen to leave the Russian company and remain in New York after the tour. The new venture was christened the American Laboratory Theatre, usually known as the Lab.

There were three aspects of the total training: (1) development of the actor's body and voice, which Boleslavsky called the outer means of expression; (2) refinement of the inner means of expression which enabled the actor to live through – in his imagination

– the situations conceived by a playwright; and (3) enlargement of the actor's intellectual and cultural awareness. (Willis 1964: 113)

The first aspect was provided by specialists in ballet, interpretive dance, eurhythmics, fencing, mime, voice, speech and make-up; the third by specialist teachers in theatre history, art, music, literature and 'ideas of Western culture'. Boleslavsky and Ouspenskaya specialised in the second aspect, and the work was derived from Stanislavskian practice, totally unknown in America until this time.

The aim was to train an ensemble for three years before letting them perform publicly, though this was eventually compromised. As the Lab repertory theatre occupied more of Boleslavsky's time, Ouspenskaya adopted responsibility for teaching, focusing on small group improvisations, one-minute plays and character work. Her improvisations, often animal or object characterisations, stressed observation but also tried to explore aspects of characterisation alien to the actor's own personality – something the MAT had resisted. Her work was closer to Stanislavskian practice in its use of given circumstances:

Improvised situations, such as waiting at a train station, were often complicated by varying the given circumstances suddenly to force the student to adjust and react flexibly to different situations while remaining true to the basic *données* of his character. During improvisations students were urged to connect with each other – to become sensitive to one another's subtlest changes in attitude or behaviour. (Willis 1964: 114)

This is the core of the New York style: derived from Stanislavsky but with subtle differences, used in the development of characterisation, and basically a system which functions *intra-actively* – between the actors in the scene. The Chicago system derives from a different, not originally theatrical tradition, and stresses *inter-action* between the performers and the audience. The New York style, like its Russian original, strives to keep its intentions 'upstage of the footlights', inside the scene. The Chicago style crosses the boundary into the auditorium, both ways.

The Lab, which Boleslavsky ran from 1923 to 1929, was profoundly influential. Among its approximately 500 members were

Stella Adler, Ruth Nelson, Eunice Stoddard, who studied acting; the critic Francis Fergusson (Boleslavsky's assistant for a while); Harold Clurman and Lee Strasberg, who studied directing and whose ideas were to profoundly affect the development of American acting, writing and drama teaching via first the Group Theatre and later the Actors' Studio. Ouspenskaya ran her own school from 1932 to 1936: her work bridges Stanislavsky's understanding of the improvisational *étude*, based on the given circumstances of the play, and the simplified, naturalised version of his work that would later typify the work of the Actors' Studio in New York under Lee Strasberg.

Lee Strasberg

Whereas Stanislavsky's System emphasises the continuity implicit in a 'through line' of action and characterisation, Strasberg's Method produces emotion which 'erupts in explosive flashes' (Counsell 1996: 58), often startlingly powerful, and conforming to the modernist sensibility of a fragmented rather than a coherent self.

> The Strasbergian character is fractured and schismatic, its inner self observably dislocated from its outer . . . Method techniques inscribe their characters with what we term an iconography of neurosis. (Counsell 1996: 70)

The character's 'inner self' is revealed as a damaged, schismatic psyche which struggles to articulate its hypersensitivity against the restricting confines of the playtext. Actors often resort to paralinguistic means which are frequently in conflict with the overt text. There is recurrent recourse to minor improvisation or ad libbing in performance, with actors extending the script, or truncating parts of it in favour of wordlessness. The result is often impressive: just as often it is unreadable. The neurotic inner self (in a recognizably American cultural way) is privileged over the social, interactive self – even when carried to the extreme of inarticulacy and isolation (think of De Niro's 'Travis Bickle' in the film *Taxi Driver*) – and its inability to coherently express itself is, of course, a major sign of its veracity.

Central to the process of constructing and then expressing such a character is improvisation. Rehearsal of the scripted text is regarded as secondary, as an alliance with the process of covering rather than revealing the inner self. So, both with the Group and at the Studio, Strasberg insisted on substantial improvisation in order to build for the character a detailed inner life. When rehearsing a play, for example, actors would immerse themselves in their roles by improvising scenes, acting their characters in situations that were not a part of the playtext and so building more extensive 'inner circumstances'. Improvisation played an equally large part in general training, and a Studio practice called 'the Scene' is exemplary. (Counsell 1996: 64)

'The Scene' was an unpolished presentation to the rehearsal group by one of the actors performing workaday activities (washing, cooking, etc.) *in character.*

As with Strasberg's other improvisational techniques, the Scene was sometimes the focus of more creative activity than the playtext itself – indeed, improvisation was usually undertaken before practical work on the playtext was begun . . . Although Strasberg demanded that his actors root their work in the text, at a *procedural* level his techniques required them to regard the playtext's conception of the character as an obstacle; to address it, that is, like language, sociality and so on, as an obstacle to the expression of what the Method considers most important, 'true emotion'. (Counsell 1996: 65)

Lorrie Hull, who worked under Lee Strasberg (not at the New York Actors' Studio, but at the Los Angeles Lee Strasberg Theatre Institute) for twelve years, offers a more positive assessment and quotes Strasberg:

The whole point is to learn to see behind words, to learn not to think of words as a safeguard, but always to look for imaginative comprehension which will extend the actor's own avenue of thinking. The improvisation trains the actor's willingness to act without knowing the end result and at the same time to permit fantasy. The actor's imagination is trained to perceive possibilities of thought and meaning. (Hull 1985: 147)

She points out that, like Stanislavsky before him, 'Strasberg always proclaimed that acting should appear to be happening for the first time. This means the actor must create the illusion of spontaneity . . . This is the Great Illusion of the theatre, Stanislavsky's "sense of truth" ' (pp. 131–2).

Lorrie Hull is adamant that improvisation 'in all phases of rehearsal must have a specific aim. The theme or purpose should be properly defined' (Hull 1985: 133), at least by the director. To approach that clarity of objective, she then goes on to outline very succinctly the major uses of applied improv work in the Strasbergian model. She asks:

> Is the improvisation utilized for an actor or director to deal with a psychological problem, to develop behavior to make a character-ization more believable, to develop a better sense of the charac-ter's physical life, to develop some aspect of the character not evident in the actor's work on the role, to understand a character better, to execute an intention set by the actor or director, to check how one character feels toward another and how well this feeling will work, or simply to note what instincts actors follow in stag-ing a particular scene? (p. 133)

She lists certain obvious kinds of improvised exploration. In addition to improvisation exercises in formal actor training (discussed on pp. 140ff.), in rehearsal for performance these include: running scenes in the actors' own words; exploring what has happened between char-acters prior to a scene's commencement; exploring the 'given circumstances' of individual characters; playing out scenes not in the play which allow the actor to explore particular feelings; continuing to running scenes ad lib when they first go 'off book' and are strug-gling to remember the script; and, finally, taking *elements* of impro-visation into the finished performance (in film as well as on stage).

Strasberg sensed the blockages in actors – indeed, perhaps the Actors' Studio began to attract blocked actors to it, craving liberation in personal psychodrama. In the exercises, that release could be obtained, and creativity made to flow. When some exercises were presented publicly, irreconcilable – and therefore risible – contradic-tions became manifest. The baby was washed away with the bath-water. This was a confusion that the Chicago school carefully avoided from its inception.

Chicago Bears

The first theatre in Chicago opened in 1847, and the city has been a

theatrical centre since the turn of the century. In 1912, British playwright Maurice Browne and his actress wife Ellen Van Volkenberg
opened the Chicago Little Theatre (following the Boston Toy Theatre
of the previous year) in the vanguard of what came to be known as
the 'little theatre movement' that quickly engulfed America:

> The influence of the new movement . . . was also felt abroad.
> Browne claims that Jacques Copeau told him he had found inspi-
> ration for the Théâtre du Vieux-Colombier from accounts of the
> Chicago experiment. (Browne 1956: 165)

Chicago was and is still the source of a uniquely American
dramatic energy, and the Chicago style of improvisation has its roots
in the work of a number of different people, some of whom had little
or nothing directly to do with the theatre.

Neva L. Boyd (1876–1963) was a teacher, sociologist and educa-
tional theorist. In 1921, she founded the Recreational Training
School at Chicago's Hull House. From 1924 to 1927 she had Viola
Spolin as a student living in her house. Spolin writes:

> I received from her an extraordinary training in the use of games,
> storytelling, folk dance, and dramatics as tools for stimulating
> creative expression in both children and adults, through self-
> discovery and personal experiencing. The effects of her inspira-
> tion never left me for a single day. (Spolin 1963: xi)

From 1927 until 1941 Boyd worked as a sociologist at Northwestern
University (Evanston, Illinois), teaching play theory, leadership and
group organisation. Margaret Naumburg and Boyd were advocates
of Progressive Education, championed by John Dewey and Maria
Montessori. Both had done work in the Projects (that is, tenement
housing for immigrant communities) in New York and Chicago
respectively, and had come to similar conclusions about the validity
of games in teaching communication and social skills. And both had
gifted protégées: Suzanne Bing and Viola Spolin.

In the Foreword to a collection of children's games published in
1945, Boyd writes:

> The educational value for so-called normal children of games
> dynamically played is unquestioned; their therapeutic value for
> hospitalised children has been demonstrated beyond doubt; their

use as therapy in the treatment of mental patients has proved effective; and their corrective value in the re-education of problem youth has been repeatedly demonstrated in schools and custodial institutions. (Boyd 1945: 6)

While the book in question deliberately does little more than list and describe about 300 children's games, Boyd is in no doubt about the sociological, physiological and psychological bases of games theory. Jean Piaget and Margaret Lowenfeld would, in various ways, continue to develop educational and psychological theory: the dramatic use of games was developed chiefly by Viola Spolin and her pupils in America, and Naftali Yavin, Albert Hunt and Clive Barker in England.

Viola Spolin (1906–94), trained by Boyd, began as a teacher and drama supervisor on the Chicago WPA (Works Progress Administration) Recreational Project during the New Deal years, developing a 'non-verbal, non-psychological approach' (Spolin 1963: xi) to help train students to use drama in community work – a remarkably advanced project for its time.

Her greatest single contribution was the development and systematisation of Boyd's insights about the use of games. Working with non-English-speaking immigrants and their children, she devised many non-verbal improvisations. Spolin, working primarily with children and amateur adults, was the first deliberately to open up improvisational work to include audience-suggested material. This would, in later years, become a feature of what we are calling the 'Chicago style'. Spolin uses the term 'player' in preference to 'actor' with regard to this kind of developmental work (and the term has great currency in the field of Chicago-style improv). The method centres on games: her definition of the term 'Improvisation' begins with 'Playing the game' (Spolin 1963: 383).

Her book *Improvisation for the Theatre*, first published in 1963, was the first to attempt to codify and to teach improvisational acting. The final draft had to wait until she was given the opportunity to observe at first hand the workings of America's first fully professional improvisational theatres. The central figure in the creation of both, back in Chicago, was her own son, Paul Sills.

Sills entered the University of Chicago as a student in 1948. Many gifted actors were attracted to the artistic environment blossoming around the University during the immediate post-war years; among the best known are Edward Asner, Fritz Weaver and Mike Nichols, while Elaine May and David Shepherd were among the many performers informally associated with the University Theatre.

Paul Sills joined the University Theatre group; then, in 1953, he was instrumental in setting up the Playwrights' Theatre Club, which, as its name implies, was intended to produce works of great playwrights. In 1955, Sills teamed up with David Shepherd to found the first performance group solely dedicated to improvised work: The Compass.

Shepherd's original idea was for a theatre derived (in inspiration) from the *commedia dell'arte*. Both he and Paul Sills were heavily influenced by the theories of Bertolt Brecht (Sills later studied briefly in East Germany and ran classes in Brechtian theory and practice). Shepherd wanted Compass to be a working-class theatre for culturally deprived groups in industrial centres of America, such as Gary, Indiana. In the end it was decided that Chicago University had its own cultural deprivation problem, and Compass settled in Hyde Park. The Chicago school adopted Brecht as its mentor, much as the New York school had appropriated Stanislavsky. Compass and its many successors derived their cabaret style from Brechtian 'Smoking Theatre'. Compass's political aspirations, though, were short-lived. An early associate, Andrew Duncan, describes the Compass clientele as 'lumpen-bourgeoisie' (Sweet 1987: 46), and Shepherd himself quickly became frustrated that the group seemed more concerned about fighting their Jewish intellectual parents than about fighting McCarthyism. Amy Seham notes that motives underlying Compass and its successors were always divergent:

> Spolin was devoted to improvisation's spiritual and psychological release of human potential. Shepherd wanted a political community theatre that would fight class oppression through a dialogic interaction between actors and 'real people'. Sills was interested in both the spiritual and the political, as long as improv also produced authentic 'art'.   (Seham 2001: 7)

From the start it was agreed that Compass was to have no playwright, and no scripted play: its work would be based upon scenarios which could be hung up backstage like the 'platt' in an Elizabethan theatre. The first Compass production was *The Game of Hurt*, from a scenario devised and directed by Paul Sills. Like the *commedia*, this wasn't imagined as totally free improvisation:

The original idea was to have a scenario which was – as we fondly imagined – the *Commedia dell'arte* idea. We wrote a story out, usually eight to twelve scenes written out on a sheet of paper, and we'd follow through the scenes by rehearsing. (Sills 1964: 174)[15]

In addition to the main piece, the group also performed short 'Living Magazine' pieces (reminiscent of Moreno's Vienna experiments – see below, p. 110), and rather more superficial than the 'Living Newspapers' developed by the Federal Theatre Project in the 1930s) and, most significantly considering Paul Sills's early training in his mother's TIE (Theatre in Education) work, *audience requests.*

The audience request, or the immediate incorporation of suggestions from the audience, is the most distinctive feature of the Chicago style. The troupe retires backstage and rapidly sketches out a scene or scenes in response, which they then perform. Mike Nichols and Elaine May, for example, astounded audiences and critics in 1960 by their virtuosity in using audience-determined material. John Monteith and Suzanne Rand still do the same kind of act (though not so often) – and this style also formed the basis for the radio and television improvisation game, popular on both sides of the Atlantic, *Whose Line is it Anyway?* It even underpins radio improvised comedy, such as BBC Radio 4's cult success *The Masterson Inheritance* (starring London's Comedy Store stalwarts Paul Merton, Caroline Quentin, Jim Sweeney and Josie Lawrence, together with Phelim McDermott and Lee Simpson, later of the Improbables).

In particular, the audience request characterises Sills's next venture, the famed Second City, established (by Sills, Bernie Sahlins and Howard Alk) in 1959 and still, nearly fifty years later, an important breeding ground for much that is best in American acting. A New York spin-off of Compass, Ted Flicker's The Premise (later involved in a row with the British censor) tended to concentrate mostly on one-line jokes, but Second City, under Sills's guidance, allowed 'long, complicated scenes, whole plays, to evolve ... all sorts of parodies and operas and musical versions' (Sills 1964: 175), while Alan Myerson's spin-off troupe The Committee (1963–73) would develop a more serious, politically involved type of improvised theatre in San Francisco.

The Second City original format involved the presentation of a main show (built up and rehearsed over a number of months). Regular 'characters' emerged over time because they were successful with audiences, who greeted their reappearance in the house shows or in 'spot improvs' with reincorporative pleasure. This amounted to a (more or less conscious, but untheorized) attempt to establish an American *commedia* (Seham 2001: 18–19), with recognizable type-figures (the blond all-Americans, the Jewish schlemiels, Alan Arkin's 'Puerto Rican drifter', Severn Darden's 'Madman') recurring throughout early Second City work. Funny though these characters were, they were *social* types, by and large, rather than *archetypes*, and lacked the enduring resonance of the original *commedia* masks.

The rehearsed show was then followed by audience suggestions which the players were allowed to think about and discuss for a short while: or by 'spot improvs' – suggestions acted on immediately, without reflection – treated by actors and audience alike as virtuoso feats (when they worked). At regular intervals, the best of the resultant material was then selected out, discussed, refined and rehearsed to form part of the next main show.

The 'Chicago style' (obviously no longer confined to that city) bifurcates into comic strip performance (typified by Shelley Berman, Joan Rivers, the late John Belushi, Dan Aykroyd, Gilda Radner), and quiet, totally credible naturalism (Barbara Harris, Alan Arkin, Alan Alda, Betty Thomas). The division has always been present in American acting, to some extent, with the conflicting Broadway paradigms of the musical and naturalistic drama. But the conflict was also part of Second City's make-up.

In its early days, many of the actors were university intellectuals, excited by the boundaries of their new form. But there were also those for whom improvisation was only a means of generating and developing performance material; they saw it as a form of play – or rather revue – construction. Improv was a product of the great period of satirical comedy, the era of Lenny Bruce and Mort Sahl.[16] Second City became increasingly a prisoner of its own success. It established improv classes early on, which attracted thousands of paying would-be performers, many of whom have gone on to found rival companies. Young talent was attracted to the theatre less because it was the home of improvised drama, than because it was an excellent platform from which to launch a career in comedy or, increasingly, in television. Clever caricatures began to replace the more thoughtful 'people scenes' of the early shows.

Paul Sills left Second City in 1967; co-founder Bernie Sahlins took over and ran the company until 1984 when he, in turn, sold his interest to Andrew Alexander, the producer of the Toronto Second City. Sills and Viola Spolin opened The Game Theatre in Chicago, which was followed in the early 1970s by Sills's highly successful Story Theatre. The Game Theatre was centred primarily on Viola's exercises. Leaving revue behind, the idea was to have the *audience* play the impro games, becoming their own performers. The technique of Story Theatre was related to impro, though it usually used pre-existing narrative and textual material. Sills moved to Los Angeles and set up a small company under the title Sills and Company, which continued to play the theatre games devised by his mother from Neva Boyd's work. The company included his daughter Rachel, a fourth-generation improviser. In 1986 the company mounted a five-month off-Broadway tour, which was widely acclaimed by the New York critics.

For David Shepherd, the original conception had been political, derived from Brecht. He has since continued to experiment with proletarian theatre forms. Subsequently, he became (briefly) the mastermind behind the growth of 'theatre sports' – 'Impro Olympics' – in the USA and Canada (see below).

But for Paul Sills and Viola Spolin, the work passed (like Grotowski's) beyond the borders of the theatre, into the para-theatrical world of self-discovery and self-actualisation, the creation of 'free space' in man.

> All the people who have worked with improvisational theater know that there's a free space they can come back to and they like to come back to . . . I'm not interested in improvisational theater *per se*. I'm interested in the establishment of those free spaces where people can do their own work, and I'm interested in the forms which begin to emerge in these free spaces. (Sweet 1987: 18–19)

The basic difference between the New York and Chicago styles is that the giants of the New York theatre world confined improvisation, seeing it only as a rehearsal tool or play-writing device. The actor was confined, too; like Saint-Denis they imagined the actor as primarily the interpreter of a written script. Paul Sills is the inheritor of another tradition. An irascible and difficult director, by all accounts, and occasionally uncommunicative, he is nonetheless inspired by the *idea* of communication. In Chicago, improvisation games were a way of communicating between people, especially those disadvantaged and without a social voice, long before they were borrowed by the stage.

Amy Seham points out, however, that these ideals were not always lived up to. In no other area has there been so much explosive change since our first edition appeared. At its height, before the market became saturated in the early 1990s, there were a hundred companies offering improv in Chicago alone. Between 1990 and the present, the field of North American improv has been further revolutionised. Chicago remains the source of much of its energy, but the form has spread across the continent and beyond.

Seham documents disquiet about issues of 'gender, race and power in improv-comedy' (Seham 2001: xi) especially centring on Second City. Noting an increasingly visible tendency towards sexism, racism and homophobia in the Chicago improv field generally (in which women performers were frequently sidelined, blacks, Asian Americans and gays often rendered invisible or tokenised), she charts the emergence of a 'second wave' (later followed by third and possibly fourth waves).

The second wave saw the creation of professionalised 'Theatre Sports', with major companies such as ImprovOlympic and ComedySportz, stemming largely from Keith Johnstone's Canadian initiatives at Calgary in the late 1970s. Seham notes (2001: 37) that sport had always offered improvisers useful metaphors for the experience of working together 'as a team', being 'in the zone' etc., though she adds that women often understood *teamwork* to imply co-operation, whereas men tended to see it as formalised group conflict. The idea of a team improv competition (synthesising both masculine and feminine views) was formalised by David Shepherd's 'Improvisation Olympiad' in 1981. Shepherd imagined friendly competition between 'identity' teams, made up of players representing occupations or age groups. He joined forces with Charna Halpern, a 29-year-old producer and actor, and together they established ImprovOlympic (now known briefly as I.O. or I.O. Chicago). However, before the venture got off the ground Shepherd and Halpern fell out over their aims (his political, hers artistic), and he left. Halpern struggled to keep the idea going until 1983, when she met (and latter married) Del Close.

Del Close (1935–99) had a background in writing comic books, liked recreational substances and was a legendary member of 'the first wave'.[17] He was an original member of Compass, had starred on *Saturday Night Live*, and had performed, taught at and been artistic director at Second City from 1973 to 1981 (where he had been responsible for discovering many of the great comedy names like Belushi, Radner, George Wendt, etc.). Already known for the surreal quality of his improvisational work, Close's great invention (originally while with The Committee in San Francisco) was what has become known as 'long form' (also 'Longform') improvisation, and, in particular, the 'Harold'.[18]

Rather than the 'short form' work of audience-galvanised multiple scenes, or 'spot improvs', which were the trademarks of Second City and its followers, the Harold takes a single suggestion from the audience. Players do not go offstage to discuss anything, but respond immediately with short and initially unrelated scenes until, as 'the game' or underlying idea or pattern which links them is osmotically discovered, all the scenes begin to make sense (or perhaps don't, which may still be fun). The Harold can last from twenty minutes to two hours depending on inspiration. The key to Longform, maintained Close, was the development of *groupmind*: relaxed attunement and memory – a pre-conscious sensitivity to underlying pattern leading to sustained group creativity, and the fundamental principle of reincorporation.

However, the tendency to marginalise women, blacks, Asians and gays led, in the 1990s, to a domination of the improv field (often aggressive and competitive, despite its apparent championing of co-operation) by men and a swamping of more thoughtful and developed work in favour of the quick joke – the slow-developing Harold by the quickfire short form. Thus in 'third wave' troupes (such as the Annoyance, the Free Associates, Oui Be Negroes, etc.) two tendencies become visible. One is a deliberate political attempt to reclaim lost ground: to give voice to ethnic and sexual minorities via improv, and to address issues of power, gender and identity directly. The other is a slightly weary, 'Generation X' postmodern deconstructionism of improvisation itself, leading to 'meta improv' (Seham 2001: 117–18), in which 'calling it on stage' (reflexive and recursive drawing of attention to the techniques of improv themselves) has become normative.

Seham (writing in 2001) is unsure whether a fourth wave is gathering beyond the horizon. But we can certainly point to possibilities outside the confines of Chicago theatre. One, still using narrative drama as its basis, is the participatory form of Instant Theatre, as practised by the English company Word and Action, based in Wimborne, Dorset.

Audience-led impro

Word and Action (WANDA) theatre was founded in 1972 by R. G.
Gregory, a former English and Drama teacher who had experienced
participatory theatre as a language teacher in Europe and Africa and
had worked with Stephen Joseph, the English originator of in-the-
round work, and with drama-in-education specialist Dorothy
Heathcote, from whose techniques he gradually distanced himself.
The company is still running as a co-operative under his leadership
in 2006; and, although it does use scripted plays and dramatised
poems, specialises in 'Instant Theatre' (Johnston 2006: 229–33).
Here the company describes its method of turning narrative into
participatory theatre:

> An audience is seated in the round: on all 4 sides of the acting
> area. A well known genre is chosen (folk tale, legend, horror
> story . . .) From an accessible and inclusive gathering technique,
> the audience creates a story. In this unique theatre, everyone's
> ideas are included and no idea is rejected. Its rules and forms of
> organisation represent an egalitarian model of society. The parts
> are offered to the audience (for voluntary participation).
> Everything is represented by people, including inanimate objects
> and special effects. An innovative play [lasting an hour] begins to
> unfold, with the help of the Word And Action actors. This extra-
> ordinarily rich and unique theatre form uses no props, scenery,
> lighting or costumes.   (Word and Action website, http://www.
> wordandaction.com)

The company slogan sums up the point of the work, linking individual narrative with collective transformation via participatory drama.

> Out of nothing the story. Out of the story the play. Out of the play
> awareness. Out of awareness the power.   (ibid.)

Chris Johnston views Instant Theatre as a model of participatory
theatre. He writes: 'While the better known Forum Theatre is
combative, Instant Theatre is celebratory' (Johnston 1998: 229).

    If, on stage, performers are becoming obsessed with their own
techniques and practices, outside the theatre *audiences* have taken to
a form of improvisation which is far less commoditised. Called Live-
Action Role Play (known as LARP, or LARPing) this form again

reduces actors to the role of supporters, while the true improvisers are the public themselves.

LARPing is remarkable as much for its widespread popularity throughout Europe and North America as for its formal departures from other forms of extra-theatrical improvisation. The key to LARPing is that:

> the player himself represents the role-played character, and the player's actions directly represent the character's actions. This distinguishes LARPs from tabletop role-playing games, where character actions are described verbally ('My character says . . .'), and from computer role-playing games, where characters are controlled by the player through a computer interface . . . Role-playing at LARPs is similar to acting in theatre and cinema, though character actions in LARPs are always improvised. (http://en.wikipedia.org/wiki/Live_action_role-playing_game)

At LARPing events – which may last for a few hours, a whole week-end or several weeks – players will typically spend most of their time 'in character' (known also as 'IC', 'in-game' or 'in-play'). An essential distinction is made between an active player in role and a player 'out of character' ('OOC', 'off-game', 'off-play', 'out-of-game', etc.). Players apply themselves between LARP events to making or acquiring costumes, props and skills, which they will use in the game itself. These costumes can be spectacular and complex (some games represent non-human species) and there can be a definite element of competitive display.[19]

Part of the fascination of LARPing arises from its simultaneous occupation of parallel, overlapped realities. LARPs ask their players to occupy two simultaneous realms: the actual physical location of the player and the diegetic 'setting', the world of the character. A theatrical set exists to allow the audience to visualise the setting of a play: the actors of a drama are generally aware of its falsity – they can see the backs of the painted flats. Improvisational drama uses settings in a slightly different way, to stimulate the imagination of the performer. In some impro exercises, for example, actors may be asked to reconstruct an environment into which they can imaginatively project themselves (such as the actor's own bedroom). The LARPing environment is of this latter kind. The physical events take place in a secluded rural setting (the real, or extra-diegetic setting), where participants sleep in tents. Some effort may be made to simulate the game world scenically, but most elements will remain conventional (a rope may signify a castle wall), or be natural (a real wall may be used).

The diegetic environment, however, may be remarkably elaborate (considering LARPing's origins in fantasy board games and litera-ture, this is hardly surprising). Depending on genre, it may represent an historical or counter-historical world (for example, a world in which the Roman Empire never fell); a science fiction or fantasy world; or a dystopic contemporary environment. Most frequently it represents a fantasy realm in which magic powers, spells, charms, swords and sorcery are active.

LARPing is the most extreme form of audience-centred improvi-sation; one in which the audience completely replaces the actors, as it were, or uses them merely as adjuncts and facilitators (known in the jargon as NPCs, or 'Non-Playing Characters') for its own imag-inative self-expression. Meanwhile, back in the commercial, commoditised world, improv shows are booming.

Improvising musical theatre

Despite the understandable nervousness of producers and theatre investors, improvisation can be used in the creation of full-scale and highly commercial theatre works. In 1998, *Musical! The Musical* premiered at the Royal George Theatre in Chicago and it has toured widely since. Using the favoured local technique of asking the audi-ence for suggestions (not only for plot ideas, but also for a three-note sequence which will later form the basis for a central musical number), the cast improvises a new two-act, ninety-minute sponta-neous musical theatre piece every night. To date, the company has delivered new shows such as *Moby! The Musical*; *Jeffrey Dahmer! The Musical*; *Psycho! The Musical*, *Alamo! The Musical*, and many others – including one show in 1999 about the India–Pakistan nuclear testing conflict called *Bomb! The Musical*. No show is repeated, though many are fondly remembered.[20]

The seven-member troupe was set up by actor and improvisation teacher Nancy Howland Walker (who began working with impro in 1989, was director of ImprovBoston and had previously worked on long-form improvised pieces with The Free Associates in Chicago), and musical director Luke Nelson, who improvises the score, complete with overture, on a plethora of instruments. Walker and her fellow actors have to be able spontaneously to create a narrative, act it, sing it, harmonise and improvise intelligent – and often surprisingly moving – lyrics.

Broadway experimented with the idea of multiple endings in a musical, in Rupert Holmes's 1985 Tony Award-winning *The Mystery of Edwin Drood* (based on Dickens's unfinished last novel), which ran for 608 performances at the Imperial Theatre. Since then, it has been staged in London (appropriately at the Savoy Theatre which had once housed Gilbert and Sullivan) and around the world. Holmes proudly claims that it has run, somewhere, every day since its opening.[21]

American writer and song composer, Holmes initially struggled with the adaptation – how to convey the complexities of the Victorian plot, how to increase the number of female roles, how to find an ending (Dickens's novel doesn't have one) and how, of course, to make the whole thing theatrical rather than literary. But his crucial inspiration was that:

> as a performer, I knew that a live audience delights in anything that happens on stage spontaneously . . . in the specific performance they're witnessing: an ad lib, an unscheduled song, a guest artist who drops in without warning, a genuinely unexpected unrehearsed encore. (Holmes 2001: http://www.rupertholmes.com/theatre/essdrood.htm)

From this he derived the realisation that the improvisatory principle could be *written in* to a full-scale work.

> I sat and typed the words, 'Victorian Vaudeville.' What if I didn't attempt a strait-laced musical adaptation of Dickens' *Drood*? What if, instead, I introduced the audience to a motley British Music-Hall company who are bravely overreaching their traditional evening's fare to create what they hope will be their finest achievement: the premiere performance of their own *Edwin Drood*, to be concluded in the fashion most comfortable to them – 'Give the public what it wants.' (Holmes 2001)

Rather than create his own ending, which would reduce the openness of Dickens's unfinished work to a fixed, closed form, and imply that only Holmes had intuited Dickens's original intention:

> I'd let the audience decide who was the murderer, who was the

Detective in Disguise, which pair of lovers had a happy ending, by writing an extra act's worth of material from which one of hundreds of combinations of endings could be created on the spot ... the traditional Music-Hall Chairman could ... be scripted to offer up candidates for Culprit, Sleuth and Lovers, and to host a series of genuine elections in order to create the audience's own customized conclusion to *The Mystery of Edwin Drood.*   (Holmes 2001)

Exploiting the source's incompleteness, he contrived a plot with multiple endings, presented as a play within a play, set in a Victorian music hall. The audience is asked to loudly vote on a number of things: Is Drood alive or dead? If he's dead, who killed him? – and thereby democratically determine whichever ending they want. It is, essentially, a choice of 'whodunnit', and the spectators are rewarded by a sense that they have completed Dickens's work. As, indeed, they have – for this performance.

The cast have alternative scenes rehearsed; interaction is largely a matter of multiple-choice voting (together with much cheering of heroes and hissing of villains), and the actual improvisational content by the actors is therefore relatively slight. But the piece respects the experience of improvisation, of spontaneous decision-making in performance, and gives the audience the pleasure of making explicit the fact of its own co-creativity.[22]

Chapter 2

Improvisation in Non-Western Drama

Japan, China and Bali

Improvisation is a world-wide phenomenon.[1] Though not always acknowledged, and sometimes vigorously suppressed, it underlies dramatic forms in all cultures at all times and is recognisable even where no formal term for it exists. The work of ISTA (the International School of Theatre Anthropology), led by Eugenio Barba and Italian scholars Nando Taviani, Franco Ruffini, Nicola Savarese and Mirella Schino, has led to a greater awareness of the improvisatory principle underpinning the actor's scenic *bios*, the pre-expressive universality of the actor.

This selection from non-Western theatres illustrates the ubiquity of improvisation. Some aspects display (postcolonial) traces of the European drama, or define themselves in relation to it. Others – usually dramas with a strong sense of tradition and heavily codified form – admit no use of 'improvisation', at least officially.

In *Noh*, for example, only the *iemoto* (head of a clan/school, functioning as a professional super-ego) has the right to invent, to introduce new elements into performance (Rath 2004: 248). This does not mean that *Noh* is not innovative, and there have been many examples of experimental crossovers; contemporary Japanese directors such as Yukio Ninagawa have specialised in applying the traditional forms of *Noh* or *Kabuki* to Western classics such as *Medea* and *Titus Andronicus*. But when *Noh* actors perform in their official style, they do not normally consider that improvisation in the liberal European and American sense of freedom to change anything applies. It is, however, the case that a *Noh* performance only occurs *once*: musicians and performers do not rehearse together in a European manner; knowing their roles intimately, they do a single walk-through before the event, which may then itself produce (or not) the 'flower' or *hana* of spontaneous perfection.

Improvisation also happens *historically*, and thenceforward defines a new epoch or a new school in the art. And it happens subtly, almost invisibly, in the way a *shite* or *waki* breathes and feels their part on stage, or the *shite*, sitting in the mirror room, contemplates the mask he is to animate. That is to say, it is manifested in the investment of energy, focus and expression (the *abhinaya* of Indian performance) in the moment of production. The supreme characteristic of *Noh* is, as George (1999) notes, its production of the Buddhist cognition of performance as the locus of generative action. What is 'improvisatory' here is not so much the *what* but the *how* of doing: the recognition that, most fundamentally, the improvisatory moment is that in which one accedes to the basis of form which is then produced as action. Lecoq's 'invention of languages' is exactly parallel (see below, p. 88).

The consummate *Noh* artist Akira Matsui (demonstrating at the 14th ISTA in 2005) clearly found it psychologically immensely difficult to permit himself to improvise freely in front of an audience, yet was always totally in the moment, every moment. Given (by Eugenio Barba) the stimulus of the Bob Dylan song *Tomorrow is a Long Time*, Matsui's tendency was to consciously, very deliberately, *translate* the verbal images and feeling of the music into the terms of his art – to recodify it and use the learned codes to express it. He knew no *kata* for the fan he carried through which to symbolise the exact emotions of the song, but he could approximate them, and turn the coded gestures of his tradition into symbols that reflected Dylan's themes ('there's beauty in the silver, singin' river / there's beauty in the sunrise in the sky'). Shored up by these symbols, he again knew how to perform, and to suffuse them with energy.

Improvisation in Asian forms ranges from comic business, repartee and interaction with the audience to the subtle, but significant, shifting of parameters in highly stylised work like *Noh*, *Kathakali* or *Beijing Opera*. The latter is a highly conventional form, and one that is learned apprentice-like in a very hard school to which improvisation would seem very foreign. Nonetheless, Mei Lan Fang writes:

A friend who had seen me playing the lead role in these two operas [Mei's favourite roles in *The Drunken Beauty* and *The Maid who Feigned Madness*] several times commented that I like to keep changing my gestures and movements. Actually, I do not do so purposely. As I perform a part, new understanding of it makes me alter my gestures unconsciously. (Mei 1986: 32)

His improvisation is based not on casual ad-libbing, but on a deep absorption into the role and its 'genetic' stage history (see Riley 1997, *passim*) as well as on an endless process of self-education, technical refinement and response to criticism.

Unless you really understand a character, even if you are taught how to act it, you cannot interpret it correctly. The technical skill of a performing artist improves with the years; it cannot be forced. I admit that I have improved my art by constantly revising my technique. (p. 32)

This *is* improvisation, but not as Western actors normally understand it; however, the development of such things as movement and flexibility, particular qualities of attention and availability and so on, to which we refer throughout this book, indicate that there are more parallels than may at first be imagined.

Balinese *Gambuh* and *Topeng* performers claim there is no term for improvisation in their language – the nearest equivalent means simply 'to react' – or in the lexicon of their theatre style. *Gambuh* is an ancient form, the progenitor of the better-known (and freer) *Topeng*, dating back to the fifteenth century, with fixed masks and codified gestures and dances, strongly linked to the *gamelan* music that accompanies it. *Topeng* is simpler, but no less codified, and no less impressively complex in performance. Yet these players, as *penasar* (clowns), have an obviously improvisatory aspect, particularly in their relation to the audience, with whom they joke and chat in everyday language. Ron Jenkins and I Nyoman Catra draw attention to the subtle and 'invisible' training that a *penasar* undergoes (Watson 2001: 85–91). Clowning (as *penasar* connotes) is the 'foundation' of Balinese theatre, and a *penasar* needs three skills (in addition to the highly disciplined corporeal ones). The first is *lingkungan* (attention to the environment, in the sense of observing one's predecessors, other actors and, of course, the immediate natural and social world). The second, *sastra*, refers to scriptural knowledge, especially of religion, history and the Balinese repertoire and its epic sources. The third is *penonton*, which they define as 'an ongoing interaction with the audience':

> The actors continually change their improvised dialogue in response to the moods and needs of the audience, so that no two performances of the same story are ever equivalent. Each performer is obligated to tailor the evening's story to the specific needs of the event.   (Watson 2001: 89)

The actors have to be responsive to the social and personal situation, the environment of the performance. They will eat and talk with their village hosts before performing, and the show will move freely from fifteenth-century epic to the most contemporary concerns (for example, tourism, politics and rude jokes about individual dignitaries attending the show). The result of the successful integration of these three 'invisibles' with the technical skills of the performer is that he is said to have *taksu*: 'receptivity', 'inspiration', 'flow').[2] *Topeng Pajegan* requires the portrayal of a number of different characters by the same actor, what Keralan forms call *pakarnattom* (multiple transformational acting) or Lecoq would characterise as *disponibilité*. Although there is no Balinese word for improvisation, *penonton* is clearly an articulation of the same underlying principle, and a reminder of the fundamental psychosocial importance of clowning.

Proto-drama: the Gimi of Papua New Guinea

There are emergent forms of drama which anthropological fieldwork (of a more traditional and scientific nature than Barba's or Schechner's) have revealed, and whose seeming *naïveté* is often only apparent. The *harukaru* ritual dramas of the Gimi people of Papua New Guinea are a case in point. Their 'theatre' is made of disposable materials – bodies and living spaces temporarily decorated and transformed. There are no specialised theatre buildings. Masks, make-up and costumes are sometimes very elaborate and colourful, but made only from local, natural materials, and generally made quickly rather than kept and stored and practised with. Their stages are spontaneously created around the central fires in smoky thatched houses, lit only by firelight. Gillian Gillison comments:

> Gimis possess an elaborate performing art, staging short dramas

and farces with costume and props made from feathers, marsupial furs, leaves, flowers, berries, mosses, barks and coloured clays. Though these materials are discarded or dismantled after use, leaving no collectible artefacts, Gimi theater is . . . an art form as complex and full of interest as the fabulous lowland sculptures now housed in the world's museums.   (Gillison 1993: 147)

There are no rules of dramaturgy for either performers or audiences. The actors are amateur, and rehearsal is brief. There is of necessity much improvisation. There is a rich song culture, but no extensive, normative standard of performance, other than a general sense of what plays can be about and that they are usually brief. This means that some dramas are awkward, overlong, inadequately produced by Papuan as well as Western standards. Actors may lack control. There is no codified and centrally adhered to alteration of balance to produce a performance style; yet the performers are fully *present*. There is none of what Eugenio Barba would call *luxurious balance*: indeed, sometimes, balance fails altogether, and the actors tread on the audience in their enthusiasm. The same lack of rules applies to the spectators, who are free to interject or interrupt a performance – or, in a most fascinating way, to respond to it with a rapidly rehearsed or improvised play of their own.

While we can trace elements of the *fictive body* (the clay-daubed faces and limbs, the ornate natural decorations), there is no consistency (and no *consistent inconsistency*) to this. Make-up, visual transformation – and thereby the beginnings of a system of semiotic codification – are visible and clearly felt to be important. The use of immediately available, natural materials is no barrier to the evolution of highly codified systems of costuming and make-up, as examples of Indian village drama amply demonstrate. While there is clearly *extra-daily activity* being expressed, it is equally possible to represent daily life as the Gimi experience and choose to represent it: however, there is no centrally acquired extra-daily *technique*.

This is early – but not 'primitive' – drama. Though it is formally undeveloped, and non-literate, it would be utterly wrong to think of Gimi drama as unsophisticated. And just as wrong to think of it as purely ritual or shamanistic. It offers a model of a theatre only a few steps away from its birth, yet already able to deal with the most difficult and complex issues of its society. The subject matter of the plays ranges from cosmic to domestic: Gillison saw 'portrayals of Gimi myths, old stories, and even household dramas and scandals'

(Gillison 1993: 141). Interestingly, she adds, 'those involved in the squabbles may be in the plays but never play their own parts'. This sounds very like a basic psychodramatic mechanism, the participants using drama to gain some perspective on the events dominating their lives.

What emerges is a drama that is consciously *used*: made to order for the society that consumes it, enlarging traditional themes, confronting traditional dreads, dealing with traditional conflicts. It dramatises the essentials of Gimi life, beginning with the division of *gender*, a deeply contested field in the society. Culture is highly gendered, with boys being removed from women's company at an early age and initiated into men's society, with separate houses, separate social jobs. Many men and boys live in the central barracks-like men's house at the village centre; only as performers can women transgress the taboos against entering there. But dramas can and do also occur in the peripheral and private women's houses as well as in the central and communal men's house. Men hunt, clear land, build fences. Women work in the gardens. Drama offers a space in which that separation, formalised in the laws of taboo and the rituals of pollution, can be temporarily dissolved.

> When plays are risqué, the sexes do not act together. But Gimi theater is a place where tabooed subjects can be broached, relations between the sexes ridiculed, and tensions eased.   (Gillison 1993: 163)

This is not ritual, though it happens on ritual occasions: it is clearly drama. Equally, it is not *just* drama, but an already sophisticated mechanism of social and psychological transaction, fully susceptible (in Gillison's work) of psychoanalysis, born out of and wedded to its entire anthropological and cultural context.

An essential element is the acting out of the unseen and unseeable – what Brook called 'the Theatre of the Invisible-made-Visible' (Brook 1968, 42). For Western theatre the invisible and intangible elements are nowadays psychological and profane; but in cultures like that of the Gimi, the invisible world is describable only in the vocabulary of spirits. So, of necessity, some dramas enact spirit visitations. Gillison tells of one powerful play which dramatises an encounter in the past between a white Australian officer and a Gimi ghost. The spectators respond directly. Men in the audience leave and return some hours later with a newly created play which dramatises another such encounter between Papuan coastal natives (speaking in appropriate dialect) and the white men arriving in their boats like the ancestors coming from across the sea that separates life and death.[3] Gimi theatre, apparently simple and naive, is obviously very capable of re-rendering experience as complex metaphor.

Orta oyunu and *ru-howzi*: improvisation in the context of Islam

The principal *indigenous* Near Eastern forms of comic drama are varieties of *taqlīd* (Arabic: 'imitation' or 'mimicry').[4] *Taqlīd* forms generally involve a degree of improvised or semi-improvised clown-ing, always involving the comic depiction of human or, occasionally, animal 'types'. There is no indigenous Islamic drama which sets out to copy the world of reality – *taqlīd* is not Aristotelian *mimesis* (Papadopoulo 1979: 53). The traditional Islamic understanding of drama substitutes for comedy and tragedy the laughter-raising mimic forms of *hijā* ('invective' or 'satire') and the panegyric, encomiastic art of *madīh* ('eulogy') (Frost 2000: 55). But *taqlīd* does not imply, merely, an external (or racist) mockery of type figures. Rather, it is a clear example of how a humorous and indigenous dramatic form has accommodated itself successfully to the religious demands of Islam which, strictly speaking, forbids representation.

As Clara Brakel and Shmuel Moreh note, 'medieval Arabic theatre was a popular, oral and mainly profane art, which apparently made use of improvisation in performance' (1996: 35). Early 'comic scenes' performed by itinerant clowns are sporadically recorded from the ninth century and accounts can be found from all over the Muslim-influenced world (see Moreh 1992; And 1975; Banham 1988). A seventeenth-century Iranian example illustrates:

> Entertainers in *taqlid* would normally imitate the accents and personal characteristics of well known people in the towns and villages in which they performed. These people would be seen meeting and greeting each other. After a short while they would fall to arguing and making fun of each other's accents and behav-iour, and the story would end with the two characters fighting and chasing each other. (Beeman, quoted in Banham 1988: 667)

There are many recorded versions of such entertainment. But the most developed forms of *taqlīd* comedy are the Turkish *orta oyunu* and its Persian cousin, *ru-howzi*.

Early accounts stress the rough, improvised or half-improvised and often animal-based nature of the farces which would develop into Ottoman *orta oyunu*. Turkish scholar Metin And has pointed out that in Central Asia, the word *oyun* denotes the shaman's exorcistic rite, and this may suggest a mediumistic origin. *Orta oyunu* has sometimes been seen as a Turkish fusion of the classic mime of Byzantium with *commedia dell'arte*: there was constant commerce between Byzantium/Constantinople and the Adriatic, particularly Venice. *Orta oyunu* certainly employs its own stock characters and uses improvisation. But, if anything, *commedia* took its birth from the refugees streaming *out* of Constantinople and towards Venice after 1453.

Orta oyunu[5] is primarily an open air form, played in an oval or rectangular earthen stage area – the *meidan* – some 20 by 30 metres in length. Usually the theatre site was a public square or a city park. Originally, the acting space was just the middle of a circle made by the spectators. Later, the staging was slightly more defined, and the spectators were roped off from the actors and seated on wooden benches or rush chairs. A raised acting area was never used until after the influence of Western theatre forms was felt.[6]

Onstage there are only two items, a low screen or a chair (*dukian*, meaning a 'shop', which locale they frequently represented) and a higher two-winged screen, the *ev* ('house', 'dwelling'). The shop and the house recall the street origins of *orta oyunu*. Sometimes two such *ev* screens are placed together to make a three-dimensional structure which the actor can go in and out of. Scenery is highly schematic; crude illustrations representing castles, doors, gardens – whatever scenic locale was required – are painted on paper and pasted onto these screens.

All Turkish performances are accompanied by music. The orchestra (visible, seated to the side of the playing area) integrates and, as it were, stage-manages the performance. The play is largely improvised: a known scenario can be expanded or compressed by the actors at will, with rehearsed set-pieces cleverly worked into the drama. The repertoire is occasionally written down, but is mostly transmitted memorially from generation to generation.

There are three main characters. Pişekiar, the 'leader' (whose name also implies 'conjuror' or 'clever man'), also known by the personal name Tosun Efendi, wears a parti-coloured hat, yellow robe and red trousers, begins the play proper and rarely leaves the performance space, sometimes sitting on the ground or amongst the spectators if not actually in a scene. It is as if his entrance 'conjures up' all the other characters.[7] Much of the play consists entirely of Pişekiar's improvised *muhavere* (dialogue, punning comic cross-talk) with Kavuklu ('Big Hat', from his comically huge turban). Usually the latter represents a comic trader, servant or porter who often breaks the few illusionistic conventions of the genre and enjoys talking to the audience.[8] Kavuklu's comedy is often physically adroit, but not as gymnastic as that of the *commedia zanni*: some acrobatic elements are introduced by the younger, minor actors. Plays often end with Kavuklu being comically beaten. Zenne is the generic name of the 'woman' character who represents a variety of 'dames' or female characters ranging from rich lady to Arabian slave. Zenne is always played by a man, speaking in a high register and wearing special make-up. The central trio are supported by minor actors playing (with much doubling) a host of clearly identifiable regional, social or racial types.

Actors generally face each other and move around the space while they speak so that an 'in-the-round' audience can see all the action clearly. The acting style is presentational:

> The actor does not lose his identity as an actor and shows his awareness of this to the audience. The audience does not regard him as pretending to be a real person, but as an actor. (And 1975: 14)

This accords with the Islamic proscription on representation, while cleverly infracting it. It is not an abrogation of Allah's sole right to give life, because such characters are not to be thought of as 'alive' (as naturalistic characters in Western drama might be). The audience comes to see the story-telling skill of the *meddah*, and the presentational skill of the actor. The guiding principle of *orta oyunu* is *taklit*. One of the principal sources of laughter is the accurate mimicking of these recognizable regional and social types (not to mention animals in the early farces).

Under Western influence *orta oyunu* declined. In the 1870s the form modulated into *tulûat* as a challenge to the influence, and official monopoly, of the Armenian director Güllü Agop (Agop Vartovyan) who was modernizing and Westernizing Turkish theatre as part of the *tanzimat* ('reorganisation') movement. Returning to the street roots of their form, the *tulûat* actors took a vague storyline and elaborated it with gossip, local events or current affairs taken from the day's newspapers (a street parallel with Moreno's later 'Living Newspaper' and the better-known American Federal Theatre version). Part of their success was their ability to address, through comic improvisation, contemporary political issues – always an important strand of *orta oyunu*, and of Turkish entertainment generally.

But *tulûat* had little chance to grow. In 1884, Agop's theatre was dissolved and its building demolished by order of the last autocratic Sultan, Abd al-Hamid II, who was disturbed by the actors' traditional freedom to express political criticisms from the stage. All other theatre forms found themselves equally eclipsed. The theatre was heavily censored, and spectacles often prohibited until the revolt of the Young Turks in 1908 curbed the power of the Sultanate and Kemal Atatürk's modern constitution in 1926 set Turkey on the path to Europeanization.

Nowadays versions of *orta oyunu* or its modified descendant *tulûat* can still be seen, although in Turkey the tradition can no longer be described as a living one. In Iran, however, and elsewhere, the form thrives. An Azeri language version operates in Azerbaijan while, in Iran, a related form, *ru-howzi*, thrives, even in the turbulent period since the Revolution.

Ru-howzi is similar to *orta oyunu*, but with particular differences worth mentioning. Improvisation plays a much greater role in the Persian form. Whereas *orta oyunu* is often at least partly scripted, in *ru-howzi* nothing is written down and the entire transmission of the form remains oral. Its original actors were craftsmen and shopkeepers rather than full-time professionals. Iranians believe it predates even Greek drama (though there is no evidence for this), and claim it originated as entertainment for wedding feasts. *Ru-howzi* performances are generally paid for by wealthy patrons to celebrate weddings or birthdays. It is at root an entertainment for a private party.

Most well-to-do Persian houses used to have a large circular courtyard pool (*howz*) about 30 centimetres deep, where servants would wash clothes or prepare food. The lower-class actors would set up their makeshift theatres *on* and around these pools (*ru-howzi* means literally 'on the pool'). The audience sit on all sides of the pool, and the colourfully costumed actors act in their midst. The acting style is very rapid and highly verbal, switching from literary to colloquial registers and back again with great fluency. Scene changes are purely nominative: to enact a journey actors take a few steps on the Persian-carpeted stage floor and announce they are in a new location. As with *orta oyunu*, musicians sit visibly to the side of the acting area and accompany the whole performance.

Classical *ru-howzi* was originally played by men to men. In big cities, the performers and their shows were often associated with the local brothel quarter. As recently as the fall of the Shah, *ru-howzi* could be found in the old walled city, or 'red light district', of Teheran, with many performances actually taking place in brothels. The version seen by Peter Brook's mixed-sex company in the early 1970s, and described by A. C. H. Smith, however, was actually 'designed particularly for women, the most salacious audience of all in Persia, because most confined' (Smith 1972, 149).

A recent innovation – one which can only have increased clerical antipathy, and which is believed to have been extirpated since the Revolution – has been the use of actresses:

> In relatively recent years, women, often prostitutes, have performed with the *ru-howzi* when they travel to wedding fetes, which often last from sunset to sunrise. In ancient times, women were excluded from these performances, which were done specifically for an all-male audience. (Ryan 1974: 114)

This is attested by Brook's company, too, who were taken into the old quarter to see the *ru-howzi* players in their natural habitat. The company responded to what they had seen by taking their own improvisational form, a 'carpet show', out to an Iranian village – though the Iranian company members had proper misgivings about Western eclecticism, and the 'theft' of indigenous theatre forms by outsiders (Smith 1972: 167).

Troupes traditionally tailor their performances to the taste or concerns of their patrons: wedding feasts would naturally call for a different subject matter from brothel plays. The actors may learn what the subject of the play is perhaps only half an hour before the performance, and therefore need to call on a huge repertoire of jokes and stock scenes, and to rely on humorous interchange with the audience throughout the show.

Subjects can be literary or legendary; drawn from incidents in the national epic, the *Shāhnāmeh* of Firdowsi; or they can be purely comic and slapstick scenes packed with risqué jokes. The clown is, once again, the central figure of *ru-howzi*. He has no specific name, but since his face is blackened he is usually called the '*Siah*'

('Black': *siah-bāzi* implies 'playing the black', 'clowning'). Often he plays servant characters, and is known by the personal name 'Rajab'. The second character is the *hajji* (making a similar dyad to Pişekiar/Kavuklu: Karagöz/Hadjeivat). The *hajji* is an elderly merchant, who represents respectability and traditional morality (for example, as a strict father whose daughter is in love with a boy of whom he disapproves) – against which the *Siah*'s clowning is set in relief. Here, as elsewhere, the Iranian clown fulfils a Bakhtinian, liberative function with regard to *authority* (textual as well as social and religious; for example, the clown can even burlesque the heroic and pathetic story of Rustem); to the physical *appetites*; and, especially in this fiercely macho country, to *sexuality*: actors introduce themselves as 'workmen of joy' (Ryan 1974: 114).

The success of *ru-howzi* – and all similar forms – is summed up by an old Iranian performer: he could speak for all improvisers. The form's energy, its endless ability to renew itself and to survive oppression and threatened religious censorship:

> derived from continuous group work, with an emphasis on instant creativity. We just love our work. We are only interested in putting on a comic performance that people can enjoy for its honest good fun. (Ryan 1974: 115)

West African 'concert party' and South African theatre

The most distinctive indigenous popular form of West African drama (foe example, in Togo, Benin, some parts of Ghana and Western Yorùbá-speaking Nigeria) is the 'concert party'. It occupies a liminal space between traditional forms (masked dance drama, storytelling) and modern, Europeanised theatre, alluding to tradition while addressing modern, and particularly colonial and postcolonial issues, and using hybrid, eclectic techniques. It is defined as: 'popular, modern, commercial, traveling, musical theatre which combined elements of indigenous and imported culture in a creative and innovative fusion' (Barber et al. 1997: 1).[9]

Concert party's chief mode is improvisational and humorous. No scripts exist but, as Karen Barber suggests, it is as if 'the actors themselves worked with a kind of virtual script' (1997: xiii), a discernible characteristic of most other professionally improvised forms. Its improvised elements are 'yoked, ambiguously but vitally, with literacy [in Akan or Yorùbá]: an orientation which has profound effects on the actors' notion of what a play is' (p. 5). She insists, however, that having got rid of a chiefly script-centred view of these works, we should resist 'merely replacing it with an exclusive emphasis on their immediate, emergent, provisional, and improvisational character. This would be to fall back on a sentimental valorization of "orality" which the theatre companies themselves would not recognize and which would fail to account for central features of their practice' (p. 5).

For Alain Ricard 'dramatic improvisation . . . [here] cannot be described as disorderly. The use of space and time was governed by definite rules, accepted by the group members and recognized by the audience' (Barber et al. 1997: 126). To be a successful performer in this style requires an ability to abide by the plot 'and at the same time provoke the audience'; sticking to the story and yet being able to 'take advantage of the emotions triggered by a song to pocket the money which the audience will throw to you on the stage' (pp. 131–2).

In Ghana, concert party was for a long time the only professional form. Groups are known as 'Trios' (whether there are three players or not), the actors as 'Comedians', and their improvisations as 'Comic Plays' (whether they are serious or humorous). The form is generally dated from 1920, when 'Bob' Ishmael Johnson started a youthful company called the Versatile Eight. His 1930s company, Two Bobs and their Carolina Girl, reveals the interpolation of American vaudeville and minstrel show, as well as the advent of Jolson in *The Jazz Singer* ('Carolina' was, of course, played by a man; and the African actors 'blacked up', or at least outlined lips, eyebrows, moustaches, noses with blanco to perform in that borrowed style). Trios flourished particularly in the 1960s and 1970s and still continue although, as elsewhere, they face competition from the encroachment of cinema and television.

Performances can take place in a formal theatre space, or on a fit-up stage in a village. The actor-manager assigns roles, taking account of individual performers' strengths and aptitudes in improvising and singing, and dictates the pace in dialogue with the chief musician, while the actors themselves agree on the scenes to be performed. The show itself depends entirely on the improvising skill of the actors who resemble the collaborative ensemble of a good jazz band. There are four sections, all associated with music. The first three units comprise a twenty-minute or half-hour build-up of energy (although it used to be much longer). The last section, known as 'the scene', forms the play proper and lasts about an hour. There are considerable similarities here with the south Indian *Yakshagana*, similarly 'compered' by an on-stage manager (*Bhagavata*) and featuring warm-up routines and songs and dances interspersed with 'naturalistic' scenes, often of domestic conflict or around local political issues.

Concert party features compressed use of time, non-illusionistic style (make-up 'masks'; traditional use of a female impersonator, which distinguishes concert party from other forms of, for example, Yorùbá popular theatre), explicit address by actors (and characters) to the audience to provide plot information, encouragement of audience participation (jeering and throwing coins onto the stage), and, crucially, linguistic diversity (Barber et al. 1997: 84–6). The original concert parties performed in English, the colonial language. In Ghana, the plays have increasingly used Akan, and are now likely to include a lively assortment of dialects and languages (Fanti, Twi, Ewe, Ga, English, etc.) as the actors improvise. Language is largely the point. Barber quotes one spectator's remark: '*Inú eré lèdèé kù sí*' ('It's in the plays that the language survives'), meaning the language 'in its fullest sense – its idioms, archaisms, innovations, slang, dialectical peculiarities, and its sacred and secret registers' (Barber 2000: 2).

> Concert actors know they are going to stage the mythologies of everyday life, that they are going to speak the language of cultural domination and represent the cultural and linguistic alienation of their coastal cultures. This is not an easy venture . . . The actors must therefore prepare themselves for the task. They wait for nightfall because 'masks only go out at night'. They mask themselves; they protect themselves against the spells cast by dead actors. A sort of symbolic armor is constructed which will allow them to withstand the shock of representing cultural beings from their inner world.   (Ricard, in Barber et al. 1997: 140)

Margaret Thompson Drewal characterises all Yorùbá performance, formal or informal, as ritual: 'moment to moment manoeuvring' in which 'each move is contingent on a previous move and in some measure influences the one that follows' (Drewal 1992: 7). West African theatre artists, like the renowned Nigerian playwright and manager Chief Hubert Ògúnńdé (1916–90), would take concert party as their starting point for the development of a completely new and politicised aesthetic, where, in the tradition established by the concert party, 'every moment and every level of production is a site of creative potentiality' (Barber 2000: 9).

A great deal of African, and particularly South African, theatre incorporates in large or small measure the improvisatory, both in terms of physicality and of language. As in Indian and other Asian forms, the plasticity of body and the understanding of performance as involving dance/movement, rhythm and music enable particular kinds of flexibility; traditions of storytelling and repartee extend this to verbal language. Negotiation between different forms, structures and languages is a crucial hallmark of the improvisatory, indicating that it operates across familiar boundaries and in the spaces 'in between' versions of identity, ethnicity and expression. Add to this the predominance of collaborative/co-creative work during 'resistance' periods[10] and there are a number of important streams feeding into this spectrum.

Several specifically acknowledge a debt to Grotowski's concept of 'poor theatre' and the subsequent realisation that precisely the enforced poverty of political oppression renders the nakedness of the actor's physical resources a site of resistance; the ability of improvisational work to escape censorship and closure, to make do with reduced and easily transportable appurtenances, and to require and celebrate the multi-dimensional, multi-role and multi-linguistic facility of the actor as an active example of liberation in practice are key qualities.

Recent South African work, which is increasingly cross-racial in creation, production and casting, has continued and extended the practice with blends of physical theatre, dance, shadow and other puppetry, music and song, often in conjunction with inventive multi-linguistic scripting sometimes including aspects of *grammelot*, and also featuring highly flexible acting in which performers play multiple – often cross-racial and cross-gendered – roles. Examples include the work of Magnet Theatre/Jazzart (Mark Fleishman and Jennie Resznek); Greg Coetzee (*White Men with Weapons*) and Brett Bailey (*Ipi Zombi*); the originality and high performance quality of Andrew Buckland's both scripted and co-created plays (*The Ugly Noo Noo*, *The Well Being*, *Makana*); the highly physical, environmentally oriented productions of Nicholas Ellenbogen's Theatre for Africa – which has also spawned high-quality street theatre work by Ellis Pearson and Bheki Mkhwane. The improvisatory mode also to some extent reflects in the more conventional form of the 'township' musical, popularised by Gibson Kente; but drawing on jazz, itself a pluralistic collaboration of various historical moments of 'Africa' as cultural other, refracted via the USA and the UK/Europe, and fused with indigenous modes. South African jazz is itself also both a central part of the music scene and one which gives rise to fertile collaborations and exciting new work across musical and cultural boundaries.

In the programme note to *Onnest'Bo* ('Upside Down'), Fleishman and Reznek claim that their work frequently 'explores the terrain between performance and historiography' to create 'moments and experiences that they transform and interpret through theatre'. *Onnest'Bo* uses a combination of movement, the spoken word in several languages (some of it improvised), music and set (a collection of boxes) to present experiences of forced removal, of which the most notable under apartheid occurred in Johannesburg's Sophiatown (1955) and Cape Town's District Six (1985). This is theatre on the borders of history, fiction and memory – recreated by the original directorial and performance team in collaboration, together with input from researchers attached to the District Six museum, which 'address[es] the gaps and spaces between facts' and may 'stumble across a moment in history that is porous, fragmented, a hole in the archive', in order to 'imagine, fictionalise and represent the *possibility* of the lived experience at that time'. These 'moments' represent a crossover point between the diachronic narrative of history and the synchronic in-depth illumination of a multi-dimensional performance event.

Such work archetypally positions itself 'between', and from the 'gaps and spaces' of this in-betweenness uses the ephemerality of theatre to engage with both history and theatre as practice. These gaps – nodal points in the location of imaginative possibility within historical narrative – function in the process of the creation of performance as junctions between sequences and episodes (Fleishman 2005), rather like the repeated pauses which punctuate Vladimir and Estragon's attempts to fill up time in *Waiting for Godot*: where you ask: what now? where next? Borders, junctions, gaps, hybridity offer the chance for what Maude-Roxby calls 'new combinations', and illustrate Fleishman's view of 'theatre as a crossroads' – in a conscious reference to Patrice Pavis's title. It's perhaps no coincidence that the terminology is reminiscent (but in no sense derivatory) of post-colonialist theorists like Deleuze and Bhabha, who also locate 'in-betweenness' as crucial to the production of new modes which can acknowledge the complex otherness of multicultural societies. The process also suggests a psycho-physiological renovation which works through the use of games or auto-creation in the style of Lecoq (whose companies have often produced multi-level and multi-language work). These factors suggest that the improvisatory in performance defines a mode and a space in which body, language and identity can be dis- and re-articulated, and that this is an important indicator of the possibility of theatre as a mode of re-engagement in democracy.

Chapter 3

Improvisation in Alternative Drama

Roddy Maude-Roxby/Theatre Machine

> *I think the most important moment in improvisation is when you don't know what will happen next.*
>
> (Roddy Maude-Roxby, in conversation)

The genesis of Theatre Machine is outlined by Keith Johnstone in his book *Impro*. The company was actually formed at Montreal's EXPO 67 by Johnstone, as director, and four actors: Ben Benison, Roddy Maude-Roxby, Ric Morgan and John Muirhead. Primarily interested in comedy improvised in performance, the group had worked together at the Royal Court Theatre, London, in the mid-1960s. They had given lecture-demonstrations to schools and teacher-training colleges (educationalists were already becoming aware of the value of their techniques in teaching).

There followed a period in which THEATRE MACHINE established its improvisatory style with audiences at home and abroad and also produced scripted and unscripted plays: *Clowning*, *Brixham Regatta*, *Robinson Crusoe*, *Arabian Nights*, and the Sir and Perkins plays *The Martian*, *Time Machine* and *Moby Dick*.

With the departure of their director in '71 THEATRE MACHINE's four actors formed a performance group, self-reliant, without a director, designer or author, these roles being taken on 'in the moment' during the performance. (Theatre Machine Programme 1987, Wells-on-Sea)

The company remained loosely organised, the four actors following separate careers and coming together to become 'Theatre Machine' at will. Among other events the 'company' was challenged – by Keith Johnstone from his base in Canada – to take part in one of the increasingly popular 'Impro-Olympics' contests.[1]

Theatre Machine emerged from work at the Royal Court Theatre with George Devine, who was closely associated with Michel Saint-Denis, as well as from Johnstone's own input. It has been the only professional company to present performances which are 'totally' improvised – though in recent years work by The Improbables has come close; not only is its work linked to the use of improvisation in traditional theatre – if of an 'experimental' kind, given the Royal Court's emphasis on new writing for the theatre – but it also marks a limit which even 'fringe' productions rarely approach.

> *Clowning* was an improvised show: there was no written script of any kind – though there was an extremely loose structure – and all the actors changed parts for different performances ... although certainly related to the *Commedia dell'arte*, its more immediate inspiration is the English music hall tradition. (Browne 1975: 46–7)

Clowning had to be presented officially as a *lecture* – because of the Lord Chamberlain's inability to pass improvisational work. We nowadays tend to forget the dead hand of official censorship, which was not abolished in Britain until 1968.

William Gaskill, Johnstone's colleague at the Court, has said of him:

> All his work has been to encourage the rediscovery of the imaginative response in the adult; the refinding of the power of the child's creativity. Blake is his prophet and Edward Bond his pupil. (Wardle 1981: 6)

With reference to Theatre Machine, it is necessary to define what 'total' improvisation means in this context. It does not mean a completely random and chaotic show. Rather it is a compilation of a number of *lazzi-type* ingredients: the performers have 'up their sleeves' a number of characters – some with appropriate masks or bits of costume – or fragments of sketches. Some sections may be familiar to them or quite fully rehearsed. But everything is open to change.

If you don't know the show is improvised, or don't believe it can be, then the bits that work well will seem obviously rehearsed. The bits that flop you will think 'obviously not rehearsed' – you'll think those are the 'improvised' bits and you'll wonder why they improvise, if it doesn't work. ('Theatre Machine Programme, 1987, Wells-on-Sea)

The answer is that:

THEATRE MACHINE has throw-away form, it is disposable theatre, ideas and memories get re-cycled and the best is really best because it comes out of the moment; and sometimes you were just ahead of them.   (ibid.)

This idea of 'throw-away' theatre captures the very essence of improvised drama. The term is also used by Dario Fo and Franca Rame (*un teatro da bruciare*), although in their politicised context, theatre is used, and then disposed of, in the same way as a newspaper is burnt once it has served its purpose of informing the reader. Theatre Machine's 'disposability' is simply an acceptance and a celebration of the central fact of performance – the ephemeral act of co-creation between actor and spectator 'in the moment'.

Theatre Machine's method of working depends on close mutual support by all performers. Timing is one important example: if something threatens to flag, the actors on stage are dependent on one of their colleagues taking the responsibility of entering and changing the direction. They must be sensitive to each other and to what is happening, 'present' and alert, prepared to support each other and not 'block'; whatever happens has to be accepted and used in the on-the-spot construction of a scene. Theatre Machine push the demands to the limit because there is nowhere to hide on stage: ultimately, all acting is about being able to take full responsibility for yourself and your colleagues. Improvisation is valuable both as individual training and as a way of enhancing ensemble work.

One of the key elements of Jacques Lecoq's training is the emphasis on *play*: using and enjoying the moment and what it brings. Maude-Roxby, like Viola Spolin, uses the term 'players' in preference to 'actors' in his improvisation work. This is part of a deliberate strategy, accompanied by a relaxed and apparently non-directive manner, to help participants to feel at ease. 'Playing' suggests a game in which everyone can take part, and in which there are more rewards than penalties; it takes the heat off the rather threatening nakedness of improvisatory situations. Maude-Roxby often says that his sessions are about 'not acting', a maxim which is related to Lecoq's work on clowning.[2] The basis of clowning is the ability to feel OK about being yourself and making a fool of yourself. It necessarily includes a passage through vulnerability, but it can't afford to get stuck in it. So, too, 'play' admits the possibility of making mistakes, or rather allows the chance for what we might think of as 'mistakes' (if we are thinking about 'giving a good performance') to be re-evaluated as possibilities of new directions. Everything in Maude-Roxby's work can lead anywhere, so there is no *a priori* categorisation of right and wrong. Rightness is more a question of *attitude*, not of what you do but of how you do it, whether you are prepared to play with what comes along. 'Play' in this context also has the idea of interplay, of the development of the range of the possible.

Many of the exercises Maude-Roxby uses are similar to things discussed below in the section on techniques. It's his way of using them that is particularly interesting. He seems to be open to the developing sense of structure, seeking an organic form which emerges through the activity. Collecting objects, talking about them, evolving a narrative; finding different ways of moving and building a 'scene' around their interrelationships; developing from one person/object/position to more and more complex collages or combinations, with or without speech; arranging a collection of bodies or masked players. All of these work off not knowing what will happen, building in the unexpected, allowing it to become an unforced part of a construction or meaning which emerges as part of a (group) process.

This kind of work also gives free rein to fantasy – allowing it to bypass cliché – by linking it to physical events which don't have a specific, predetermined meaning. The shape which the body adopts, or the function of an object, are not interpreted as fixed notations in a set code, as they might be in naturalistic performance. There, for instance, a chair tends to be a specific sign in a particular context – it denotes economic or social status – or a bodily position is evidence of a particular psychological state (head drooping, shoulders dropped, hands clasped = powerlessness, depression). In impro situations, the chair could become an umbrella, a bicycle, the horns of a bull; the pose could suggest a child being told off, a person sheltering from a storm and dying to go to the loo, someone praying. The sign ceases to *denote* and becomes the possibility of infinite *conno-tation*: it opens out to the play of significance.

Absence of specific meaning allows anything to be imagined – but not in a total void, because the physical event ensures a physical memory-trace. The impulse to meaning is generated in conjunction with the physical event, as the body moves and relates to itself, to other bodies or objects: the pattern of meaning evolves as a succession of such relationships and assessments. So this kind of activity is doing at least three important things at once: showing that signs are arbitrary, helping us to play with them and getting us to experience that we make meanings with the body as well as with the mind. It is also a mediation between structure and freedom, between memory and imagination, between the given and the created.

Theatre, of course, is about *physicalising* the sense-giving act, producing it as *performance*. Structuralist analysis has highlighted sense-giving as a central human activity, and indicated how different codes of meaning and kinds of discourse are elaborated and given privileged status in different usages. Structuralists tend to view the symbolic and the mythological as processes of *encoding* but, useful as this is, it to some extent ignores the role of the body. If symbolism, as Susanne Langer suggests (Langer 1959), is about giving form to *feeling*, performance underlines the equality of the mental and the physical in this process, and improvisation work particularly acknowledges that mind and body have to be treated in tandem. The work of Lecoq exemplifies this further.

Jacques Lecoq and the semiotics of clowning

Jacques Lecoq (1921–99) began by teaching physical education and sport, learned improvisation from Claude Martin, a pupil of Dullin, and worked with the Association Travail et Culture (TEC), which gave shows based on improvisation and organised spectacles for 10,000–15,000 people after the Liberation. In 1948 he went to Italy; he claims to have discovered '*le jeu de la Commedia dell'arte*' in the markets of Padua: '*Commedia* has nothing to do with those little Italian troupes who export precious entertainments. It's about misery, a world where life's a luxury ... If you're thinking of *commedia*, forget about Italy' (Hiley 1988).

In 1951, Lecoq created the Theatre School of the Piccolo Teatro in Milan, and worked as both director and teacher; here he developed his speciality in mime and dramatic choreography, and gained experience of many other theatrical styles, assisting on Strehler's early productions of Brecht, and choreographing the young Dario Fo and Franca Rame in revue work.

In 1956 he returned to Paris to found his own Ecole Internationale de Mime et de Théâtre, which he ran until his death in 1999. Lecoq's Paris school has given rise to some of the most important developments in performance style to have occurred during the last five decades. His original interest in movement in sport has remained at the basis of his work. He worked with Michel Saint-Denis and Jean Dasté, and thus has direct links with the tradition of Copeau. He represents, however, an important modification and development of what Copeau began, both in terms of approach and of the organisation of a coherent curriculum.

The overall aim of Lecoq's work is: '*découvrir les règles du jeu théâtral par une pratique de l'improvisation tactile à tous les niveaux (du réalisme à l'abstraction)*',[3] which might be glossed as: to discover the essentials of play and interplay in theatrical performance by the practice of improvisation using the whole range of tactile possibility at all levels (from realism to symbolic condensation). The significance of '*règles du jeu théâtral*' and '*improvisation tactile*' – key phrases in Lecoq's method – will be touched on further below.

Four things figure prominently in most of Lecoq's courses: (*a*) the establishment of the 'neutral body', including use of the neutral mask; (*b*) the concept of 'play'; (*c*) observation and research, both of 'realistic' detail and of rhythm and movement; (*d*) the *auto-cours*, or 'do-it-yourself', work, in teams or groups towards producing various kinds of performance.

The structure of the courses themselves typically involves work which can be classified into three areas: (*a*) basics of dramatic performance; (*b*) the play of styles; and (*c*) movement and plasticity in terms of the architecture of space.

Running through Lecoq's presentation of his work is a metaphorical complex related to the activation of space in performance; starting from '*la récolte de rhythmes moteurs*' (a gathering or harvesting of fundamental rhythmic impulses, dynamic rhythm, or the basic rhythms of life), going on to suggest that moods and emotional tones can be identified according to the orientation taken by the body in space (melodrama is 'oblique', as is jealousy, whilst pride elevates and shame seeks to lower itself), and finally engaging with '*l'architecture invisible du drame*'.

Lecoq breaks down movement and gesture structurally, using anthropological and physiological criteria. For him, *'l'homme pense avec tout son corps'* (Lecoq 1987: 17), and these criteria enable him to offer his students a way of analysing and reproducing the dynamics of action. There may well be interesting parallels here with, for instance, the work of Laban[4] and the approach to movement teaching in other schools. But what we are concerned with here is the relationship to improvisation.

Impro work is a central part of Lecoq's courses: a typical four-hour session will contain one hour of movement, an hour and a half of improvisation and an hour and a half of *auto-cours* work in groups, which aims to use the results of the first two areas in building up group presentations.[5] So there is a very close fusion of movement and improvisation in developing the 'play' of performance. And perhaps nowhere else do we find such a precise intellectual and practical structure to movement work in the context of improvisation. For Lecoq, theatre is an *'acte essentiellement physique'*, and it must thus deploy its range of meanings through the movement of bodies in space. Every organism has spatial coefficients of position and direction; each mood or style may also operate like an organism in this sense. Lecoq's method is directed towards the identification and physical assimilation of these relationships, so that they come to form a 'vocabulary' on which the performer may call as appropriate. Lecoq calls it the *'saisie du réel qui se joue dans notre corps'* (1987: 17): performance always occurs as immediate experience within and across bodies and their emotional and physical sensibilities, be they of actors or spectators, prior to categorisation or assimilation into discursive categories. I know *only and directly* because I know 'before' what is conventionally defined as knowledge. It is the job of any serious actor training to get performers to that condition. In other words, real knowing always has to be a surprise, an amazed 're-cognition': for producers and receivers.

Simon Murray describes the major aim of Lecoq's school as 'to investigate the corporeal basis of creativity' (Murray 2003: 158). Fundamental principles of the exercises presented by Murray are (*a*) movement generates emotion; and (*b*) the body remembers. So in targeting a 'site to build on' (McBurney, cited in Murray 2003: 63), Lecoq is interested not just in the physical flexibility of his early sports training, but more crucially in the body's potential for engendering, registering and remembering experience at subtle and profound levels. For Lecoq, the body moves and speaks as it moves.

Its speaking is an act of memory and an act of creation, an invention of corporeal, imaginative and theatrical languages. To arrive at that capacity, which is in fact something like a 'pre-expressivity' prior to the 'physical score' sought by Eugenio Barba, Lecoq's practice adds to rhythm and flexibility the 'economy and simplicity of movement' of Georges Hébert (see Murray 2003: 165), which feeds into work with the neutral mask. (This is not 'affective memory' in the Stanislavskian sense, but the *production* of a psychophysical 'trace' which can be incorporated into a network of performance signs.) Neutral work opens to that sensitivity towards the least perceptible impulse or sensation, it is the most basic level of Lecoq's work of 'preparation'.

This preparedness leads to a 'read[iness] to be surprised' (McBurney, cited in Murray 2003: 106), which in turn stimulates the capacity to become aware of how bodies move in space (see exercise section on work with elements, pp. 146–7), how they play and interact with each other, and how they produce meaning. Its rootedness in the materials of production enables performers to explore the relationship of their bodies to other kinds of body and to the ways these together can reconfigure the space in which they operate: both in the 'optional extra' LEM (*Laboratoire d'Etudes du Mouvement*) course which seems to have in many ways encapsulated much of his most astute thinking and which has become if anything even more integral to the school after his death, and in the productions of the companies Murray describes in some detail, Théâtre de Complicité and Mummenschanz. The latter – Murray calls them 'sculptors of the imagination' (Murray 2003: 115; see 110–26) – use a vast range of materials to produce 'a redrafting of the boundaries between masked performance and puppetry' (115). Complicité's work in *The Street of Crocodiles*, *The Three Lives of Lucie Cabrol* and *Mnemonic*, specifically produces a linkage of personal and cultural memory out of the interaction of bodies and the objects of daily life – desks, cloth, buckets, books, agricultural tools. *The Street of Crocodiles*, for instance, draws on the fragmentary and evocative narratives of Polish writer Bruno Schultz, and Complicité's transformations of themselves and their surroundings embody the experience and the location of threat, marginalization and intense desire.

It is thus in this context that we need to see Lecoq's use of improvisation, and the way in which the concept of 'play' is central to it. Lecoq uses the term to signify the energy that is shared between performers on stage and in rehearsal – the ball that the game is played with – which is why for him improvisation is very much a matter of physical activation. 'Play' also means the *inter-play* of this activity, emphasising the relationships which spark off or create new combinations: people, movements, moods or styles meet and collide, giving rise to different possibilities. Structuralism's 'play of the signifier' is relevant here, suggesting the idea of verbal play and inventiveness. Other appropriate shades of meaning include the hint of 'bringing into play', and the sense of 'possible movement or scope' as in the degree of play in a bicycle chain, for instance. This picks up another useful angle, namely the balance between freedom and restraint; 'play' here indicates a fruitful tension within reasonably precise limits.

All of these usages are underpinned by the sense that 'play' is a salient feature of mankind's capacity for the production of symbolic form, signalled primarily in Schiller's *Aesthetic Letters* and in Huizinga's *Homo Ludens*. Thus it also implies *playfulness* – the pleasure derived from discoveries in the moment of creativity. Thus for Lecoq 'play' is very much a question of developing the physical articulation of mimetic possibility; for him 'mime' signifies all the resources available to the actor including his use of text, and the function of improvisation is to set those resources in play. Therefore, the outcome is in and through performance, that necessarily improvisatory moment when imagination composes new shapes and makes active the knowledge that resides in the body.

'*Le style est un esprit de jeu*', says one of his course descriptions ('style is a way of playing/a sense of play/a kind of playfulness'): the body of the actor has to be 'disponible' (open, available, ready; see Part III below) to engage in different styles which demand that he or she be capable of '*changer l'espace, la vitesse et la matière de son jeu*' – that is, to transform the various coefficients of performance, whose 'content' (*matière*) then becomes something quite different. The 'spirit' of play which emerges is precisely the ability to *activate* a particular configuration, to enter the game of its structuring: an acute mental and physical condition permitting creation to occur: '*provoquant (l')imagination à inventer des langages*'.

Lecoq uses the *masque neutre* as the first and fundamental stage in the development of this condition; through it he aims at a physical condition ('*état neutre*'; '*état de disponibilité silencieuse*'; '*masque du calme*') which is at the basis of dynamic extension in space (*l'espace*), time (*vitesse, rhythmes moteurs*) and matter (*animaux, éléments, matières, couleurs, lumières*).

His work then proceeds via the *larval mask*, which offers nascent expressive states, towards an incorporation of the passions in melodrama and *commedia*. For him, improvisation is less about psychological liberation (though that is, as it were, taken for granted) than a matter of building up resources of physical awareness about how people move, how the body develops certain attitudes when it is in certain modes, about the acquisition of precise mimicry which can then be activated in the construction of scenarios, at first more realistically imitative, then involving more elaborately imaginative forms.

For Lecoq, knowledge comes about *through movement*: so 'he attempts to return the mime to the precognitive state, freeing him to gather a new set of sensory impressions in a neutralised state of naiveté' (Felner 1985: 148). He works (via the neutral mask) towards what he calls *mime de fond*, the 'gestural rendering of the essence of reality' (Felner 1985: 153). This reflects an Artaudian belief in the ability to discover a pre-verbal level where, after passing through the *silence de fond* – the first phase of his work, Lecoq says, is about forgetting – one may begin to: 'find the gesture of the word, the actions for the verbs in the profound silence in which they were born' (Lecoq 1967).

Anthropologically and anatomically, movement precedes language, and Lecoq seeks to return students to that situation where they discover emotion and meaning through gesture: the *mime de fond* is also the *mime du début* – of the beginnings of all knowing and all articulation.

The *disponibilité* Lecoq seeks is a situation of balance which can draw upon an extensive range of possible movement and action which has been internalised in the preparatory work. Here as elsewhere, then, 'neutrality', of mask and of the whole body, is not a kind of blankness; it is highly charged. The body has a wide range of available resources; neutrality engenders a state in which they are ready to go into play, but not programmed to operate in a predetermined way. The 'waking up' exercise often used by Lecoq and others in neutral mask work (Eldredge and Huston 1978) indicates the desired condition: it's rather as if the whole body were 'full of eyes within' and they are all opening to an unfamiliar world.[6] The coefficients of action have to be drawn anew. But if it works, this kind of alertness as the basis of performance can produce inventive and delightful play.

Lecoq uses the Clown to illustrate this. (The Clown is the *'esprit*

de jeu' par excellence: Lecoq says that clowns operate 'at a point
where all is blunder' – where the unexpected is the rule, therefore.)
The semiotics of clowning rate a closer look in this context.[7]

A clown emerges from behind a screen. He wears a red nose, but
otherwise has no props. He looks at us. And for some reason we
laugh. He looks at us again, pleased to see us. We laugh louder. He
takes delight in our laughter, and that pleases us too. The clown has
done nothing – except *notice* us. And yet we are laughing. He has
told no jokes. He has performed no 'routine' to amuse us. So why
have we laughed?

That red nose? It is iconic. It looks stupid, and the clown is happy
to wear it. He is not afraid of making a fool of himself. He is vulnerable, and happy to be so. His face is a disarming icon of happy
stupidity.

It is indexical. It draws attention to the eyes and mouth, the
expressive parts of the face, pointing that expression and at the same
time defamiliarising it. The nose magnifies the movements of the
face, alerting the spectator, informing him that the gesture is being
presented, is on display, is to be watched.

It is symbolic. The very entrance of that nose arouses in us the
expectation of laughter to come, predisposing us to judge the clown's
actions in a certain way, making us willing to laugh at the slightest
provocation.

Only partly; for the true clown doesn't need the false nose. He
could have made his entrance without it, looked at us, and we would
still have laughed. Ah, but he *entered*: the clown's entrance is unique.
It has only one purpose, to make us start to laugh. The fact that the
clown was *aware* of our presence was vital. He made *contact* with us
directly and openly. So the clown has included us in his game; right
from the start we are implicated in whatever he is doing. He is doing
it for us; if we laugh he may repeat the action. If we don't laugh he
will almost certainly repeat it, insisting that it is important, magnify-
ing its significance until its very triviality becomes the occasion of
our mirth.

The clown plays. The clown plays the realities of what and where
and with whom he finds himself to be. He cannot know these realities in advance, for so much of it depends upon us, the audience, that
it cannot be pre-planned. Everything is *new* to the clown. Of course,
the clown always has 'an act' up his sleeve, a sure-fire set of gags and
jokes and routines. But in good clowning he may never have to use
them. The clown has to 'find the play' in the immediate context. The

work is hard and, especially in the early stages, fraught with fear of what Lecoq calls *la tasse* (the 'cup') – in other words, catastrophic failure.

Clowning is one of the purest forms of improvisation. None of the things the clown does is ever guaranteed. Everything is on the brink of *la tasse* – because everything is real. The successful clown plays *his* clown:

> For several years now, the clown has taken on a great importance; not in the sense of the traditional circus, which is dead, but as a part of the search for what is laughable and ridiculous in man . . . We put the emphasis on the rediscovery of our own individual clown – the one that has grown up within us, and which society does not allow us to express. (Lecoq, cited in Towsen 1976: 353–4)

This exercise requires the student to leave aside habits of performance and find what is genuine in the moment. It asks the student to be truthful about himself. It asks that he be happy to go on, unarmed (in Grotowski's sense), expectant, open to the context in which he finds himself. Once, if ever, that condition has been discovered – through trials and many errors – the clown is ready to develop a more studied 'act'; which he should be equally happy to abandon as he begins to work with his partner, the audience.

Neutrality, play, rhythm; and the offering of himself, fraught at any moment with not just the possibility, but almost the necessity, of failing and looking silly: the clown incorporates all of these in the 'encounter' (to use Grotowski's term) with the audience, and always underscores the frailty and the miracle of creation. At any moment his act is on the verge of dying, and yet somehow he rescues it, and another fragile construction of gesture or words is launched.

Beckett perfectly understands the condition of the clown, and that of the improviser. The final words of his novel *The Unnamable* express, though in the context of the writer rather than the actor, the fear of self-revelation, of being *true*, of finally encountering oneself:

> it will be I, you must go on, I can't go on, you must go on, I'll go on, . . . it will be the silence, where I am, I don't know, I'll never know, in the silence you don't know, you must go on, I can't go on, I'll go on. (Beckett 1979: 381–2)

Beckett's world is like Lecoq's in its utter absence of self-pity (the protagonists are totally 'unheroic' and going on is the only thing they can do). And in both cases the attitude overrides any tendency to dwell on the 'blocks'. 'Where I am', in a neutral mask or a red nose, is 'the silence you don't know'. If you let that silence go on, it stops being a silence in which you don't know, and becomes an introverted embarrassment crowded with self-accusations, justifications and excuses jostling each other into impotence and leaving you rooted to the spot. What Beckett and Lecoq emphasise is the need to act (speak, write) *immediately* from the silence, from the unknowing. For Lecoq, the actor is not an interpreter.

His work has spawned many exciting companies and solo performers whose style reflects his concern with plasticity and physical precision. Among them are *Théâtre de Complicité*, whose work relies on exact observation and subsequent stylisation of movement and mood, sharpened by the interplay between idiosyncratic rhythms developed by each performer. From this they construct a texture of emotional situations inscribed in time and space as shape and rhythm and counterpointed by expressive *grummelotage*: their show entitled *A Minute Too Late* deploys their impeccable timing via a series of reflections on attitudes to death – and is itself a comment on the improviser's art. In contrast, Footsbarn Theatre's inventiveness has led to a manipulation or restructuring of Shakespearean texts.

Lecoq trainees have produced shows based on a variety of mime styles and movement, using a range of masks and exploring to the full the possibilities of 'physical' theatre. All of Lecoq's protégés are different; and all of them work in differing fields of theatre. Ariane Mnouchkine, Stephen Berkoff, Peter Brook and Dario Fo have all learned from and with Lecoq. The British group I Gelati made a speciality of *commedia* work, yet a major project, for example, was a five-actor version of Brecht's *The Good Person of Szechwan*. The American Avner the Eccentric presented shows which were a mixture of circus skills and clowning. Moving Picture Mime Show gained their greatest successes using 'larval' mask work and mime. Footsbarn are most noted for their vigorously physical reinterpretations of Shakespeare.

What links these very disparate groups and individuals – apart from time spent with Lecoq in Paris – is not that they all follow Lecoq's precepts. They don't. In the end, like all students, they take from their training the things that have impressed them most; and, like all creators, they use the things that serve their own artistic needs and discard the rest.

What links them, then, is not a stylistic unity. Each group has its own artistic integrity. Each is making its own vision of a future theatre. They are not all, by any means, devoted to improvisational work: yet all of them share a common theatrical vocabulary, and that internalised repertoire of physical and imaginative skills which marks the successful Lecoq graduate.

In some forty years Lecoq's school claims to have taught 4,000 students from more than sixty countries, and many of them are well known in Europe and the USA. They return occasionally to Paris, and Lecoq has acknowledged with a certain pride the existence of a kind of 'mafia' of his graduates. Certainly they recognise and value each other's work, and attribute much of its success to their training.

Lecoq himself occupies a major position in the history, theory and practice of improvisation in theatre, particularly in terms of the growing importance of clearly conceived and precisely executed physical expression. In his work, improvisation and mime become ways of developing highly focused capacities for generating richly iconic texts which articulate an extensive internalised vocabulary of gesture, shape, rhythm and sequence in continually inventive patterns and structures.

For Lecoq, the occasional resurgence of the improvisatory (that is, the *mime de fond*, for him) marks periods of redefinition when theatre returns to its roots. From here it can emerge, as does his own work and that of his students, in new forms, and it does so because his training most centrally focuses on: 'pitting the student face to face with himself in a state of perpetual discovery' (Lecoq, n.d.: brochure of L'école Jacques Lecoq).

Le Théâtre du Soleil

Ariane Mnouchkine's Paris collective Le Théâtre du Soleil, formed in 1964 as a workers' co-operative, reflects a clear development of the tradition of Meyerhold and Copeau (Mnouchkine also attended Lecoq's school in 1966) both as aesthetic practice and as a form of politics of and in theatre.

In 1969 the company mounted *Les Clowns*, a production which was their first real attempt at group creation, the result of an investigation of the circus as a form of popular theatre, intended to break away from the constraints of socialist realism and what the company referred to as *psychologisme* (Kiernander 1986: 196).

Les Clowns continued the use of *lazzi*, together with the 'ebullient, physical style' and 'frantic rhythm' which had marked their production of Wesker's *The Kitchen* in 1967. This was followed in 1970 by perhaps their most famous piece, *1789*, 'a group creation based on improvisations'. *1789* was premiered in Milan at Giorgio Strehler's Piccolo Teatro, then performed from 1971 at their now famous base, the Cartoucherie, until 1974. By this time, the group had established their commitment both to popular theatre forms, and to collective, improvised creation around a powerful political statement.

In working on their next project, *L'Age d'or*, the company (partially) succeeded in doing what Copeau had dreamed of, creating a contemporary form of *commedia* that could speak to the twentieth century. Not *la comédie nouvelle* exactly, for the actors of the Théâtre du Soleil had no intention of developing their Masks for the rest of their careers. But to the extent that the work addressed contemporary themes (exploitation, poverty, sexual politics) and did so via the reinvention of *commedia dell'arte* (without attempting any historicist reconstruction of it), Copeau's vision was fulfilled.

In the resultant play, Pantalone becomes a real-estate promoter; Abdullah-Harlequin a cheap construction worker who is bribed to work on a high scaffold in a fierce wind. He dances his death fall to Verdi's 'Requiem'. Pantalone tries to stop the show, tries to cover up the scandal.

Like Copeau's own company, the Théâtre du Soleil went on retreat into the countryside, contrasting the reactions of the villagers of the Cévennes with those of the Parisian critics. Unlike the latter, the villagers simply accepted the work in its totality, making no distinction between the formal elements and the political content. The Théâtre du Soleil's discoveries about the creative relationship between a community theatre and its patrons via improvisation exactly parallel those of Copeau and Saint-Denis:

> The actors improvised every day in various village meeting places, both outdoors and indoors, around themes proposed by the people, who were very receptive to the masks, costumes and physical movements of the performers, as well as to the accuracy of what was expressed about their lives. (Williams 1999: 171)

Mnouchkine and her company read Copeau for the first time (as his *Registres* were being published) in 1974, during the rehearsals for *L'Age d'or*. But their inspiration also goes right back to Meyerhold's early conception of a reborn theatre of the *cabotin* and the *balagan-schik* – and includes Meyerhold's political as well as theatrical fervour.

Mnouchkine (who is happy to be thought of as the artistic 'midwife' rather than director of the group) works almost entirely through improvisation. She provides visual materials, imaginative prompts, research materials; and the work grows out of lengthy discussion and careful repetition. From Lecoq, Mnouchkine centrally derived the early emphasis on *création collective*, the desire for performers to acquire a plasticity particularly in their relationship with space and bodies in it, and some of her use of masks in rehearsal and performance. These principles – which, as we shall suggest in Part III, emerge from much improvisation work to similar effect – underpin her concern to require performers and audience to validate and engage with the 'other', as artistic process and political imperative (see Bradby and Delgado (2002) and Williams (1999) for a fuller account of Mnouchkine's work).

Dario Fo and Franca Rame

The improvisational style that stems from Lecoq's work is well illustrated, in addition to the examples given above, by Dario Fo and his wife Franca Rame. But English-speaking audiences have a multiple-distorted view of Fo and Rame's work. We need to clarify those distortions – recognise them as such, at least – before proceeding to look at what the Fos' real achievements are.

1 We only know a relatively small fraction of their work, in spite of increasingly available translations and productions of their plays. Fo is one of Europe's most popular dramatists, with consistently more productions in more languages than anyone else over recent decades. Still, it is true that most people outside Italy associate the Fos with a limited number of works: *Can't Pay? Won't Pay!*, *Accidental Death of an Anarchist* and *Female Parts*.

2 The plays do not have the political bite that they do in Italy. English versions, divorced from their original context, often seem cleverly satirical – but sometimes merely whimsical. There are, of course, parallels between political injustice or governmental corruption in Italy and in

Britain, but translations do not always render specifics and may distort the sense by virtue of different cultural assumptions. British farce is almost exclusively a bourgeois form of lightweight sexual innuendo (except in the hands of Joe Orton), whereas for Fo the term implies a particularly acerbic form of satire readily accessible to 'the people' (the '*piccolo populo*' as he refers to them in *Accidental Death*). Fo wrote to the director of the Washington production of *Accidental Death*:

> Don't call my play a comedy. I call it farce. In current language, farce is understood as vulgar, trivial, facile, very simple. In truth, this is a cliché of Official Culture. What they call comedy today has lost the rebellious strain of ancient times. What is provocative and rebellious is farce. The establishment goes for comedy, the people for farce.   (Fo 1974: 121)

3   Non-Italian speaking audiences primarily regard Fo as a playwright. Fo is not present to them in the theatre, any more than Shakespeare is. All they have of him are the plays which bear his name (though, as suggested below, they are the work of translators and adaptors as well as Fo). In Italy both Fo and Rame have long been celebrated as performers of their own works rather than as writers. Fo's primary aim is to create

> a throwaway theatre [*un teatro da bruciare*], a theatre which won't go down in bourgeois history, but which is useful, like a newspaper article, a debate or a political action.   (Fo 1974: 58)

Like Theatre Machine, Fo and Rame produce disposable drama. Not in the consumerist sense, but theatre 'to burn', like a newspaper when its purpose has been served: plays of the situation, activist responses to a social and political context. The techniques are farcical, the structures often loose, looser than would be the case if they were crafted only at the keyboard rather than in the theatre. The 'play', for Fo and Rame, is not finished when its author stops typing – in fact, it has only just begun its process of being wrought. It will be rehearsed, will change and develop throughout that period, as with traditional plays; but then the next, perhaps most important, phase begins. The play is offered to an audience, and will continue to change and develop in response to that audience's reactions during and after the performances. *Mistero buffo*, for example, always relied on improvisation, since the audience is involved in it and doesn't play a passive part, since it imposes its rhythms, and provokes off-the-cuff lines. This type of theatre is recreated from performance to performance, and is always different, and never repetitive. (Fo 1977, trans. Mitchell 1984: 18[8])

Fo is much more than a playwright. He is a director, teacher, stage designer, student of architectural and theatrical history, song-writer; most importantly, he is a political activist and a theatre performer.

4 The act of translation itself means that the play becomes a fixed script. It loses its improvisational relationship to the audience. Stuart Hood writes:

> Franca Rame and Dario Fo work within a tradition of improvisation which means the texts of their plays are difficult to 'fix'; they change according to the changing political situation . . ., different audiences. They are like living organisms but within them there is a hard skeletal framework of radical criticism of our society and of relationships within it. (Hood 1981: vi)

Accidental Death of an Anarchist, for example, was first produced at the same time that Inspector Calabresi, implicated in the 'defenestration' of the anarchist Giuseppe Pinelli, brought a libel suit against the left-wing paper *Lotta Continua*. These court hearings were the immediate context against which the play was first received. The play was constantly updated, and each night included a report on the day's proceedings in the case. *Mistero buffo* is re-created from performance to performance. Franca Rame speaks of developing her one-woman show with audiences in the same way,[9] rather than having a fixed script to which her performance nightly adheres. When the play is translated (*a*) to another country, (*b*) to another language, (*c*) to a different political context and (*d*) to another performer – all that Rame has gained experientially is lost. The play may become by default a 'text' to be rehearsed and performed, alien to its original conception as having a living relationship to a contemporary theatrical and social context. Yet, despite these inevitable distortions, Fo and Rame's reputation has grown. Enough of the spirit and theatrical power of their work remains to excite audiences and performers all over Europe and America.

Sources and origins

Dario Fo was born in 1926 near Lake Maggiore in Lombardy. His father, Felice, was a staunch socialist and keen amateur actor. As a child, Fo would repeat the tales of the local storytellers to his brother and sister, and built a puppet theatre to act out stories. He also studied and imitated the gestures and techniques of the *fabulatori*, descendants of the medieval *giullari* – 'essentially *pre-commedia* . . . popular, unofficial mouthpieces of the peasant population' (Jenkins 2001: 34) – and came to be regarded by the locals as an expert. Tony Mitchell points out how large a part first-person storytelling plays in almost all of Fo's plays (Mitchell 1984: 36), and Fo regards the techniques of the *fabulatori* as 'a structural storehouse' for all his later work, celebrating their love of paradox, of contradiction and contrariness; de-sanctifying, demythologizing – always and quite naturally political.

Fo believes his work goes back to a tradition of itinerant comedy deriving directly from the *mimes*. As an authority on *commedia* technique, he is perfectly aware of the tradition of the *comici dell'arte* (professional 'court jesters' taken up and given official recognition by the ruling classes); and consciously uses techniques such as *grammelot*, an onomatopoeic theatre language derived from *commedia* theatrical practice.[10] Such techniques develop the quality of *souplesse*, and help the actor to discover physical ways of relating to his audience. But he always tries to relate the origins of those techniques to their social context.

Fo worked with Giorgio Strehler at his Piccolo Teatro, where he created *A Finger in the Eye* (*Il dito nell'Occhio*), a piece which broke new ground theatrically: zanier, more satirical and more political. Fo designed the sets and costumes. Franca Rame was in the cast (they married two years later); Strehler did the lighting. But, most important, it introduced Fo to a French associate of Strehler. The choreography for *A Finger in the Eye* was done by Jacques Lecoq.

Lecoq taught Dario Fo

> mimic and vocal technique to shape his spontaneous improvisations. Lecoq trained Fo to use his physical defects (long arms and legs, uncoordinated body and flat feet) to advantage rather than hiding them, instructing him in the different forms of laughter, while also introducing him to *Grammelot* and character transformation, ingredients which were to come into their own in *Mistero buffo*. (Mitchell 1984: 40)

Fo, a natural improviser, nonetheless needed to learn the theatrical skills of performance. Lecoq taught him how to find 'his' clown, his personal comic style. One might say that, although their encounter took place before the school was founded, Fo is the most distinguished alumnus of L'Ecole Jacques Lecoq. Their acquaintance continued (despite various disagreements) with Fo giving special classes to Lecoq's students.[11]

Franca Rame also taught Dario Fo: she, too, is a gifted improviser, coming from a touring theatre family (Teatro Famiglia Rame) with a repertoire of popular farces.[12] Fo attributes his education in improvisation to working on stage with Rame. She shares in the traditions of the *fabulatori* and the *giullari* – perhaps even the *cabotin*. David Hirst reveals that her attitude to improvisation is that of all strolling professionals: nothing is left to chance (Hirst 1989)! She records her performances and makes detailed notes of which ideas and jokes worked and which did not. Her style (and hence Fo's) returns to the kind of improvisation that rests, like that of the *commedia*, on solidly prepared and rehearsed foundations. Fo directly credits Rame with teaching him how to improvise (Fo, cited in Jenkins 2001: 80):

> The kind of improvisation Rame advocates is not a digression but a way of personalizing the text and creating intimacy with audiences by making them feel that the performer is responding to the specific circumstances of time and place in which the play is happening. (Jenkins 2001: 83)

Fo and Rame conceive of theatre as direct intervention in, rather than detached comment on, political life. That abrasive, urgent struggle, which has often brought them into conflict with leading figures at different points on the Italian political spectrum, is rarely so visible in English versions of their plays, even when presented by left-wing groups. Sexual politics are central to Rame's self-expression, too. She is at the forefront of the women's movement in Italy, and her monologues are performed by actresses across Europe and America.

The jester of the people

The piece that exemplifies the style they have evolved together, and which ties together many historical threads, is Fo's long solo *Mistero buffo* ('comical mystery play'), a dramatisation of a collection of medieval texts deriving from the strolling secular performers and street entertainers of Europe. It is a *bouffonerie* – a grotesque spectacle – a carnival version/inversion of sacred events mingled with *lazzi*, *canovacci*, *grummelotage* and mime – bound together by Fo's modern *discorsi*, which contextualise the pieces and serve as prologues and discussion prompters.

Mistero buffo is not a static text: it has undergone innumerable revisions, and there are several versions of it. The play is created every time it is performed. The pieces Fo performs as *Mistero buffo* now are not necessarily the same as those he performed in 1969. It is as if one man has created and performed an entire medieval cycle, an epic conception. The pieces cohere around the idea of undercutting the repressive structures of church and state; by taking an officially accepted form and casting it back into the language of the peasant, he reveals what is grotesque in those structures themselves.[13]

The piece with which Fo usually opens *Mistero buffo* is called 'Zanni's Grammelot' ('*Il Grammelot dello Zanni*'). Zanni, the prototypical *commedia* character, is here played without a mask (although in an *Arena* documentary Fo demonstrates how to play the traditional *lazzo* on which it is based in a mask: see 'The Theatre of Dario Fo'). The theme is peasant starvation, but typical of Fo (and his sources), it is treated as bitter farce: Zanni is so hungry he imagines he is eating himself. He then dreams of an enormous feast. Finally, waking, he catches and eats a fly. Each detail of the scenario is physically portrayed with great virtuosity, accompanied by the onomatopoeic sounds of cooking, eating and digesting.

The pieces are introduced by *discorsi* in which Fo – using the familiar *tu* form – addresses the audience directly, explaining, expanding and improvising. Fo's intended audience is the industrial working class, just as the *giullari* played to the rural peasantry. In Italy, he achieved this aim, playing in occupied factories as often as in 'art houses'. He listens to that audience both during and after the show. Listening during the show means responding to their laughter, shaping and reshaping the text, breaking the frame to incorporate topical or local allusions. Listening afterwards, in the 'Third Act', means incorporating political and social, as well as dramatic, criticism. He has been attacked by the Church for blasphemy in the way he inverts Gospel narrative to reveal the Church's underlying message of political servitude; he has been attacked politically from all sides. For the terrorists he is too moderate, for the PCI (the Italian Communist Party) he is too militant, for some other political dramatists (like the late John McGrath) his style is too disorganised to be

politically effective, and for the conservatives (in art as well as politics) he is simply unspeakable. But

> When I relate the origin of the *giullare* in *Mistero buffo*, I'm able
> to tell the story in a convincing way because I believe in it, I
> believe in the mission which the *giullare* originally chose for
> himself as the jester of the people. I also believe in it because I've
> experienced what it means to be the jester of the bourgeoisie.
> (Mitchell 1984: 21)

Dario Fo, the politicised clown, inheritor of the traditions of the
giullari and the *comici dell'arte*, stands as the embodiment of the
improvisational style of performance and audience relationship that
grows from Lecoq's work. That relationship and that style are crystallised in Fo's use of *tu*. From the moment the clown enters, his relationship with the audience *is* a familiar one. What Lecoq's work
centres on – above and beyond the acquisition of technique – is the
necessity of *complicité*. Linguistic familiarity is more than cliché.
The improviser's relationship to the audience (in Martin Buber's
terms) is that of 'I and Thou', not 'I and It', because in this style of
work more explicitly than in any other the performer and his audience create the piece *together* (see Buber 1923).

Performance and the grammar of participation

The processes Fo employs are, according to him, similar to montage
and cutting between cameras (the use of millimetrically precise
gestural detail to create close-ups forms part of the grammar of his
acting); or to the sixteen-line structure of blues:

> I also improvise in a sixteen-line structure. When I invent an
> action, you can count it out, and you'll see that it fits into that
> rhythm. If I insert a new gesture, a discovery for achieving a
> particular effect, I have to take out something else. I can't add a
> line with impunity. (Jenkins 2001: 135)

This quality of precision and rootedness in the specifics of place
and situation is what enables Fo to 'play' the interaction with the
audience in musical terms. This is technically achieved by breathing
– and that rhythm in turn determines the interrupted style of the
performance on the microcosmic scale – which in turn leads naturally to the interrupted, epic style on the macrocosmic level:

> The tempo of breathing . . . comes from the necessity to listen to the reaction of the public. To be able to do this you have to interrupt the flow of the performance with a pause that allows you to observe the tension of the room.   (Jenkins 2001: 136)

> I take the same breath you are taking. We breathe together so that you have enough breath to make the sound of laughter. You laugh and we continue on together . . . We are telling the story together. (Jenkins 2001: 145)

'Interrupting', like 'accidents', gives a clue to the generative mechanics of Fo's improvisatory style: it identifies the points of suspension and renewal at which the chance to make new sense is available. That is the only way to ensure that what you do is a new creation. The shifts of perspective, Jenkins claims, are intentionally Brechtian, in order to stimulate understanding from a variety of perspectives: rhythm here is not just a musical device but a way of moulding a psychodynamic response. The gap, which is in many ways a crucial signal of the improvisatory attitude (What next? Where next? Who next? Why?), is used as a means of treating the audience democratically, inviting them to become co-creators. Jenkins continues:

> The theatrical jump-cuts in Fo's performances suggest a complex interaction between history, economics, religion, morality, and mundane current events. Fo's comedy exists at the overlap between the private and the public domains.   (Jenkins 2001: 266)

'Gaps' (rhythm is syncopation around silence) are structural holes or moments of in-betweenness which mark important opportunities for intervention and sense-making by the receivers; they offer the possibility of alternative vision, border-crossing, bypassing of taboos; they are the synapses of new connections, but these connections are not only performative and active (important enough in itself as a mode of engagement with the audience) but also moments of political and ethical recognition[14]

Chapter 4

Beyond Drama – 'Paratheatre'

Jerzy Grotowski

Jerzy Grotowski (1933–99) came into contact early in his career with the work of Stanislavsky (at the Polish State Theatre School in Cracow, and at GITIS in Moscow, where he did a one-year directing course, learning also about Meyerhold and Vakhtangov). Visiting France in 1957, he learned of the works of Jean Vilar, his teacher Dullin and Marcel Marceau (a pupil of Decroux, who was taught by Suzanne Bing). Thus, he was open to the traditions of Stanislavsky, Meyerhold and Copeau, in addition to those of Polish writers and directors (for example, Witkiewicz, Slowacki and director Juliusz Osterwa, who founded one of the first theatre *communities*, similar to Copeau's and Stanislavsky's experiments and prefiguring those of Grotowski himself).[1]

In 1959 Grotowski became the director of 'the only professional experimental theatre in Poland'. The 'Theatre of the Thirteen Rows' had a small company, dedicated to ensemble work from the outset. It began in Opole with nine actors, three of whom were to remain to form the nucleus of the later Teatr Laboratorium group. These were the actress Rena Mirecka and the actors Zygmunt Molik and Antoni Jaholkowski. In 1961, these three were joined by Zbigniew Cynkutis and Ryszard Cieślak. (Stanislaw Scierski joined in 1964, Venezuelan actress Elizabeth Albahaca in the late 1960s.) This group – together with Ludwik Flaszen as Literary Director – were the co-creators of most of Grotowski's work after that time. In January 1965 the company transferred to Wroclaw, where it nominally remained until its final dissolution in January 1984, after twenty-five years of performance, teaching and research.

Jennifer Kumiega describes the theatrical situation in Poland at the time as being largely dominated by the director, and (as with Western theatre) by literature (Kumiega 1985: 11–12). Right from the beginning (despite his increasing status as *auteur*) Grotowski wanted to re-establish the primacy of the actor, and of communication via the actor's body:

> To create theatre we must go beyond literature; theatre starts where the word ceases. The fact that a theatrical language cannot be a language of words, but its own language, constructed from its own substance – it's a radical step for theatre, but Artaud had already realised this in his dreams.   (Flaszen 1985: 12)

The company moved gradually towards this goal, both through discussion with the 'Friends of the Theatre of the Thirteen Rows' and through performances such as Mayakovsky's *Mystery-Bouffe*, a stage version of *Shakuntala*, and *Dziady* ('Forefather's Eve', with words by Mickiewicz). This production saw the beginning of Grotowski's relationship with Eugenio Barba, later to found Odin Teatret, who came to see one of the performances, stayed on as Grotowski's assistant for two years and was largely responsible for popularising his work outside Poland. Then followed the major productions which established the Theatre Laboratory as an internationally respected group of theatrical pioneers and extended the frontiers of theatrical possibility in their use of space and their demands on the performers' bodies, voices and minds: *Kordian*, *Akropolis*, *Faust*, *The Hamlet Study*, *The Constant Prince* and *Apocalypsis cum Figuris*.

Jennifer Kumiega discusses four main areas of development during this period:

> (i) the emergence of the principle of 'poor theatre'; (ii) the attitude to, and treatment of, literature and text; (iii) spatial construction and relationships (environmental theatre); and (iv) the actor-spectator relationship.   (Kumiega 1985: 17)

These are the four main planks on which Grotowski's early work rests. In 'poor theatre', the actor's body is the primary resource. Everything else can be dispensed with: text, costume, lighting and so on are revealed as 'accidents' rather than 'essentials' in the act of performance. The actor can be and do anything and everything. (For instance, if a mask is needed, the actor's own facial muscles can create a mask). Everything needed for the production is there in the performance space throughout, objects are transformed simply by the actors' use of them. Text is used but it is reformed, deconstructed and reconstructed text; displaced and given new meaning by the way it is employed by the performers.[2] The performance space envelops and includes the audience – they and the actors share the same space and time, the same event.[3] In the end, for Grotowski all performance is an encounter between the actor and the spectator – and between the actor and himself. Throughout the early work there develops the idea of the actor making a 'total gift of himself' – the 'total act'.

Grotowski's *theatre* practice – as distinct from the *paratheatrical* work which we shall discuss shortly – is implicitly based on a theatre of signs: a semiotic theatre, in which texts, objects, actors are infinitely redeployable. Words are relexicalised; texts are intercut and their intertextuality made evident – often blasphemously: the actor searches for the archetypal physical sign of the character's condition. But, beyond the semiotic, even in the early days we can see the quest of the actor to escape from role: to be himself. The theatre exercises (described first in *Towards a Poor Theatre*) and the daily training routines give a slightly misleading impression of Grotowski's aims. The exercises were not a 'training' for the act of performance. They used improvisation in training, certainly, developing remarkable physical and vocal skills, but the aim was not purely to develop bodily and imaginative *skill*, but rather to bring about the spiritual condition in which

> the body would not resist the actor . . . For as long as the actor has the feel of his body, he cannot attain the act of divestment. The body must totally stop resisting; in effect, it must cease to exist. (Grotowski 1979: 36)

Part of Grotowski's aim, then, was to *subdue* the flesh. The body is seen as an obstacle to be overcome, and the harsh yogic exercises are as much a means of fighting the body as training it. The same stricture applies to the mind of the performer (at least as it is evident in the teaching work of Rena Mirecka): the mind's desire to shape, to form, to 'script' the event, the intellectual ambition to create 'meaning' (by making intertextual references), hampers the ability genuinely to experience the event. The famous *via negativa* approach of Grotowski's rehearsals is an attempt to prevent physical or mental habits from interfering with the process of *giving* oneself utterly to the event. Acting in 'poor theatre' is not dressing up and pretending: it is divesting – sometimes physically, always spiritually – and being. One is aware of the actor as an actor, not in the Brechtian manner of calling our intellectual attention to the fact, but in the sense that, beyond the matter of the play, the event is an encounter with the actor as a human being. He is not so much a *character* of the play, as the *subject* of the play. His skill may amaze us, but what moves us is the actor's gift of himself.

Grotowski believes we use art 'to cross our frontiers, to fill our emptiness' (Grotowski 1969: 21). For him this is a slow process in which we 'peel off the life-mask', and the theatre thus becomes (as, in somewhat different ways, for Artaud and Brecht) 'a place of provocation'. Workshops and performances are a confrontation with the vulnerability of feeling and experiencing which lies behind public and private roles. We often avoid this exposure: we screen ourselves by adapting our feelings to the image we have of ourselves, or that we would like others to have of us. Actors, even or especially in (dangerous) impro situations, are prone to this: it's much easier to adopt a stereotyped role. This easy route out is tempting precisely because the alternative is frightening: facing up to the fact that I don't know who or what 'I' *is* or how it might respond if it abandons all *a priori* models. Before filling our emptiness we have to experience it, and that is uncomfortable. But until we do this we can only go on 'acting' what we think we ought to feel.

> We arm ourselves in order to conceal ourselves; sincerity begins where we are defenceless . . . if a method has any sense at all it is as a way to disarmament.   (Grotowski 1973: 121)

Grotowski's 'obstruction exercises' aimed at locating and neutralising individual blocks or tendencies to hang on to comfortable habits; one technique used by Rena Mirecka in workshops illustrates this. As soon as the participants become aware that they are no longer fully 'with' whatever they are doing (that is, starting to decide what they ought to feel or do instead of doing it), they must immediately do a backward roll (without looking behind) and come up facing in a different direction. This physical breaking of the situation allows a fresh start.

In Grotowski's process, we find many of the basic assumptions of improvisatory work in theatre and outside: work on actors and audience, in the awareness that their relationship creates theatre, and centred on the establishment of a state which may be called neutrality, being wiped clean, deconditioning. This last aspect is comparable with Copeau's neutral mask work mentioned earlier, and involves an element of fear and crisis. It is only moving through this that allows us to experience without the familiar filters of habit. (When you put on a theatrical mask, especially a neutral mask, the body suddenly 'sticks out', all its awkwardnesses revealed; you can't 'hide' it behind the attention-catching expressions of the face.)

If we *do* move through, if we abandon ourselves to what may seem like chaos, to the totally unknown, we may find that there is an unsuspected order to feeling. In the backward roll exercise, people rarely bump into each other: the body orientates itself in space without conscious thought (just as blindfold trust exercises, or the 'eunuch/pauper' game described in Part II may produce an extension of spatial awareness and other subtle operation of the senses). We may begin to 'know' and to 'behave' in different ways, which change our patterns of relationship to others and to the environment.

Grotowski's work – with performers and audience – thus implicitly moves beyond the boundaries of what we conventionally designate as 'theatre', and seeks to set in play fundamental physical and psychological capacities. But it arises in the first instance from a concern to establish a more acute experience *in* the theatre, and from an understanding of what that involves. In his later Theatre Laboratory performances, the audience (strictly limited in numbers) is assigned a role (accomplices, judges and so on) which inhibits the passive or detached gaze. Provocation is physical and psychological, and thus personal and political. It affects the audience as a whole, making them uneasily aware of collective responsibility, and, as individuals, making them confront the limits of their capacity to understand and respond. What is created first is the sense of panic at being cut off from familiar behaviour, which is exactly paralleled by the demands on the actors: Grotowski 'stresses the moment of surrender ... the extinguishing of individuality, and then the elation and regeneration involved in the recognising of "another" reality unobtainable in everyday life' (Grotowski 1973: 121).

Grotowski's work with the Theatre Laboratory, in its various phases, always focused on small groups (of actors and audience members) exploring or being subjected to very intense experiences and sometimes reaping rewards in the form of profound personal 'breakthroughs', revelations of suddenly liberated or unblocked capacities for doing and understanding. There is, in addition to the emphasis on psychological process, something slightly esoteric, hermetic and elitist about this kind of activity, necessarily largely self-selecting in terms of participants. Of course, all intense work with actors requires relatively small groups, and improvisatory work is certainly no exception: but there are many instances in which that work aims to open itself up to a wide public and to formulate its presentation in a 'language' of directly accessible physical or symbolic signs. Grotowski's approach is even more 'difficult' than, for example, *commedia* or Lecoq's work. But it's clear that Grotowski himself was aware of this, and that this awareness contributed to the move towards 'paratheatre'. In the course of this move, the boundaries between performers and spectators are broken down; thus, although the total number of participants at any one event is not necessarily very different, their function and relationship to each other changes significantly. *Performance* as psychophysiological process opens itself to a wider clientele, but in doing so performance as theatre is left behind.

The charge could be made that by moving out of theatre, and ultimately out of Poland, Grotowski confirms the 'solipsistic' or even 'narcissistic' direction of his work as opposed to practitioners like Kantor and Róŝewicz. Grotowski's response to the political situation can be seen as a form of retreat. However, that should not obscure the significance of his work with actors, within the contexts of bodies, links between mental and physical action, and the importance of focus, generosity and openness.

After *The Constant Prince* in 1969, the search for technical mastery becomes less important, and the exploration of personal authenticity through group activity becomes central.[4] The major focus is on the discovery or disclosure of the full self (or Self, to give it its Jungian emphasis) through group activity. In its various phases and locations (for example, USA, Australia, France), the work is seen as 'research' (the 'University of Research' operated in Warsaw in 1975), sometimes with a small select group, sometimes with participants from a slightly wider public, though these too were carefully screened and selected. The aim is to achieve a condition of personal and interpersonal behaviour where 'a man does not impose himself . . . He comes forward and is not afraid of somebody's eyes, whole. It is as if one spoke with one's self: you are, so I am' (Kumiega 1985: 144).

Activities include work on aspects related to acting (release of vocal and physical blockages); the use of language to penetrate to, rather than conventionally mask, the personal; exploration of the 'oscillation between game and play'; workshops leading to interpersonal contacts. The experience of paratheatricals directly fed the later work of the Laboratorium: in 1981 Ryszard Cieślak directed *Polish Thanatos*, in which the audience was informed: 'It is possible for those present – without constraint – to enter the action. Your participation in the particular life of this group may be active, vocal, or simply by being with us' (Kumiega 1985: 208).

From 1976 onwards, Grotowski's attention turned towards a new focus, which he called the 'Theatre of Sources': a multicultural exploration of the ritual, communal roots of the theatrical experience, and an attempt to study their foundation techniques, or sources. In many ways, his study of non-Western ceremonies, liturgies and ritual forms seeks a return to the original, shamanistic experience of inner transformation – of making over one's body and one's self.

The latter two phases especially work towards this 'meeting' between ancient modes of performance score (song, dance) and the highly personal associations which these evoke in the performer through physical response. This process raises lots of questions – for instance about how particular stimuli, which are necessarily culture-specific, may resonate with performers from other cultures. Does this quest for some kind of (historical or material) 'origin' in the realm of the pre-expressive resemble Barba's claims for 'universal' kinds of extra-daily balance across cultures? (Schechner 2002: 297). But it is a form of 'improvisation' which fits into the spectrum of work which uses impro to engage with kinds of otherness or extension of the self.

Although there are some parallels, the use to which Grotowski puts improvisation is, in the long run, clearly different from that of Copeau and Lecoq, and even, though to a lesser extent, from the direction taken by Johnstone and Maude-Roxby. For all of these people, theatrical performance is still the issue, whereas for Grotowski it has been superseded by other concerns, however much these arise originally in the context of performance. But Grotowski's way of thinking and working has had important effects on developments in theatre, and perhaps most of all on the theorisation of theatre – thinking *about* it, developing an aesthetic and a range of theoretical approaches which account for its influence in various spheres. Improvisation is now used widely in other contexts, ranging from 'psychodrama' as a recognised form of therapy, to various educational and developmental applications (role-playing in language learning, in project-centred work in schools, in the acquisition of interpersonal skills in counselling, in training for management or negotiation situations in business). The bibliography lists publications which deal with some of these areas. Part II sets out some of the techniques and exercises available, and we will discuss the implications of the use of improvisation in a wide variety of contexts in Part III. First, we shall consider three key examples of its use in the situations we mention above.

Jakob Moreno: *Stegreiftheater* and psychodrama

Jacob Levy Moreno (1889–1974) was, among many other accomplishments, a renowned confabulator. He liked to embellish the story of his life, making biographical statements about him at best somewhat provisional.[5] As far as can be discerned, he was born as Jacob Levi into a Sephardic family in Bucharest; he preferred to claim he was born aboard ship during a storm on the Black Sea. His mother moved the family to Vienna, where he studied medicine – hearing Freud and Jung lecture – and began his career. He was for a time a tutor to the family of Elisabeth Bergner, later a leading Austrian actress. At medical school,

> he became interested in social issues and started to experiment with ways of facilitating social change, most of which were either weird (he grew his beard long, wore strange clothes and gave up worldly goods) or revolutionary (he worked with prostitutes), or both. (Gale 1990: 85)

After graduating, he divided his practice between lucrative paying clients and the poor, whom he treated without charge.

His association with theatre began while tutoring the Bergner children. There are accounts (perhaps true) of his attracting a crowd of children in Vienna's Augarten park, and regaling them with stories which he improvised dramatically for them. And when they told stories of family problems, he would encourage them to act them out.[6] In 1921 he founded *Das Stegreiftheater* (the 'Theatre of Spontaneity', located in Vienna's Maysedergasse) which operated as a prototypical improvised 'Living Newspaper'. The actors – among them future international stars like Elisabeth Bergner[7] and a youthful Ladislav (László) Löwenstein (who later changed his name to

Peter Lorre) – would improvise in public upon the day's newspaper articles. According to one source:

> *Mit seinem Theater der Spontanität schuf Moreno ein Forum, in dem aktuelle, tagespolitische Fragen, aber auch persönliche Probleme der Teilnehmer nicht nur erörtert, sondern unmittelbar verkörpert und erfahren wurden.*

(With his improvised theatre Moreno created a Forum in which topical socially relevant questions could be examined, as well as personal issues of the participants, which were not simply mentioned but directly embodied and experienced.)[8]

The painter and actress Anna Höllering was a leading member. Her husband, the writer Georg Kulka, told Moreno that she was difficult to live with, though sweet and charming in public. Moreno noted that Anna tended to avoid seedier, darker, riskier roles in performance and suggested to her that she consciously try to confront them. In analysing her responses, they noted that the more she acted out anger and violence on stage, the happier she was at home. This is the key observation from which grew the psychodramatic cathartic process, which Moreno took to America when he emigrated in 1925.

In 1931 he founded Impromptu Theater (more or less a translation of *Stegreif*) and the review *Impromptu*; he was naturalised in 1934. In 1936 he opened Beacon Hill Sanatorium in upstate New York, the site of his most famous theatre of psychodrama, and became associated with New York University (where one of his colleagues was Margaret Naumburg). In 1942 he founded the Sociometric Institute and the Theatre of Psychodrama in New York City. Most importantly, he married his third wife, Dutch-born Zerka Toeman Moreno, in 1949. Derek Gale believes the method

> owes as much to Zerka Moreno as it does to J. L. Moreno. It is no insult to Moreno's memory to say, that he was the visionary and thinker and that Zerka tidied up and developed his vision.   (Gale 1990: 88)

The principal techniques of therapeutic psychodrama – often confused with other practices, both psychiatric and dramatic – require a private space. Beacon Hill had a circular undecorated stage;

some chairs, seating blocks, cushions; a reinforced back wall covered in carpet (against which chairs, etc. could be harmlessly thrown if necessary); a balcony above and behind it; and seating for the spectators. The formal stage is regarded as necessary to form a therapeutic boundary between participants and audience, but its actual shape matters little. Sessions are only ever facilitated by a trained, experienced therapist called the 'Director', who, after a warm-up, elicits from the watching, participating group by a variety of techniques someone who wishes to work on themselves, a 'Protagonist'. This protagonist, the client at the centre of the psychodynamic transaction, tells their story and is then helped by the Director, assisted by volunteer 'Auxiliary Egos', to act it out. The director effectively 'interviews' the protagonist, encourages the re-enactment of a 'scene' and instructs him to 'role reverse': in other words, to play the other pole of a problematised relationship, while an auxiliary takes his role. In a dramatised conversation with a deceased mother, a daughter may be encouraged to put herself in the mother's role for a time. By an intuitive and empathetic process which Moreno called '*tele*' (pronounced 'tay-lay'), the facilitator knows when to intervene and when to suggest role reversal or invite a soliloquy from the central actor and guide the protagonist safely towards 'catharsis' – usually the liberation of affect in tears – after which there is a cool-down period of 'sharing' in which the significance of what has transpired may be discussed and realised cognitively.[9]

Moreno's beliefs and practice are linked to a network of artistic and theatrical work spanning more than a century, whose key points might be Jarry, Brecht and Boal. He begins in resistance: disagreeing with the emphasis Freud – whom he met while at university in Vienna – places on the (bourgeois) individual and instead construing humans as social beings, working with prostitutes and refugees; and, like a cross between Zürich Dada and Alfred Jarry, mounting an All Fools' Day carnival in the Vienna Komödienhaus in 1921, in which he appeared 'in [his] king's boots, king's beard, and king's hat' (Pörtner 1967: 11) and invited the audience to join in creating a 'sacred apocalypse'. The particular target of his '*Konflikttheater*' was the 'historical theatre' which he termed a 'resurrection cult' merely justifying the past, designed for those who 'don't want to live but to be lived' (Pörtner 1967: 11). In 1923, as well as his manifesto *Das Stegreiftheater*, he published *Der Königsroman* (*The King's Novel*), which denounced the deadening influence of Fathers, Kings, Prophets, God and Therapists.

His legacy might also conceivably include Artaud and the Situationists, both of whom influenced the body in performance and the nature of the performance event in significant ways, but for our purpose there are two more immediate and interlinked lines to pursue. They are his work on spontaneity and his attitude to the spectator.

For Moreno, the sign of being fully alive is to be a complete player, to *play* your life to the full. He who plays is most powerfully himself: '*Die Lebensmächtigsten müssen de Spielmächtigsten sein*' (Pörtner 1967: 12). So the spontaneous is a mark of the ability to escape inculturation and all forms of social programming and indoctrination, manifested both externally and internally (for example, as super-ego, for which Moreno constructed the balcony in his psychodrama theatre). *Stegreiftheater* aims to articulate the unconscious, and in order to do so it needs to overcome both gestural/physical and verbal inhibitions: it thus goes further than Freud's 'talking cure' and is closer to the kinds of process Keith Johnstone targets in work to overcome conventions and taboos. (Moreno viewed *commedia* as too stereotyped and conventional: he said it tended to cover up the 'free space for improvisation' with events.)

Playing requires people to join in. Moreno asked Rudolf Königsfelder to design him a 'theatre without spectators' for the 1924 Theatre Technology Exhibition in Vienna, and his intention here was '*die Wandlung der Zuschauer in Zuschauspieler*' (Pörtner 1967: 11), which, with a degree of hindsight, might be translated as 'to change the spectators into spectactors'. Like Augusto Boal (see below, pp. 115–17) too, Moreno saw the 'safe' fictional space of theatre as affording '*Freiheit des Handelns*' ('freedom of action'), and the possibility of articulating what it has not been previously possible to speak. Although the emphasis in Moreno's case is more immediately on the therapeutic than the communal or political, there is a progression in the work of both men, although in a reverse direction. Where Moreno starts with individual process (not forgetting however that he conceives the individual as a group member in a social context), Boal finds a need to address this dimension when concerns which might initially be thought to be only 'public' reveal their roots in the experience of individuals. Moreno's scenarios usually developed by using a number of co-performers to assist the protagonist in materialising his or her situation, often in rapid (staccato, succinct, 'image'-like) succession; Boal's 'Cop in the Head' and 'Rainbow of Desires' work similarly uses a 'row of bodies'

(Pörtner 1967: 12). Moreno particularly emphasises the need to play not the passage of time, but the 'moment'.

The liberating function of spontaneity and play, and the injunction to engage the spectator in the theatrical process, conceived as both social and individual events, mark an important understanding and practical use of the methods and implications of the improvisatory: it can, as many of its practitioners recognise, be simultaneously an aesthetic, a psychodynamism and a politics.

Jonathan Fox and Jo Salas: Playback Theatre

Playback Theatre was founded (also in upstate New York) by Jonathan Fox and Jo Salas in 1975, and has become an international success, with major branches in Australia, Germany, the UK and around the world. The form acknowledges debts to both Moreno and Augusto Boal, and both Fox and Salas were briefly connected with a Connecticut 'improv' group called 'It's All Grace' as well as having experience of travel in the Far East, thus synthesising from many of the different strands of improvisational work we have discussed (Fox 1994, Salas 1993).

Playback is distinguished from psychodrama and from Boalian methodology. Its format is ritualised. The 'Director' of psychodrama is replaced by a 'Conductor' who facilitates the event, and solicits stories from the audience. The protagonist is replaced by a Teller. The auxiliary egos of psychodrama are here formalised into professional actors. The space is kept deliberately open and simple, and reflects the psychodramatic arena (though without the reinforced back wall and balcony of Beacon Hill). The actors sit upstage, on chairs or on boxes. There may be a rail with a selection of coloured scarves, which are the basic props of Playback. The Conductor sits downstage right, with the Teller on a chair beside him or her. When a Teller has been chosen, and has recounted a personal story (the story must *belong* to them in some way), the Conductor will assign actors to roles and say 'Let's watch'. The actors will then enact the events which have been recounted: sometimes from the Teller's point of view and in a naturalistic mode; sometimes in a more stylised form, or from a perspective that the Teller lacks. The events are referred to the Teller for confirmation ('Was it like that?') and may be adjusted or reviewed, before an aesthetic closure is conferred on the performance by the troupe.

For Chris Johnston, Playback is relatable to Keith Johnstone's

Lifegame (with which Phelim McDermott and Improbable have had such theatrical success) in which improvisations cohere around the life stories of a particular individual, rather than to psychodrama (Johnston 1998: 240).

In fact, Fox and Salas's key insight has been to position Playback away from the psychodynamic pole of therapy towards a cooler, cognitive affective approach; from personal, emotional action centre-stage to a more detached, observational stance at stage-right. The Teller does not violently re-enact (with all the potential problems known to therapy of transference and reinforcement) like the Protagonist, but instead *watches* a skilful re-enactment; avoiding metaxis, but gaining the ability to redirect problematised experience from the sidelines.

Playback theatre thus offers the individual the same chance to rescript personal experience that Boal's Forum offers social groups.

Augusto Boal

Boal conceives of theatre as a politics: a practice which unites performers and receivers in an interactive and dialogic mode of engaging with the personal, social and ideological parameters in which we live, in order – as with Bert Brecht, but in a manner more reliant on the process of making theatre than with analysing its product – to open up possibilities for change.

Boal's well-known *Games for Actors and Non-Actors* is a compilation of games and exercises (sometimes referred to by Boal as 'gamesercises' – as in much improvisation work, the two things tend to merge). It is extensive and has become widely used in many countries and many forms of what might be called theatrical process work in which participants are encouraged to articulate their situation. Paul Heritage speaks of 'the most systematic and widely used techniques by which non-actors can discover a means of making theatre' (Heritage 2002: 151). Ultimately the games aim to enable actors and 'spectators' to engage in the various forms or stages of activist theatre promoted by Boal – image theatre, invisible theatre and forum theatre, which later develops into legislative theatre. In the process, however, they draw on improvisation, on an understanding of the liberating personal and collaborative effects of theatre games and the exploitation of the ability to signify and express through and with the body; in short, on an awareness of the outcomes of impro not dissimilar to those suggested by Johnstone, and a sense of its importance in actor training, which itself can be made available to 'non-actors' as a kind of personal empowerment, development or therapy in ways similar to those promoted by Barker, Lecoq, Grotowski and others.

In Boalian practice, improvisation is also a necessary ingredient of Forum theatre, in which a short play or sequence of scenarios depicting a situation of social or political 'oppression' is shown once and then repeated with an invitation to the audience – who ideally recognise the situation as one affecting their own lives – to intervene and speak or act out alternative responses in order to work towards a potential improvement – thus becoming 'spectactors'. The second (and any subsequent) run is compered by a 'Joker' who engages the audience, helps volunteers to make interventions, and decides how far to let each one continue. S/he will also further engage in debate with the audience about the effectiveness or otherwise of the intervention, and lead them in recognising each spectactor's contribution through applause. This is the first example of the need for improvisation skills: a high order of interaction with both audience and performers is required, and each intervention demands a different response. The second example relates to the performers in the scene. Normally the victim of oppression is replaced by the spectactor, though it is also now not unusual to allow the replacement of other characters, so long as this does not result in an unrealistically 'magic' solution (for example, an unmotivated change of attitude on the part of an 'oppressor'). The other actors need to respond in character to the intervention, and to play the scene out in order to test the effectiveness of the suggestion. Here they will naturally have done some preparatory rehearsal of the most likely kinds of intervention to occur in each particular situation; but how the spectactor produces this is largely unpredictable, and they will be required to improvise appropriate responses on the spot. What is required therefore in Forum are two forms of improvisation skill: semi-rehearsed but remodelled character work, rather like that used in 'hot-seating' exercises; and spontaneous interaction with audience, play-situation and play-event. Frances Babbage says: 'Forum Theatre is playfully combative' (between actors and spectactors); and 'elements of unpredictability and creativity make Forum Theatre at its best highly entertaining and challenging' (Babbage 2004: 69).

So the games and exercises which Boal suggests lead towards both of these, in similar ways to those which we outline in Part II: they develop the ability to respond rapidly mentally and physically, to be alive to the dynamics of the play-situation, to work together as a group, and to be able to develop the substance of a character to the extent that it is possible to respond to modifications in the 'script' without being thrown. Babbage indicates the following categories of preparatory work (see also Part II):

Theatre of the Oppressed	*Games for Actors and Non-Actors*
Stage 1: Knowing the body	Feeling
Stage 2: Making the body expressive	Listening
Stage 3: The theatre as language	Dynamism
Stage 4: The theatre as discourse	Seeing
	Sense memory

Key features of Boal's method set out clearly in Babbage's book, which contextualizes his development and both explains the principles behind the training methodology and offers a clear track into his process, have already been indicated in terms of links with Moreno (see above). They include the belief in the power of theatre *process* as personal and psychosocial liberation, which is grounded in the awareness of the role of play in the sense both of group dynamic and of observable modelling of a situation which may subsequently be changed. The use of short scenarios (images, snapshots) to encapsulate key transactions and situations, and the role of a 'facilitator' ('Joker' for Boal, 'witness-director' for Moreno) to construct, comment on and solicit reflection or contribution from audience-participants is common to both (it may however be more accurate sometimes to speak of a 'difficultator', since his or her role is often to prevent easy outcomes and open up alternative possibilities) (Boal, cited in Paterson 1997). Both are noted for their aggression towards what they saw as the repressive or pacifying function of conventional theatre practice – Moreno in his antagonism to 'historical theatre' and Boal – following Brecht – for casting Aristotelian catharsis as an 'Aunt Sally'; and both believe that theatre can be a personal and public/political form of 'therapy' – though Boal might also be suspicious of the use of this term, and Moreno's work becomes almost entirely centred on the dynamics of groups and individuals in social, rather than political, contexts.

Much of the debate around Boal has focused on his somewhat cavalier use of theatre history for his own ends (see Milling and Ley 2001: 147–72) and on his potential status as a 'guru' figure. In the present context, it's worth saying that his use of improvisational strategies is what is paramount for us, and that stands or falls according to its effectiveness in practice. The problem might be if – related to the second issue – this usage were to crystallize into rigidity, which runs counter to the entire basis of improvisatory work. However, whether Boal likes it or not (sometimes he has said that it's fine, at others he has sought to limit the *contexts* in which 'theatre of the oppressed' is practised, though not the selection or use of the components), both the structure (games > image work > scenarios > Forum) and the games and exercises themselves have been very widely used and frequently adapted to particular circumstances and particular cultural contexts. The choice of games and the kinds of 'therapeutic' or 'political' issues which are raised through them need to be very carefully evaluated according to such contexts; the way for instance in which Augusto's son Julian works with urban populations in France is different from how he works with the Indian company Jana Sanskriti, which for over twenty-five years has been using Boal's methodology in rural West Bengal (Ganguly 2004; Yarrow 2007).

Boal's work is conceived as personal and political liberation, as a means of activating response to environmental, social, cultural, doctrinal and political restrictions: a theatre of, by and for the oppressed. The fact that a large part of the training he envisages is made publicly available as 'games' indicates his place among significant practitioners of the improvisatory in theatre and establishes the link between the personal dimension of theatre-based work and its insertion in social and political life. In particular, his concept of 'the cop in the head' identifies oppression as internal as well as external, signalled also in the development from *Games* to *The Rainbow of Desire*, in which Boal focuses on methods of liberating suppressed emotion as a fulcrum of personal and subsequent collective empowerment. The penumbra of Boalian work is now (2007) very extensive, both geographically (well-known groups in France, UK, Germany, Scandinavia, Austria, India, etc.) and generically, and in terms of the impact on the perception of interventionist theatre practice around the world as an ethico-political praxis.

Part II

What? The Practice of Improvisation: Improvisation Exercises

Introduction

This section describes in greater detail the kinds of practice outlined in Part I, and is intended as a summary and source of reference for both students and theatre practitioners.

There are a number of techniques commonly used by teachers and directors of improvised drama. Individuals place different emphasis on different exercises. Some are important only for specific types of work (for example, for creating a very structured piece); others are fundamental to all acting. One thing is certain: techniques cannot be adequately learned from books. Improvisation is learned experientially, in the rehearsal room and on the stage. The improviser learns from his or her mistakes (and, if he or she is clever, from other people's mistakes).

What follows, then, is not a DIY manual on 'How to Improvise', but a discussion of techniques and approaches: those we consider to be part of the improviser's repertoire and others central to the work of some of the most distinctive teachers of drama and practitioners of improvisation. The techniques fall into a number of groups, although they ultimately run into one another, so that distinctions of grouping soon dissolve. Equally, many of the techniques discussed are by no means specific to improvisation work, but are common to all types of drama and actor training. The first group, in Chapter 5, is about *preparation* for work:

Relaxation
Games
Balance and 'body/think'
Space and movement
Concentration and attention
Impulses and directions

The second group, in Chapter 6, is about *working together*:

Trust and respect
Making a machine
Showing and telling
Entrances and exits
Meetings and greetings
Blocking

The third group, in Chapter 7, is concerned with more difficult exercises, *moving towards performance*:

Senses
Tenses
Status
Masks

The last group, in Chapter 8, is about *applied* improvisation work:

Who/where/what?
Objectives and resistances
Point of concentration (focus)
Memory
'Set'
Character
Narrative as generative structure

The exercises lead towards particular *objectives*, which develop psychomotor, cognitive and affective skills in individuals and group relationships. These objectives imply an underlying network of processes and significations inherent in improvisation work. These *active meanings* are generated through impro activities, indicating that improvisation keys into fundamental ways of creating the structure of human existence. In the following chapters we outline the practice; in Part III we will follow up the implications.

Chapter 5

Preparation

Relaxation

Experimental work in drama has always been underpinned by movement theory, by a fundamental system explaining how the body is organised, and how its performance can be rendered more in harmony with nature, or more efficiently controlled. A line (exactly parallel to our history of improvisation) links François Delsarte to Emil Jaques-Dalcroze, to F. M. Alexander, to Rudolf Laban, to Georges Hébert and to Moshé Feldenkrais. Each innovator in theatre or dance improvisation has been influenced by a leading movement specialist, or has adapted their own movement training from a pre-existent movement tradition, such as yoga or t'ai chi ch'uan.[1]

Beginning with Stanislavsky, an insistence upon relaxation is the prerequisite condition, the starting point, from which to improvise or perform:

> One of Stanislavsky's first discoveries was that muscular tension limits the actor's capacity to feel as well as move. A body totally free from tension is essential for stage creativity.   (Gordon 1987: 241)

The actor's primary resource is the body. It has to be fit, flexible and capable of a great range of expressive movement. Everything the actor communicates is expressed through the body, through conscious and unconscious tensing and relaxing of the musculature, which controls posture, gesture, movement, breath and vocal expression. If the body is inappropriately tense, the channels of communication will be interfered with, or blocked altogether.

Relaxation does not mean 'to go limp'. Going limp means that the actor falls over and lies like last week's blancmange on the floor, without the energy or the inclination to get up and do anything. Tension is necessary for balance: the calf and neck muscles are contracted (that is, under tension) when we stand naturally, with the head in its normal, raised position.

The principle of *relaxation*, therefore, in Feldenkrais, gives way to the idea of *eutony*:

> which doesn't mean lack of tension, but directed and controlled tension with excessive strain eliminated. (Feldenkrais 1966: 121; see also Callery 2001: 39)

Clearly, what is implied by 'relaxation' is the elimination of *unwanted* tension – or habitual and inefficient muscle use. This can be temporarily relieved by a 'draining exercise', where physical tension is imagined as a liquid pooling in the body's extremities and is made to 'flow' towards the centre, from where it is 'drained away'. Laban- or Alexander- or Feldenkrais-based techniques for understanding and correcting posture are extremely valuable, as are yoga or t'ai chi exercises. They leave the actor physically composed and mentally refreshed – in the perfect condition to begin work.

Currently the most significant theorist and practitioner of movement is probably Dr Moshé Feldenkrais, whose practice has somewhat eclipsed Alexander and Laban in actor-training establishments. The two methods that bear his name are Functional Integration (a direct manipulation technique used to assist with injury or disability); and Awareness Through Movement (a verbally guided system which liberates students from habit in order to increase self-perception and free movement). His ATM work was introduced into contemporary theatre practice largely by Monika Pagneux in the 1970s; and through her it has come to support the practice of *inter alia* Peter Brook, Jacques Lecoq, Philippe Gaulier, Jos Houben, John Wright – and through them generations of physical theatre companies (for example, Complicité, Trestle, Told By An Idiot and many others).

Games

Theories of play, and the usefulness of games in actor training, are major studies in themselves. We can trace the impact on Copeau and, especially, Suzanne Bing of the time spent at Margaret Naumburg's school in New York; and at approximately the same moment, the development of Neva Boyd's work in Chicago. Both Naumburg and Boyd can claim to be originators in the use of play-based methods in drama teaching worldwide. From their pioneering work – through Bing, Copeau, Spolin, Barker, Yat Malmgren and countless other teachers of drama – games have become a standard, orthodox approach to drama training and to rehearsal.

Clive Barker, in *Theatre Games* speaks of 'taking the pressure off the actor' (Barker 1977: 69ff.). The ideal way to do this is through game playing. One of the primary functions of childhood play is the acquisition and development of motor skills. Games are a heritage we all share, a language we can remember with the minimum of prompting. Most of all, games are *fun*. 'Opening the pelvis', freeing the pelvic joints to facilitate movement, is very difficult to learn, and painful to practice. But sit the actors in a ring, legs outstretched and wide apart, feet touching those of the people on either side, and let them roll a ball at each other's feet, scoring and losing points if the ball makes contact, and the exercise is accomplished automatically. Actors and students *will* stretch their arms, backs, hamstrings to prevent the ball touching them, or to sweep it away to score off someone else, without complaint.

The game takes away the pressure of formal training, and replaces it with a focus which is external and purposive. It *socialises* the training. The body becomes more supple; but so does the awareness. The actor's energy is directed outwards, towards the world and towards other actors. The work is in harmony with the body, and the body responds by flowing naturally. The spine stays erect, the head lifts, the posture straightens, the actor laughs rather than grimaces.

Chris Johnston offers a practical definition of play as:

> Directed activity, engendering liveliness, interaction, imaginative exciteability and the reduction or removal of conventional spatial and temporal boundaries, in an exercise which is releasing and rewarding, often merely for its own sake.   (Johnston 1998: 5)

Games can be played over and over again. The more proficient the players become, the more they become free to experiment and to develop. Games have myriad uses in actor training. Barker's book (subtitled *A New Approach to Drama Training*) offers a wealth of examples of ways to tackle difficult scenes, to encourage social interaction or to release the imagination.[2]

Balance and 'body/think'

Eugenio Barba speaks of the 'extra-daily' or 'luxury' balance central to all performers of codified form (the Western ballet danseuse '*en pointe*'; the Indian *Kathakali* dancer poised on the outside edges of his feet so that his soles partly lift from the ground; the *manis/keras* duality of Javanese movement; even the less obviously codified, apparently naturalistic balance of Western actors, nonetheless trained to erect and centre the posture, orient themselves towards the audience and, sometimes, hold unnatural reserves of breath). He asks:

> Why do all codified performance forms in both the Orient and the Occident contain this constant: the deformation of the daily techniques of walking, moving through space and keeping the body immobile? This deformation of daily body technique, this extra-daily technique, is essentially based on an alteration of balance. Its purpose is to create a condition of permanently unstable balance. (Barba and Savarese 1991: 54)

The answer is that this deformation, this flirtation with instability, dynamises the body and charges the performer's being with energy in the eyes of the spectator. It creates a 'dilated body' – which Barba also terms 'a body-in-life' (Barba and Savarese 1991: 54) – a perception of the performer's presence, and readiness to perform.

The practitioner who has perhaps most developed this principle into a training and performance technique is Tadashi Suzuki (*b.*1939), whose essay 'The Grammar of the Feet' suggests:

> The way in which the feet are used is the basis of a stage performance. Even the movements of the arms and hands can only augment the feeling inherent in the body positions established by the feet.   (Suzuki 1986: 6–8)

Suzuki suggests exercises for contemporary actors which energise the feet and legs (stamping to rhythmic music, squatting, moving in crouched positions, walking pigeon-toed, or on the insides of the feet). They are partly about exploring different forms of balance; but equally they concern the apportionment, direction and reservation of the performer's energies. The lengthy continuous stamping sequence, for example, which is often regarded as Suzuki's trademark exercise, targets the relationship of the upper and lower body, the transfer of energy between them, and the conservation of breath. It is a way of teaching the performer to self-organise, in order to make the whole body speak (Suzuki 1986: 8–9).

Two very simple games can be used to develop balance, and that awareness of the self in space that Clive Barker calls 'body/think', or the *kinaesthetic sense* (Barker 1977: 29). Barker was one of Joan Littlewood's Theatre Workshop actors, and worked alongside the Laban-trained Jean Newlove, who offers a fuller explanation of kinaesthesis.

> Information is relayed to the brain about the state of the body and its ongoing relationship with the outside world. This constant awareness of the current 'state of play', enables the brain to assess the situation and take appropriate action, i.e. unity of mind and body (gestalt).   (Newlove 1993: 63)

Balance is essential to the improviser who cannot prepare to change direction in advance, but must instinctively respond to each new impulse fully and openly. Japanese swordsmen long ago realised that there is no ideal, preset position in which to stand before a fight. To adopt any one stance reduces the possibilities of all other stances, and therefore creates a potentially fatal weakness. The ideal position is 'no position' – a condition of alert or 'armed' neutrality – containing all potential within it. If the attack comes from the left the sword *sensei* can move right and counter-attack instantly, and vice versa. For the improviser, too, balance is that 'armed neutrality', expressed physically as well as imaginatively. The best game for developing it is itself based on the idea of swordsmanship (though Chinese rather than Japanese): the Fight in the Dark.

The game comes originally from a favourite scene of the Peking Opera. Two men armed with lethally sharp swords hunt one another in a room supposed to be pitch dark. The actor has to convey to the spectator the idea of darkness, though his eyes remain open throughout. The swords slash the air centimetres away from the opponent's body and face as the actors manoeuvre in a terrifying and wholly credible dance of danger.

The game version of the Fight in the Dark (under the title the Pauper and the Eunuch) is a little safer. A square or ring of chairs facing outwards forms the outline of the room, perhaps 15 ft × 15 ft, with a single chair missing somewhere around the circumference to provide the only entrance and exit. On the chairs sit all the members of the group except for the two players. In the space lies, somewhere, a bunch of keys – which the players are told represents 'a jewel of great price'. The room is 'totally dark', and in the room, guarding the treasure, which he is unable to see, waits a Eunuch armed with a scimitar (the lights are on, and the 'scimitar' is a rolled-up newspaper). Into the room comes a Pauper – sometimes armed, sometimes not. The Pauper is starving and desperate enough to try to steal the jewel. He knows the Eunuch is there, and he has to find the jewel, and then find his way out again without being 'killed' (that is, dealt a hefty whack with the rolled tabloid). Those are the rules.

The game is played in three stages, with other group members watching in total silence (as far as possible), and commenting later on what they have seen. First, Pauper and Eunuch try to imagine themselves in the dark room, with their eyes open. They *act* the darkness. Then they play the game again, after hearing the comments of their peers (or they can watch two others play), but this time the combatants are blindfolded. They *experience* the darkness. The third stage repeats the first, assimilating what has been learned. When the players are blindfolded, there are a number of marked changes.

The actor's personal space extends to include the other player. The head is raised, the posture of the spine naturally corrects itself, balance improves, the actor tunes in to the slightest vibration in the air around him. The distance between the two players becomes very clearly defined as dangerously close, and the watchers thrill as the 'swords' come ever closer to the players' bodies. The tension generated is often cathartically discharged as laughter in the culminating collision. In the open-eyed version the actor is concentrating on a *result*, on playing the darkness. Blindfolded, he is forced to enter the *process*. His body relearns how to 'think'; how to balance; how to wait, poised and still for the slightest betraying rustle. The audience cannot help but be drawn into the same process, holding its breath with the actors. The final version tries to use what has been learned, with the eyes open once again.

Play is innate. It links directly to the actor's experience, and has pleasurable associations, lessening the actor's resistance to the exploration process. Sometimes, though, it is essential to contextualise the use of play and games. This should always be done *after* the practical session rather than during it, unless absolutely essential. To explain what a game is useful for actually changes the objective of the game: the players begin to strain after what they now see as the desired results, instead of just playing the game and letting the process provide that result naturally and organically. Sometimes students and actors do need to know why what they see as precious rehearsal time is being 'squandered' on games, however pleasurable. Once they understand the intrinsic value, and are aware that there is a justification for each and every game, this resistance vanishes.

Space and movement

The individual actor's space intersects with that of his fellow performers, and with that of the audience, however large that may be. The actor's skill is to *fill* his space, to inhabit it fully: to be *there*, totally, in the moment of performance. This is what relaxation and 'body/think' enable to happen, and allow to be seen happening.

Improvising pure movement in space is difficult. The body quickly loses orientation, and movement becomes aimless, unless some way of imaginatively coping with the surrounding void is internalised. Up and down present few problems; movement works with or against gravity, and the floor is the primary reference point. Now imagine a large, invisible cube, centred on, and moving with, the performer's body. A movement can be seen to grow from the actor or dancer's centre and flow outwards towards a given point (say, the top right-hand corner of the cube). The idea of the cube encourages both spatial precision and the fullest possible gestural extension: it formalises the idea of the kinesphere, and gives it clear spatial coordinates – angles, diagonals, diametrals – towards which the body can reach. Every movement, every foray out into the void, is accompanied by a *recovery*, a return to inward poise and stillness preparatory to the next exploration or offering.

This Laban-derived work is totally compatible with Lecoq's teaching, which also centres on the actor's body in space:

> You can't talk about movement unless you have equilibrium. You must know about the horizontal to undertake being vertical. What we give the public comes from within. There's a link, a reverberation between inner and outer space. If I make a physical action – pulling or pushing – it's analogous to internal emotion, love or hate . . . I indicate passions in space. (Lecoq 1988: 40)

Both methodologies get students to observe things with and in their own bodies, and thus to develop an active vocabulary of appropriate signs in movement.

Concentration and attention

The central principle of 'presence' is mental and imaginative. It is a matter of concentrating without straining, attending and behaving in accord with the situation. Copeau's and Lecoq's work with neutral masks, or relaxation exercises, are ways of tuning up in preparation for this. Stanislavsky, in *An Actor Prepares* (better translated as 'An Actor's Work on Himself') underlines the importance of the principle of 'concentration of attention':

> The eye of an actor which looks at and sees an object attracts the attention of the spectator, and by the same token points out to him what he should look at. Conversely, a blank eye lets the attention of the spectator wander away from the stage. (Stanislavsky 1937: 78)

Stanislavsky's Circles of Attention exercise is very useful for overcoming this. Using first a spotlight in a darkened room, he placed objects within the circle of light, allowing the actor to examine them. The surrounding darkness contrasted with the brilliant illumination of the objects makes it easy for the actor to ignore everything but the objects of concentration. Using a larger circle, including other objects, the actor finds it at first more difficult to concentrate, to attend only to the illuminated area. The largest 'circle' is the whole space, fully illuminated. Now everything competes for the actor's attention, and focus is dissipated, unless the actor learns how to regain the original sensation of 'public solitude', imaginatively selecting the smaller circle out of the large one, and concentrating wholly upon it. The actor's *attention* replaces the spotlight. As soon as concentration wavers it can be regained by this act of imaginative focusing.

A related but slightly different exercise can be done with sound. The actors lie still on the floor and listen. First they listen to the sounds emanating from their own bodies, their breathing perhaps, or the noises of digestion. Imaginatively, they are listening to the sound of their own heartbeat. The actor is still and silent, but concentrated and aware. Next, without losing the first set of sounds, if possible, they expand their awareness to include other sounds from within the room. The sound of others breathing, most especially, as well as the incidental background noises of the plumbing, and from time to time the quiet, reassuring voice of the teacher or director. Then, the actor listens to *all* the sounds from within the audible range. He admits into consciousness the noise of traffic from outside the room, bird-song, people talking along the corridor, whilst trying not to lose the original sets of sounds. This magnified consciousness is too diverse at first, and so the actors are asked to come back to the middle stage, of listening to all the sounds within the surrounding room, and stay at that level for some time, making occasional forays into the smaller and larger regions. Actually, it is the middle level that the actor must learn to operate in. He has to be aware, albeit subliminally, of the whole space within which he operates, and of all those who share it with him. Whenever concentration is destroyed, or misaligned, it can always be pulled back by regaining the sensation of alert stillness, or 'armed neutrality'.

Stanislavsky's Grasp or 'Empty Space' exercise involves each actor getting the other in his or her *grasp* (Merlin 2003, 65–6, 159). Every facial gesture, every physical movement, every sound is instantaneously noted and responded to by each actor, leading to a constant state of inner (and outer) improvisation. If the actors are 'in each other's grasp', the audience will be drawn – like magnets – towards the on-stage action. In this way, they also become part of the communion or grasp of the live performance.

For Michael Chekhov, the working definition of concentration was simply 'being with something' (Chekhov 2000, 30). Franc Chamberlain summarises a sequence of his exercises in developing and maintaining concentration. Picking any object in the room, the student *pays attention* to it; taking in its shape and colour and imagining 'a current of energy' connecting them to it. They then imagine that they are close to the object, and can physically touch and manipulate it. Severing this imaginative connection with the object, the student notices the different quality of interaction when they do not maintain the imaginative focus. Working with a partner, imagining a current of energy linking them, the students explore the range at which they can maintain their connection, and what happens when they break it and resume it. Finally, they work on concentration's opposite, distraction. One partner tries to listen to an internal melody, while the other sings aloud to try to distract them (Chamberlain 2004: 120–1). The exercises themselves are simple, but they operate on the recognition that the connection between self and other (whether person or object) has to be made visible, to each other and to the spectators. It can be imagined as visible and tangible; and the act of imagining this helps to reify the connection.

Impulses and directions

Direction in movement and speech once begun can be worked on. But what starts the movement? Every movement starts with an impulse to move. Whether voluntary or involuntary, all physical movement originates with nerve impulses that activate the muscles.

There are exercises which develop the motoric and impulsive functions, like 'The Starfish'. The actor lies on a mat, curled up, closed and protected. On some agreed signal – say, a sharp noise – she instantly (and without thinking about it first) flings herself into a starfish shape, arms and legs fully outstretched. It doesn't matter whether she is face down or face up. At the next signal, the exercise is reversed. A soft fall-mat is essential if the actor is to feel confident about this.

In this exercise, the impulse to move is both controlled and liberated. The actor knows what movement is to be made, but the random timing of the signal means that the impulse has to be generated and obeyed instantly, without the intervention of 'insurance policy' thoughts of personal safety (which is taken care of for her by the mat, and by having properly warmed up first!). She learns to obey the impulse. The 'backward roll' exercise used by Grotowski's actress Rena Mirecka (described in Part I) is another example of impulse work, involving a sudden shift of relationship.

Jacques Lecoq's structural analysis of movement includes the principle of *eclosion*, a more controlled and fluid movement training sequence, which

> opens up from the centre. It starts from a crouched position down on the ground, the body occupying the smallest possible space, and opens up to finish on the 'high cross' position, upright, legs together and arms extended above the horizontal. Eclosion consists in moving from one position to the other without a break and with each segment of the body following the same rhythm. Arms and legs arrive simultaneously at the extended position . . . The difficulty is to find exactly the right balance and an unobstructed dynamic. Too often the upper part of the body reaches the end before the arms, simply because more attention is being given to it. Eclosion is a global sensation which can be performed in both directions: expanding or contracting.   (Lecoq 2000: 78)

Other key exercises in movement are derived from Lecoq's own experience of sports training, where he identified 'undulation as the principle of all physical effort . . . the human body's first movement . . . underlying all locomotion' (Lecoq 2000: 75), and 'inverse undulation', which leads from the head rather than the feet; between which two poles eclosion is situated. The use of such primal exercises in drama training is to 'lay down circuits in the human body, through which emotions flow' (p. 75). Lecoq, even at this preparatory stage, allows the performer to make a *liaison* between the external and physical and the internal and emotional, because 'in the theatre making a movement is never a mechanical act but must always be a gesture that is justified' (p. 69): movement contains meaning, and movement liberates meaning. *Tout bouge.*

> I ask the students to adopt these positions one after the other . . . to experience passing through the different ages: infancy, adulthood, maturity, old age. The body in forward position, back arched, head thrust forward, suggests an image of childhood or the figure of Harlequin. The vertical position, with the body upright, takes us back to the neutral mask, to the mature adult. The autumn of life, or digestive phase, makes us incline backward from the vertical axis. We fall back into retirement. Finally, old age hunches us up so that we become, once more, like a foetus. (Lecoq 2000: 77–8)

Once moving, the performer can explore and, by exercising, extend what Rudolf Laban called the 'kinesphere', the space that surrounds and is reachable by the performer's body; The improviser has to be able to react within the space to any stimulus, changing direction instantaneously – literally and figuratively. An exercise which prepares for this is to ask the group to walk rapidly across the space and then, on a given signal (a clap, a whistle), always careful to avoid collision with others, abruptly and increasingly radically change direction. This can be modulated into Chris Johnston's 'Walk, Clap, Freeze' exercise, which enhances concentration as it develops spatial confidence:

> The group walks around the space at will. Their task is to respond in different ways to different commands. The commands are given by clapping or verbal instruction. One clap might mean 'walk', two claps 'stop'. Three, 'reverse direction'. The purpose is to fulfil the commands with speed and discipline. (Johnston 1998: 119)

Finally in this section, a couple of Strasberg exercises which promote spontaneity of response in the individual.

> The *one-word improvisation* teaches the student spontaneity in acting. Here the student is told that he will be given a word [either by the instructor or by members of the group] in response to which he must stand up at once and react to the word with action, speech or both. The reaction may be silent or verbal, so long as it is brief, impulsive and unplanned. The word should be a noun: perhaps the name of a country or a word with broad implications such as 'religion' or 'politics' . . . This exercise helps the actor follow his impulses to achieve a feeling of true spontaneity that can be applied to a script.   (Hull 1985: 146)

Augusto Boal uses a similar game, specifying that the response must be in the form of a body image.

Hull describes at length Strasberg's invention of the 'Song and Dance' exercise, originally devised for teaching acting to singers but later used to deal with all manner of acting problems (Hull 1985: 117–30). She quotes Strasberg's often repeated 'Anyone who can do the Song and Dance exercise can do anything on stage' (p. 119) because it is designed to release and make the actor aware of blocked impulses and emotions which it links with vocal and physical expression. It is a strange exercise, quite unlike any of the others we have looked at.

The 'Song and Dance' exercise (which actually has nothing to do with singing or dancing) deliberately disrupts the habitual connection 'between music and the verbal pattern, between rhythm and movement' (Hull 1985: 117). It begins with the student standing still and alone, balanced and relaxed, centre stage. Hands by sides, the actor begins a simple song (a nursery rhyme or 'Happy Birthday' is fine) in a monosyllabic fashion. Syllables are given roughly equal time, ('reduced to rhythmless, single sustained tones': p. 117) and the song may use the melody or be in a monotone, with the relaxed singer aiming for a full and resonant, open-throated tone. Each tone should be stopped before the breath is exhausted. Once the song is finished,

> the student executes a spontaneous movement [which] should be larger than life and should involve the whole body, if possible, though the feet usually remain still. The relaxed arms will natu-

rally follow the body movement. The movement may be explosive. The first movement lasts only a few seconds, but the student then repeats it five to eight times. During this repetition the actor vocalizes syllables of the song fully [sounds, not words] in an irregular, explosive monotone, letting the sound erupt occasionally through the movement ... After several repetitions [with directions from the instructor] ... the student initiates a new movement, which can involve the feet moving (jumping, marching, skipping in place or whatever).   (Hull 1985: 117–18)

The student initially responds to commands from the instructor: with practice, he or she initiates his or her own changes. The new movement is also repeated five to eight times, with the student continuing to erupt the sound as before, and the exercise continues until he or she has worked (or been guided) through at least three different movements. At that point, the instructor halts the exercise and asks the student, still centre stage, to relax and 'to think about what he is *now* feeling' (p. 118), and then to share the thoughts and feelings with the rest of the group.

Given the mechanical disruption induced by the exercise, it is not surprising that the request to examine and discuss one's own feelings often produces 'a flood of feeling and expression connected with the student's own life' (Hull 1985: 118). The exercise appears closer to a psychodynamic therapeutic intervention than a conventional actor-training technique – clearly related to the Method's fascination with 'true emotion' and 'psychic fracture' (of the actor rather than the character). Its benefits are that it encourages the actor's self-awareness, releases inhibitions and liberates blocked affect, opening a dialogue between the student and teacher, or actor and director. It can work diagnostically to identify a student who finds it difficult to let go of habitual physical movements, or whose jerky, involuntary movements may reveal an inner conflict 'between spontaneity and repression' (Hull 1985: 120). The exercise is good at identifying motor problems, physical tensions in stance or motion, and body habits.

The principle underlying all such basic preparation work relates to what Eugenio Barba calls the *pre-expressive*, by awakening and strengthening the performer's body, and establishing scenic *bios*, the actor's presence. Style is a creation of the performer's culture; it may therefore involve highly specific training in a particular performance form. But the *condition* of performance requires a universally identifiable preparation; an internal organisation of physical prerequisites, which training can address.

> Theatre anthropology postulates that there exists a basic level of organisation common to all performers and defines this level as pre-expressive. ... It is the doing and how the doing is done which determine what one expresses. (Barba and Savarese 1991: 187)

The activities we have here classified as 'preparation', or 'training', then, open out physical and mental skills, get the system balanced and alert, begin to work on focus and presence and leave the actor in a state of readiness to work for himself and with others.

Chapter 6

Working Together

Trust and respect

When an improvising actor gets into difficulties, he or she has to *know* that somebody will come to their rescue, take what they are offering and develop it. Every member of the group is responsible for every other.

One way of developing this is the use of 'trust games'. In the 'Trust Circle', the group stands in a circle, facing in, shoulders touching. Each member in turn (and all of these exercises include the director or teacher) enters the circle, closes their eyes, relaxes and leans in any direction. The surrounding circle takes the person's weight and passes him or her upright across the circle. The one in the middle has to do precisely nothing; the group takes the weight, and the responsibility for not letting him or her fall. The actor in the middle gives up responsibility to the others.

The necessary corollary of trust is respect. So much of this work is personal and difficult to learn. The group – and it is almost always *group work* that we are talking about – has not only to trust its members equally, but to have respect for them, for the work and the ultimate goals of that work.

When an exercise is in process, some people will finish before others. They should go quietly to the side of the room and sit down, or remain silently where they are and wait. They cannot just walk out or start chattering to one another. They have to respect the needs of those who are still involved in the process.

Making a machine

One of the simplest ways of getting a group to start working together is the 'Making a Machine' improvisation. One member of the group is asked to make a mechanical and repetitive movement; others join in, fitting in with the original movement one by one, adding their own until the whole group is physically involved.

As well as being about personal responsibility, and following impulses, the 'Machine' exercise encourages listening and observing, and the practising of rhythm. The combined noises are often very musical. If the exercise is repeated, and the students or actors are encouraged to relate physically to one another, by contact as well as by isolated movements, the exercise helps to break down tactile inhibitions. If the first person to begin, once the entire 'machine' has been assembled, is told to move or adapt within it (followed by all the others in sequence) then the 'sterile' machine can suddenly become an organically living 'monster', sinuously writhing and moving as one. This can lead to a whole series of related tactile explorations involving the whole group, which can evolve towards emotional work (victory, joy, anger, control, love, violence, etc.) as the group nears performance.

Another example of this is the 'Laughing Snake'. Everyone lies on their back on the floor with their head on someone else's stomach. If they haven't done it before, don't tell them what it's about. It takes time to get everyone arranged (either in a serpentine diagonal line or, if possible, in a circle, or two lines or circles if it's a big group), so ask them to do nothing, just lie still and compose themselves. After a while someone will giggle. When people lying on their backs giggle, their abdominal muscles vibrate. The head resting on their stomach begins to bounce up and down. The owner of the head usually begins to giggle, too, infecting the next person in the chain. The sound of giggling is enough to set off some of the others and, in no time, there is a room full of people cackling away dementedly, heads bobbing up and down on each other's stomachs. It goes quiet, and then somebody's stomach rumbles, right beneath someone else's ear – and the laughter bubbles up again. It's an excellent exercise for de-inhibiting a group (and, when necessary, for stopping a workshop becoming too serious).

Work with *sound* can extend the feeling of interconnectedness. A group can build up a rhythmic weave from different individual noises (percussive, vocalised, clapped and so on), or explore relationships between the close proximity of sound and physical distance (start far apart, with a range of different pitches and notes; move closer together, shifting through harmony towards unison). The effects of chanting and choric work can be very powerful, and specifically in terms of improvisation they create a strong physical sense of unity, as well as freeing the voice – a significant method of de-inhibiting and relocating the sense of self and its potential.

Exercises from teachers of musical theatre (who use improvisation too) are useful here. A simple 'group clap' exercise very rapidly establishes concentration and a sense of unity. Standing in a circle, relaxed, everyone touches the tips of their middle fingers to the person on either side. 'The object of the exercise is for everyone in the group to clap at the same time' (Burgess and Skilbeck 2000: 54).

The actual object (or 'destination' in Burgess and Skilbeck's terminology) of the exercise is relaxed concentration. The cue for the clap can be overt or subtle, or completely absent, and the game can be played with eyes open or shut. Their 'Concert' exercise explores 'aural awareness', via 'rhythm, vocal improvisation, relaxation'. Singers lie on their backs with the soles of their feet flat on the floor, their heads towards the centre of the room. Everyone simultaneously vocalises an 'ah' sound at any pitch until breath runs out. Each time a new breath is taken, a new pitch is randomly chosen. When the leader calls 'Concert!' the group finds its way to a single note; then, on another signal, the group again returns to random pitches (Burgess and Skilbeck 2000: 61). 'Jets and Sharks' (the name deriving from *West Side Story*) splits a large group into subgroups of between three and six. Each 'gang' devises its own 'code' (a sequence of 'vocal sounds, claps, stamps etc. . . . to last exactly eight steady beats'). The groups have to cross the space, passing through other groups, while maintaining their code as a group at all times. The games teaches 'co-ordinating complex rhythms using the whole body' via 'imagination, co-operating, eye-contact' (pp. 90–1).

Dymphna Callery details a number of rhythmic exercises, citing Fo's maxim that 'theatre is rhythm' (Callery 2001, 118). It makes sense to unify a group through musical means, and she stresses the usefulness of Meyerhold's tripartite structure of *otkaz/posyl'/tochka* (Pitches 2004: 76); *otkaz* is the preparatory counter-movement or 'recovery', *posyl'* the action itself, and *tochka* the completion, preparatory to a new sequence. The arrangement is used to develop the inner rhythmic sense of the actor, or the group, and Callery also lists clapping and sound exercises ('body rhythms', 'clap-clap', 'rhythm-scapes') which employ the Meyerhold structure and lead on to more advanced work on character rhythms.

Franc Chamberlain very usefully digests many of Michael Chekhov's psycho-physical exercises. Chekhov was concerned that we are afraid of ourselves and of each other, and devised exercises – simultaneously imaginative and physical – to overcome this barrier to co-operative work. One sequence which is helpful for group work is that headed (by Chamberlain) 'Making Contact' (Chamberlain 2004: 117). The sequence begins with holding hands in a circle, looking calmly about the group – opening oneself to being looked at as well as gazing at others. When ready, the hands are released, but the feeling of contact is maintained. The group is asked to imagine a giant golden hoop on the floor inside the circle. They squat together and lift it, stretching upwards to release it skyward. Next, the group chooses a variety of energetic actions to perform:

> (e.g. jumping three times in the air, quickly touching all four walls of the room, sitting on the floor, standing still or shouting nonsense loudly). Without planning, and keeping a sense of open-ness and contact, the group should try to sense which action to do as a whole.   (Chamerberlain 2004: 117)

The sequence of actions and interactions continues, building and dissolving groups and partnerships and exploring tempi and rhyth-mic movements. Throughout, performers are asked to invest imagi-natively in the situation, location or action; and to 'radiate' warmth and acceptance to each other, as they attempt to attune themselves as a group, and as creative individuals.

> Chekhov suggested that we need to keep this sense of contact in performance, even when we're offstage. If we stay in touch with our partners, we'll enter the scene at the correct tempo. But we can also have this sense of contact with the set, props, and audi-ence.   (p. 118)

Showing and telling

One of the hardest things to grasp is often the difference between 'showing' and 'telling'. 'Telling' avoids the full physical involve-ment of the body. It substitutes codified signs (words, pantomimic gestures) for full body response. An actor can 'tell' the audience he is 'walking through a doorway' by miming reaching out and turning a door handle and stepping forward (or by saying 'Oh look, here's a door. I wonder what's through here . . .'). The audience understands what is happening but they won't *believe* it. The actor 'shows' us the doorway by first imagining the door (creating its reality in his mind) and then changing his whole posture as he steps from one visualised space into another. When a person steps from a small room into the open air, the spine lifts, the head rises, the eyes change focus. This happens naturally in life. As long as the actor imaginatively re-creates the circumstances and obeys them (creates the 'set' – see below – and conforms to it imaginatively), he will 'show' the audience where he is. If, through haste, he just wishes to signal the change, he will 'tell' the audience.

Exercises to develop the imagination of mind and body are primarily non-verbal. Roddy Maude-Roxby and others use variations of the 'Mime-stick' exercise. The student is given a simple stick (or equally basic object, such as a jumper) and has to assign it a reality other than its own. The stick may become a telescope; the jumper may become a baby. But, whatever the transformation, the new reality of the object has to be conveyed physically, and truthfully, within the improvisation. In early stages, transformations tend to be signalled rather cheaply (we read the stick held to the eye as a telescope almost without the actor needing to do anything else). Notions of 'showing' and 'telling' can then be brought in, and the actors encouraged to use the object as an imaginative trigger for a scene. When the actor's whole body begins to conform naturally to the imagined reality, 'showing' replaces 'telling'. At that point the prop itself will be subsumed into the scene which has been created from it. The audience's attention, like the actor's, will no longer be on the sign but on the signified. We will forget the telescope and, with it, see the ships in the distance.

Entrances and exits

The entry of a new character signals an intensification of energy. The audience knows that the playwright has sent him or her on to *do* something – that is, a new action is about to develop. (Hence the neoclassical system of scene division in play texts.) So entrances are vitally important.

In improvisation this is equally true. In rehearsal, the group watches a scene developing and is encouraged to join in as soon as possible with it. As each actor joins in – that is, enters – the energy of the scene lifts. As soon as it begins to flag, someone else *must* come in to help out. The actors mustn't be left stranded. That is the First Cardinal Sin in improvisation. The new action doesn't have to be highly significant, as long as it's sensitive to either the demands of the developing scene or the energy level of the situation. If this is learned as a principle, then there is very little difficulty in sustaining the spontaneity of improvisation. Actors learn to look after one another, to take the pressure off each other rather than increase it.

Entrances physically signal a change of space. In a development of the 'showing/telling' exercise, placing two chairs in the centre of the rehearsal space, about three feet apart, creates a natural 'door-way'. Stepping back and forth through this doorway, the actor must imaginatively see and respond to new environments each time. The exercise can be done alone, first, so that the actor simply feels the impression of each imagined space. Later, the exercise can be done with onlookers, who should be able to understand from the bodily expression of the actor what kinds of environment are being traversed.

Exits, too, are important. They finish the scene: ending the action for the person departing (though not necessarily for those who remain). Encourage people not to hang around once their contribution has run out, but to think up a good reason for leaving and to play it. This can develop a sense of shape in the actor's mind; making the actor work through every moment of a scene. Sometimes, of course, this will be used as an excuse to get off as fast as possible, but just as often it will open up a whole new reason for staying on.

Meetings and greetings

All theatre is an act of encounter. Characters meet each other and we understand from their meeting how they relate to one another: this is a husband greeting his wife upon awakening; that is an underling receiving his boss into his home; these are two lovers who have been apart. But there is also a deeper level of encounter implicit in the act of theatre. Clive Barker writes:

The theatre is the art of human relationships in action. This defin-ition will apply to modern unstructured forms of improvised drama and rituals as well as to older established forms. In the theatre people meet, and plot is the result of their interaction. At the end the situation is not what it was at the beginning, because human beings have experienced a process of change. Change takes place in the audience individually through their meeting with the actors/characters/dramatist. (Barker 1977: 124)

There are a number of implications here. On stage, *people* should meet, not machines repeating the fixed formulae of lines learned in rehearsal. In one type of theatre (say, the Chekhovian) the implication is that *characters* encounter one another. In another (say, in *commedia*) the *actors* meet – and so do the *masks*.

Exercises about meetings and greetings abound. They include sitting in a circle and introducing the person next to you to the rest of the group; walking round the room and stopping first to acknowledge silently, then to greet, finally to introduce oneself to each other person; throwing a name (maybe accompanied by a ball) across the circle, focusing total attention on a chosen person for an instant. Here the idea of meeting is enhanced by a directing of energy and purpose. In Lecoq's school (just as in Copeau's) the neutral and other masks are used to facilitate genuine encounter. The openness of the neutral mask (discussed below) and the childlike curiosity of the expressive masks makes them (and of course their wearers) especially apt for exploring and meeting the world around them because they encourage the laying aside of preconceptions and emotional 'armour'.

But in performance work the audience, too, encounters the actors, and through them the characters, and beyond them the dramatist, or the idea of the play. This is the deepest level of encounter; an audience comes to meet itself; touching physically (at the elbows if nowhere else) and touching spiritually via the play's depiction to the audience of their own concerns. And the individual audience member encounters herself, recognises some truth about herself in what she sees.

Blocking

'Blocking' – the second cardinal sin of improvisation – is a denial of the possibility of encounter (Johnston 1998: 190–2). Blocking occurs when an actor tacitly refuses to accept what another actor is offering (or, indeed, when he refuses to accept the impulses and ideas of his own psyche). Keith Johnstone calls it 'a form of aggression'. He sometimes uses video to record improvisation sessions. It's difficult at first to show people (even those watching) how the blocking is inhibiting the development of a scene. On video it becomes obvious what has been offered and either missed or denied:

> Each actor tends to resist the invention of the other actor, playing for time, until he can think up a 'good idea', and then he'll try to make his partner follow it. The motto of scared improvisers is 'when in doubt, say "NO" '. We use this in life as a way of blocking action. Then we go to the theatre, and at all points where we would say 'No' in life, we want to see the actors yield, and say 'Yes'.   (Johnstone 1981: 94–5)

There's a good reason for wanting to hear the actors saying 'yes': it offers us a chance to experience those aspects of our 'character' and those possibilities of action which we do not feel confident about trying for ourselves in normal situations. The freedom of the stage action allows us to live a little more fully, and that is also what can happen through improvisation.

As Johnstone says, good improvisers develop action, even when they aren't sure where it's leading; bad improvisers block it. And in blocking action, they deny the possibility of any kind of encounter happening between the actors, and between actors and audience.

Some useful exercises which promote unblocking (though almost everything done in impro works towards this) focus on response situations: making machines and body-sculptures, telling stories one word or sentence at a time, adding noises or gestures to a partner's story. In 'Yes/Yes, but' scenes, one actor is allowed to say no more than 'Yes' (twice in succession) and then 'Yes, but' every third response. There is a version of this which figures in Indian folk-theatre such as *Yakshagana*, where the narrator-cum-director (Bhagavata) (or another character) intersperses 'comments' into an actor's speech, for example, 'Um', 'Ah', 'Eh', 'Oh' and so on. With very little or no vocabulary, the interlocutor can incite all kinds of interesting possibilities depending on tone of voice, timing or inflection.

Gibberish exercises may also be useful here. One used by Strasberg is playing a scene in an invented nonsensical language which has to make sense. A good way to begin is to ask one student to give a gibberish talk on a subject, which another student will translate for the audience. The translator does not invent the meaning, but attempts to derive it from the gibberish speaker (Johnston 1998: 125; see also Fo's *Grammelot*) In full scene work, importantly, the aim is to communicate with the acting partner: it encourages the rest of the body to become involved in signifying; and it makes the actors listen to each other. Each actor forces the partner to become clearer before the scene can proceed.

Strasberg noted that gibberish exercises were particularly useful when working with actors who could feel the emotion of a scene, but found its expression difficult. One actress, experiencing such a blockage, was encouraged to play through her emotional scenes in gibberish, 'and in using sounds and words that broke away from her conventional and habitual tightness, she exploded' (Hull 1985: 115).

Blocking is both a physical and a mental problem (discussed in Part III as censorship and psychodrama), and everything from gentle warm-ups to the most intimidating Grotowskian encounter strategies can be appropriate to tackle it, depending on the context. The things we have referred to here relate mainly to working in pairs or groups, that is, to the importance of unblocking in developing the ability to work together, which is basic to all acting.

Chapter 7

Moving towards Performance

Senses

The actor's senses are of paramount importance in order to be fully responsive to fellow performers and to the audience. They are the actor's only means of experiencing and contacting the world around. Sight and hearing are crucial, of course, but smell and taste and, particularly, *touch*, are equally important. Sight is the primary means of spatial location – remove sight (with a blindfold) and the actor has to reorient physically, and reach out through space. Learning to extend oneself spatially with eyes open leads automatically to becoming more physically expressive – less 'bound' or 'closed' (as the 'Fight in the Dark' game demonstrates).

But the senses also have an imaginative dimension. We have sensation memory, which Stanislavsky used as the key to 'emotional recall' – allowing the actor to get in touch with memories of child-hood, say, by recalling the smell of soap, or the roughness of school clothes. It is impossible to say whether 'emotional recall' is actual recall – or an imaginative creation of the present.[1] But the use of recalled sensory information is certainly central to the process, personalising and concretising the imaginary reconstruction. The group can be taken on a mime 'journey', for example, through an imaginary sensory landscape.

Lecoq makes the journey involve a passage through each of the elements – water, fire, air, earth – and an exploration of how the body functions in relation to weight, speed, balance and so on.

The four elements ... are approached through their different manifestations. When it comes to water, we have to discover ponds, and lakes, and rivers, and the sea. For example, we observe the movement of a body in relation to the sea: it is lifted by the water, thrown back by the waves . . . Water is a moving, resisting force, which can only be experienced by struggling with it. It is only from the pelvis that this overall sensation can be transmitted to the whole of the body. We emphasise the involvement of the pelvis so as to avoid arm- or hand-gestures which would tend to 'signify' the sea without experiencing it. (Lecoq 1997/2000: 87–8)

Lecoq's work is rooted in movement; in mime, he directs the performer away from 'telling' and towards 'showing' through experiencing. The exploration of the elements has far more to do with the performer's body than with the external world, with sensing inner, physical realities than imagining external ones, and it is a highly systematised, structural, even structuralist, approach.

Fire is born from within. It flows from breathing and from the diaphragm. In fire, two movements can be distinguished: combustion and flame . . . Air is found through flight. Running across the room, arms outstretched like a glider, we can sense the possibility of getting leverage on the air, which is not a vacuum but an element that can give support. The whole body is drawn in . . . Finally we work on earth, in the form of clay which we can compress, smooth, stretch. Here the sensation begins from the hands, before spreading to the whole of the body. (Lecoq 1997/2000: 88)

Michael Chekhov's training scheme – disciplining the body to liberate that 'higher ego' which he feels to be the core of the actor's creativity, sensitivity, morality – also makes use of the four elements, but with different nuances. He speaks of 'moulding' (earth), 'flowing' (water), 'flying' (air) and 'radiating' (fire). In the 'moulding' exercise, for example, the mime of moulding clay (in fact moulding the air itself around the actor) is enlarged, and repeated, step by step, so that it becomes less naturalistic, and involves the whole body. Each movement is precisely delineated by the actor, and performed without tension, ruled by the 'sense of ease' which underpins Chekhov's work. The actions are then reduced again, until the smallest of gestures conveys the sensory idea perfectly.

In the 'flowing' exercise, movements lose their isolation and begin to merge into each other, while in the 'flying' exercise the body seeks a sense of lightness, and the movements continue outwards from the actor's centre as if continuing indefinitely. The 'radiating' exercise – deriving from Sulerzhitsky's *prana* yoga work – asks the actor to imagine him- or herself radiating, projecting and receiving energy. Franc Chamberlain, in his book on Chekhov (Chamberlain 2004: 64–8), considers these exercises at proper length and notes that, once the basic physical forms have been mastered they are then also connected to the 'ideal centre', located for Chekhov in the actor's chest (as a Chinese performer or martial artist may speak of *chi*, or energy, being centred in the solar plexus). Through such exercises:

> Chekhov hoped that students would develop a sense of the impor-
> tance of form for the actor and learn to be dissatisfied with 'vague
> and shapeless' work in themselves and others. (Chamberlain
> 2004: 65)

For Ruth Zaporah, 'presence' has something of the 'decided' qual-ity of the Barba body, but little to do with charisma. Zaporah uses it in a more Buddhist sense; her work is concerned with 'how to focus attention on the body's awareness of the present moment' ((Zaporah 1995: back cover). The exercises she presents in this book are in themselves relatively familiar – work on time, space, shape, dynam-ics, sound, movement and rhythm via moving and freezing, mirror-ing and pair work, exploring properties of phenomena like rocks and leaves. Each set culminates in a 'performance score', and 'we must notice what inhibits our freedom, be willing to give up all precon-ceptions, be truthful, and relax in order to act from lively emptiness' (p. xxii). What characterizes her work – as a teacher and performer for over thirty years, starting in late 1960s California where impro was part of 'the march toward feeling' (p. xx) – is a focus on being aware of what you are doing and how you do it, and letting impulses, emotions, movement, interaction and a degree of verbal interchange emerge from the attention to nascent sensation: 'clear, spontaneous expression is not the result of how much you do but rather of the quality of attention you give' (p. 41).

Tenses

Acting occurs in the present tense. It is experienced in the moment of its creation – the 'now' of the performance. That is another reason why we speak of the good actor as having 'presence' – his or her concentrated attention fills the space, and fills the time. It doesn't matter whether the play is set in the remotest past or the farthest reaches of some imagined future: in order for it to be experienced it has to be performed in the present.

But Clive Barker (following Brecht) has importantly qualified the process of acting 'in the present' in a way which throws light upon one of the basic principles of improvisation: the actor's use of the imagination. The performer can vary the tense – and the person – to produce a clearer mental and physical narrative of the action being portrayed. The actor moves from the understood 'I, the character, am doing this', via 'He, the character, is doing this', to, ultimately, 'The character did this' – which the actor then *re-enacts*. He explains it thus:

> The activity of the actor is not the illusory *reliving* of an imaginary event, but the *re-enactment* in the present of an event which we accept as gone for ever, in which we personally had no part, and which is no longer a direct issue. Whatever terms we work in, the actual event is the performance of a play by actors. (Barker 1977: 162)

Actors can discover for themselves the 'tenses of acting' and have little trouble with changing person from first to third, or tense from present to past. But how do you act in the future? Through dreams, prophecies, visions which take you forward into the future, just as memory takes you back into the past.

One director and theorist principally concerned with re-enactment is Richard Schechner. He is concerned with 'restored behavior', or with 'strips of behavior', as the essential material of the actor, separate *from* the actor:

> Restored behavior is living behavior treated as a film director treats a strip of film . . . [It] is used in all kinds of performances from shamanism and exorcism to trance, from ritual to aesthetic dance and theater, from initiation rites to social dramas, from psychoanalysis to psychodrama and transactional analysis. In fact, restored behavior is the main characteristic of performance. (Schechner 1985: 35)

The behaviours themselves, originating outside the performer in society, are the material with which the performer's process concerns itself (whether a Broadway actor in rehearsal, or a shaman).

> Because the behavior is separate from those who are behaving, the behavior can be stored, transmitted, manipulated, transformed. The performers get in touch with, recover, remember, or even invent these strips of behavior and then rebehave according to these strips, either by being absorbed into them (playing the role, going into trance) or by existing side by side with them (Brecht's *Verfremdungseffekt*). The work of restoration is carried on in rehearsals and/or in the transmission of behavior from master to novice. (p. 35)

That is to say, the means with which we work, whether on scripted plays or via improvisation, are drawn from a repertoire of pre-existent and re-membered behaviours.

> Restored behavior is 'out there', distant from 'me'. It is separate and therefore can be 'worked on', changed, even though it has 'already happened'. Restored behavior includes a vast range of actions. It can be 'me' at another time/psychological state as in the psychoanalytic abreaction; or it can exist in a nonordinary sphere of sociocultural reality as does the Passion of Christ or the reenactment in Bali of the struggle between Rangda and Barong; or it can be marked off by aesthetic convention as in drama and dance; or it can be the special kind of behavior 'expected' of someone participating in a traditional ritual . . . Performance means: never for the first time. It means: for the second to the *n*th time. Performance is 'twice-behaved behavior'. (p. 36)

The implication is that although improvisation is never entirely 'pure', in the sense of being created *ex nihilo*, it may still be spontaneous and unplanned, and draw upon these inculturated repertoires which have nothing to do with theatre, and everything to do with living in the world.

While Clive Barker's 'actor-re-enacting-character' theory is demonstrably true, both as a description of what the actor does and as a method of approach, it is rather problematic for improvisers to work in this way. In pure impro there is no past, only the immediacy of the present. There is only action, not re-enactment. Barker's work does have relevance to improvisation, but of a specific kind. His criticisms of improvisation (which he is at pains to point out he regards as both productive and creative) reveal a fundamental separation between two understandings of improvised acting – that which is 'pure' and that which is 'applied'.

While Schechner remains open to the manifold possibilities of pure performance, as excited by the theatricality of a political demonstration as by a shamanic performance, Barker doesn't acknowledge *pure* improvisation at all. He regards it only as a valuable rehearsal device (if properly used) in the service of the traditional play, a process of *programming* the body/think to respond and adapt instinctively:

> If it has not been programmed with a mass of material about the play, the situations, the characters and their interrelationships, it will only produce the material it has, which will naturally relate directly to the here and now, the situation in which the actor is actually present, along with a mass of cliché responses he has learned from other situations. This is not improvisation. It is 'mugging', 'fooling about', a totally self-indulgent activity. (Barker 1977: 89–90)[2]

Barker is right; the production of cliché responses is not improvisation, and improvisation does demand enormous technical prowess. Where we disagree is with the dismissal of the 'here and now', the real situation of the actor. 'Impro' makes that situation its subject. This encapsulates a central concern, to which we will return in the theoretical section of this book, that, when I 'act' in theatre (as performance, rehearsal or improvisation), I both cause something significant to happen in the present and repeat something which has already happened (either historically or conceptually). Improvisation, like all theatre, is both past and present – an enactment of that conjunction. Every time we 'repeat', 'rehearse', 'restore' or 're-enact', we make present the significance of what is repeated but we also, crucially, change it (we *re*-make it) and render it alive in its new incarnation. The improvisatory partakes of and underlines this quality of liveliness, and that's why it's central to much, if not all, inventive performance.

Every actor is the sum of his or her experiences (real and imagined) learned from other situations in life and on the stage: the collection of behaviours to which he or she has personal and cultural access.[3] To draw upon them (often unconsciously) is not to submit to cliché: every actor does it. If the actor is responding genuinely, truthfully, to the here and now of his or her situation, improvisation can be divorced from the preparation process and become the performance itself.

Status

The two chief sections of Keith Johnstone's *Impro* are devoted to *status* interactions and to *masks*. Both are extremely complex subjects and the reader is advised to consult Johnstone's book directly.

Status, for Johnstone, implies far more than just given power relationships, or questions of submission and dominance. The word 'status' is best understood as both noun and verb. It does not simply define a state or condition, the social status, it is something one *does*, or plays.

> TRAMP.   'Ere! Where are you going?
> DUCHESS.   I'm sorry, I didn't quite catch . . .
> TRAMP.   Are you deaf as well as blind?

Audiences enjoy a contrast between the status played and the social status . . . Chaplin liked to play the person at the bottom of the hierarchy and then lower everyone.   (Johnstone 1981: 36)

Status is a dynamic interactive process of continual adjustment. One can work to raise or lower oneself and those around one – what Johnstone calls 'the see-saw principle'. In Johnstone's view, people train themselves in life to become 'status specialists', manoeuvring themselves in any social situation into their preferred position and feeling uncomfortable when asked to play the alternative position. So a lot of his work consists in training his students to recognise and to adapt their preferred social positions. His exercises often centre around scenes in which pairs work together on status transactions. First both will lower status; then both will raise it; then one will raise while the other lowers; finally status will be reversed during the scene. He emphasises that the chosen position should be just a *little* bit higher or lower than the partner's; this means careful observation and delicate modulation. The actors have to learn the subtle dynamics of transition.

Status can be played to the space, and to objects as well as to people. One can, for example, play high status to an empty room – rubbing a finger over surfaces and finding dust will raise one's status and lower the room's. Or one can play low status to a chair – avoiding it because it looks too posh lowers oneself and raises the chair.

One very important point about status information is that it may be all an actor needs to begin improvising. Talking of the 'Method' actor's wish to know all the 'given circumstances' in detail before attempting improvisation, Johnstone says:

> In order to enter a room all you need to know is what status you are playing. The actor who understands this is free to improvise in front of an audience with no given circumstances at all! (Johnstone 1981: 47)

There are many exercises which explore status relationships. Simple ones using distributed numbers or playing cards work well. A large group is divided into players and watchers. Players are dealt a card face down. On it is their status: King is high; Ace is low. As an ensuing improvisation (say, a playground scene, or a courtroom drama) unfolds, they have to play their relative status, and defer to characters they imagine to be higher than themselves while acting high status to their presumed inferiors. At the end of the improvisation, the watchers have to come on stage and line up the players in their status order. It's easy to get the King and the Ace right; trickier for audience and actors to get the subtler distinctions between fives and sixes without practice.

Variations include a number of 'party' games in which participants have a status allocated by the facilitator and spelt out on a card stuck on their back, or on a Post-it note attached to their forehead. They can see other people's but not their own, and each actor has to guess what s/he is from the reactions of the others.

A similar exercise works extremely well for exploring status with creative writers (or for re-animating a scene that isn't working). Cards are dealt to the writers, who are then given a fairly neutral but dynamic starting line to which they have to write a single line response, for example 'Read the note and give me the money'. If the card is a high number, then the 'bank teller' plays high status to the 'bank robber' (for example, 'Your spelling is appalling, young man: you should be ashamed!'). The scene can be developed with further lines/cards. If a scene isn't quite working, then asking oneself abstract questions about the status interactions *might* help: reaching for the cards and writing a high or low status response *will* animate the scene, or clarify the issues within it.

The basic status game is 'Master–Servant' (Johnstone 1981: 62ff.) in which each plays the status of his respective role to the limit, so that the interaction becomes a battle (by grovelling to the utmost, the servant implicitly attacks the master, who has constantly to reassert himself). This game and its variants allow actors to recognise and begin to use status as a part of their repertoire. Like other improvisation games dependent on a rapid response, it liberates the player from any one habitual mode and moves him towards becoming a kaleidoscope of available choices. Important for actors, of course, but equally so for actors as people, because it produces an extension of the range of existential choice, which is the most serious and far-reaching effect of the play element in culture.

Masks

Masks are used in various ways in improvisation and related forms of teaching. Copeau, Lecoq, Johnstone and Maude-Roxby all made or make extensive use of them. We have described some of this in Part I, particularly from the point of view of the aims of mask work. In what follows, aims are naturally also relevant, although here we are more concerned with different techniques or ways of working. Of all the teachers we have mentioned, Lecoq is most systematic in this, since he incorporates work with five different kinds of mask into his training, although recently, Sears Eldredge has systematised his own mask training into a complete course (Eldredge 1996).[4]

In his curriculum for studying and teaching mask technique, Eldredge says:

> Mask improvisation training is an actor training method that sensitizes and frees the imagination stored in the psychophysical being of the performer.   (Eldredge 1996: 17)

The intention behind it is 'to train actors to be more effective in their acting *without* masks', and it starts from 'the . . . "breaking down" of the actor [as suggested by trainers like Clive Barker, following Rudolf Laban] as a precursor to learning methods of transformation' (pp. 18–19).

Eldredge sees the mask as operating this 'freeing of the imagination' in five ways: he lists 'The Five Major Functions of Masks' as: '*frame, mirror, mediator, catalyst* and *transformer*' (pp. 4–5). Both the Lecoquian scheme or progression – moving from neutral to larval mask, and then exploring character masks and finally the red nose, and the ritualistic use of mask to assist shamanic trance or access the ways of being of 'gods' or 'demons', are covered by this taxonomy. Eldredge suggests that the bi-polar either/or view of trance obliteration or acute self-consciousness might be more profitably regarded as 'an experience of convergence' – that is to say a new, synthetic condition to which the transforming mask gives access: the creative '"both/and" duality of divided consciousness' (p. 8). Eldredge is emphatic that

> work in the Neutral Mask always underlies the work in the Character Masks – and, in fact, all performance work, with or without masks. (p. 19)

Neutral mask

Lecoq starts with this; in *The Moving Body* he writes:

> The neutral mask is unique: it is the mask of all masks. After our experiments with it, we go on to work with a great variety of other kinds of mask, which we group together under the heading of 'expressive masks'. While the neutral mask is unique, the number of expressive masks is infinite. (Lecoq 1997/2000: 54)

It is the mask most fundamental to improvisatory work because learning to wear it is learning to achieve the state from which new creative structure can arise. It works as a kind of 'unlearning', liberating the performer from preconceived notions, from any 'recipe'. It requires – almost like a Grotowskian *via negativa* – a complete letting-go in order to reach a condition of unprejudiced being, whilst at the same time one must remain acutely focused and alert, ready to respond with the whole organism.

Lecoq regards the process as a *via negativa*, a process of discovering 'the "yes" of neutral by a series of "noes"' (Eldredge 1996: 50). The neutral mask

> depersonalizes the wearer [while at the same time] it essentializes

the wearer. You discover more of what is distinctly 'you' . . . what is elicited is actually your *individual* neutral. (p. 50)

Lecoq uses this mask as part of the process of 'forgetting': 'Neutral . . . means without a past, open, ready' (Felner 1985: 158). He aims for 'a liberation that permits the mime to rediscover the world in a newly attained state of nonknowing' (p. 158). In this condition 'the individual becomes a blank page . . . Everything is erased so he can start from scratch, seeing things for the first time' (p. 158).

The typical exercises on 'Waking Up' (in which one imagines waking on the ground, without memory, without fear; then slowly rises, looks around, explores), or the improvisation 'Farewell to the Boat' (in which the actor rushes to the end of a jetty to wave good-bye for the last time to a dear friend (Lecoq 1997/2000: 40–1)), ask actors to explore movement and expression from a situation of no prior knowledge, evading preconceptions. Although the features of the mask itself are simply of a male or female in repose, without particular characteristics (latterly, Eldredge has challenged this Amleto Sartori design[5]), it is actually almost impossible to 'behave neutrally' – and this is the first discovery one makes. The body 'sticks out'; one's habits of stance, movement, energy are thrown into relief by the mask's simplicity even in these first, basic exercises. Out of that self-discovery, with patience, the ability to recognise and discard habitual postures and gestures begins to emerge.

> You take on the neutral mask as you might take on a character, with the difference that here there is no character, only a neutral generic being. A character experiences conflict, has a history, a past, a context, passions. On the contrary, a neutral mask puts the actor in a state of perfect balance and economy of movement. Its moves have a truthfulness, its gestures and actions are economical.   (Lecoq 1997/2000: 38)

True 'neutrality' is, of course, unobtainable: 'The image of the individual neutral figure, like the concept of neutral, is obviously an intellectual construct – a compelling and powerful image that can function as an agent for the psychophysical transformation of the actor' (Eldredge 1996, 55). Eldredge suggests six characteristics of the ideal neutral body which would unite the body with the neutral mask:

1 symmetrical
2 centered
3 integrated and focused
4 energized
5 relaxed
6 involved in being, not doing

and, when observed in motion, the neutral body would appear:

7 economical in its use of energy, and
8 coordinated, with every part of the body engaged. (See Eldredge 1996: 53.)

This is the all-important process of getting back prior to habitual reactions and fixed notations, including language. Acting comes later. Lecoq goes on to use exercises derived from Copeau and Bing:

> We play people, elements, plants, trees, colours, lights, matter, sounds – going beyond their images, gaining knowledge of their space, their rhythm, their breath through improvisation. (Lecoq 1972: 41)

All Lecoq's work on rhythm, matter, plasticity and relationships in space is rooted in the improvisations he does with the neutral mask, examining or refusing to allow each *dérive* (detour or digression) that emerges. It is interesting that he also uses this mask for work on the Greek chorus, both in terms of the way it responds as a single organism rhythmically and spatially balancing the protagonist, and because he regards it as incorporating a neutrality that is 'all-knowing'. What Lecoq sees in the neutral mask is precisely this leading into a kind of total and potent organic knowledge.

> Once [the actor] has achieved this freedom, the mask can be removed with no fear of falling back on artificial gestures. The neutral mask, in the end, unmasks. (Lecoq 1997/2000: 39)

Expressive mask

This mask represents a fixed psychological type – rather like Pirandello's *Six Characters*. Wearing this full-faced, unspeaking mask forces the body to find gestures and emotions in direct response to the stimulus it offers. (Some *commedia* masks may be of this type: the difference lies in the degree of intensity with which they are invested.) Masks should never be form-fitting, argues Lecoq:

> masked performance requires an indispensable distance between the mask and the actor's face ... [and so, including the neutral mask] the mask must be larger (or smaller) than the wearer's face. An expressive mask tailored to the exact dimensions of the actor's face or, even worse, a mask moulded onto his skin, precludes playing: it is a dead mask. (Lecoq 1997/2000: 55)[6]

The expressive mask is allowed its detours and digressions:

> Anything that is not neutral is the beginning of a characterization – a turnout with the left foot, or a cocked-back pelvis, a head tilting down, or a loping walk, a movement centre in the chin, or a shallow chest with hunched, curving shoulders. Each of these is a character. (Eldredge 1996: 55)

Lecoq also uses this mask for *contre*-masque; perhaps Eldredge's greatest contribution to mask acting is his use of the *countermask*: not a distinct type of mask, but a method of playing counter to the 'givens' of the mask one is wearing (only, of course, after the actor has discovered them in rehearsal or training).

Beginning with the 'nested mask' exercise – wearing one mask on top of another and shifting one's performance between the two (Eldredge 1996: 97) – actors are taught to use this doubling imaginatively when carrying only one mask: they are asked to play the visible mask, and then switch to playing an imagined, invisible, opposite mask: the countermask.

Observers unite the two contradictory systems (that derived from seeing the visible mask, and that derived from watching an opposed physicality carrying it) into a successful synthesis: a more complex character.

From the performer's perspective, rather than developing two separate characterisations, the actors quickly discover that there is a unsuspected relationship between the inner and outer masks.

> The actor can use the work in the countermask to develop different characterizations or a synthesized, single characterization ...

Mask/countermask is therefore a useful technique for creating characters based either on Stanislavsky's psychological model or on Brecht's dialectical model. (Eldredge 1996: 99)[7]

Impro work with this mask thus leads to the experience of what it feels like to be a 'split' character with an internal conflict; one whose inner sense of himself is always at odds with his appearance, for instance. The multiple possibilities of self-regard and self-deception begin to emerge as physical experiences.

Commedia

In Lecoq's teaching, the essence of *commedia* lies in the fact that it takes stereotypes to the extreme, and is always played at the highest level of intensity. Here too 'fixed external movements and the mask create the internal character' (Felner 1985: 164) so it's a matter of working off the mask through the body, not of thinking up suitably typical actions (or words, since the *commedia* half-mask has a voice; it uses language) in advance. Lecoq progresses towards use of *commedia* masks both through work on breathing and through exercises which raise the level of intensity of expressing emotion: each feeling, for instance, can be progressively 'scaled up' by every new character entering a scene.

Working with expressive or *commedia* masks involves particularly energetic preparation; it can even lead to trancing, as the writers can testify. Fifteen minutes under the Mask of Arlecchino can seem like hours of relentless pressure. When the mask is removed it can take an hour or two to 'come down' from the high induced by intense physical and mental concentration, and perhaps also by changes in breathing due to the mask's demands. This type of work is, in the end, a validation of Johnstone's claims for Mask states of consciousness rather than a negation of them. However, where Keith Johnstone and Roddy Maude-Roxby's work is relaxed and exploratory, this style of mask improvisation is intense, physical and highly technical.[8]

The first half of a three-hour session consists of a devastatingly thorough physical warm-up, designed to inculcate professional discipline, and to work on all parts of the body, especially the legs and the torso. The exercises stress co-ordination, flexibility and rhythm. The aim is simple. Under a mask, it is the rest of the body which must be expressive. The thorough bodily warm-up aims to awaken each part of the body, leaving it ready to become expressive, preparing it to help to *carry* the mask in an appropriate way.

Having selected a mask, the actors are asked to walk around the acting space. At first it is evident that the masks do not 'belong' to these bodies. There seems to be a discrepancy between the mask and the body that is failing to 'carry' it appropriately. So the work proceeds by requiring instantaneous organic response. Snap changes of bodily position, direction of gaze, gesture and so on have to be found in response to the beat of a drum or tambourine. Then the actors are asked instantly to assume a posture which (*a*) involves the whole body and (*b*) seems to suit the mask. As the actors adopt specific, grotesque positions and freeze them, the masks do seem to flicker into life. With the masks 'alive', and all the group working together, the session proper begins. The method is simple enough. Verbal instruction, coaching, comes continually from the sidelines, punctuated by cues from the drum: the group is at a zoo, looking at the exhibits. Over *there* is a magnificent bird of paradise on a high perch. At first the actors imagine the bird and 'pretend' to see it. But then the description from the sidelines becomes more precise.

The imagined bird has a sharp crest with three upright feathers. The actors' heads begin to lift three times in unison as the eyes of the masks – and the *always open eyes* of the actors (for to close the eyes for longer than a blink is to close out the watchers, to introvert the mask) – begin to trace the imaginary plumage.

The beak is long and angled down to the left, ending in a sharp point. The heads and bodies turn, following the line; noises begin to come freely from the masks, expressing the shape vocally and ending up in a sharp point of sound. The actors are beginning to show us, physically, what it is that they are imagining and responding to.

The bird has a magnificent swirling tail that reaches the floor. The actors' heads swirl downwards, and then bob back up again so as not to lose the whole image, and so as not to lose contact with the watchers.

The bird of paradise exercise illustrates a number of key ideas. The mask is a *frontal* medium. It is often difficult to see properly when wearing a mask, and improvising in one is made more difficult by the fear of losing contact with the audience – letting the mask 'go dead' – while trying to keep contact with one's partners on the stage. The answer to this problem lies in a 'whole-body awareness' of the other performers, rather than in the 'eye contact awareness' appropriate to other forms of improvisation (for example, the exercises of Michael Chekhov alluded to above) and, indeed, naturalistic acting.

The whole body listens: it isn't necessary to look at one's inter-locutor in order to convince an audience that one is paying attention, nor to establish and hold eye contact in order to communicate with a fellow actor. It *is* necessary to give one's attention totally and to communicate; but in the frontal style that communication is always mediated via the audience.[9]

The mask has to *show* the audience what it is seeing, with the whole body. It is carried by the physical being of the actor – which starts from a physical posture in some way appropriate to that mask (Il Magnifico's beaked nose is naturally avian and everything else is consonant with that; Arlecchino's mischievous agility goes with the feline smile on his black face). In Dario Fo's famous master-classes, Il Magnifico (Pantalone) is rendered as a fantastical kind of chicken, an ageing rooster whose power has gone for ever.[10] Thus the mask comes instantly alive for the spectator but, as Fo (and Bertolt Brecht) would remind us, there is also a powerful political *gestus* inherent in that incarnation. It is part of the conception of the role, not a gloss upon it. Together with the physical there is also a mental set, and a specific attitude to the character. The mask remains dead without it.

Physical considerations matter a great deal. The half-mask, for example, may depress the actor's upper lip, or the large cavity behind a grotesquely extended nose may create an extra resonator, both of which will naturally transform the sound of the voice, adding and subtracting tonal qualities, and these changes have to be accepted, used and developed. To do anything else is to attempt to deny what the mask is demanding of the actor. Finding this physiological qual-ity is a measure of integration of actor and mask.

Once the technical skills have been inculcated, the teachers home in on each mask in turn, providing the performer with a constant source of stimulation. They instruct ('Keep that voice'; 'Look at us!'). They ask questions ('What's that you're holding? Show it to us. Do you like it? Aren't you proud of it?'). Sometimes they cajole and flatter; at other times they seem to want to belittle or humiliate the mask ('You're boring!'), until the mask responds with something new, or something true. Sometimes the sideline coaching is more belligerent; they refuse to accept an explanation, say, or demand that it be sung first, or spoken like Shakespeare, or danced (while keep-ing the basic posture). This serves to renew energy and continually to pull the focus outwards, away from any relapse into introversion.

They pick up on every little thing the mask is doing, or failing to do, and instantly suggest a way of extending or developing what is happening. 'Camera Two has packed up and we didn't quite get that, love. Could you do it again for Camera Three over there?' The mask loves being the centre of such attention and happily repeats and enlarges the activity. Or they suggest that the mask freezes certain moments ('A few shots for the publicity people'). The mask, happy to oblige, naturally begins to find those fixed points, those moments of stillness which allow the action to be clearly read.

This form of mask work is difficult and initially scary, in that it involves overcoming resistance (arising from a lack of trust in oneself, but liable to be transferred to the teachers and the work) and operating at intense pressure under constant 'nagging'. It also requires discipline: once the mask is on, the actor has to stay within that mental set.

But if these conditions are accepted – and in the end they represent that willingness all improvisation work aims to initiate, to prise open the protective shell of the narrowly conceived self – the results can be exhilarating. Some students reach and sustain a high level of creativity very quickly. One mask, on trial for the theft of a can of soup (from a soup-ermarket), spontaneously made up and performed a rhyming aria on the merits of various brands of broth, while another operatically demanded the soup-reme penalty for the malefactor. Students who find it difficult to give their whole body to a performance (scripted and rehearsed as well as improvised) can be coached through a revelatory learning experience while wearing a mask.

Larval mask

Larval masks are abstract forms. A subcategory of the expressive mask, naive and non-human yet evoking psychic and emotional states, they lead, like the neutral mask, to a kind of precognitive situation where physical gesture precedes emotion and both precede conceptualisation. Larvals usually focus facial characteristics on one feature – a bulbous nose, bushy eyebrows – which thus stands out and 'speaks' for the whole face/personality: wearing them, actors experiment with the position of different parts of the body and discover that emotional changes may result. Lecoq's hierarchy, similar to Copeau's, runs from gesture through emotion and then to thought and finally language. The *mime de fond*, which Lecoq also calls *mime du début*, arises at the gesture level. The Lecoq-trained Swiss company Mummenschanz use larval masks (which derive in part from the masks of the *Fastnachtspiel* of Basel) which are power-fully evocative, working at a kind of pre-verbal level. The English troupe Moving Picture Mime Show also centred their work on the larval mask, as do the celebrated Trestle Theatre Company.

Trestle have used masks, particularly larval masks, since their inception. Gill Lamden's book on devised drama has a useful section on Trestle, describing their working processes and use of masks. (Lamden 2000: 19–29) Toby Willsher ascribes importance in devising to 'letting go'; and explains that 'what masks do best is interact'. Painstaking choreography results in freedom to play; scenes are built around kernels, called 'coathangers', with minimal verbal description (Lamden 2000: 20, 27, 29, 21).

Callery comments that, despite a drift towards whimsicality in later years,

> Trestle's highly legible, visual style forces the audience to 'read' the thoughts of the character in movement, as the masks do not speak . . . [Their] genius has been to see the connection between the emotional charge of mask work and naturalism. (Callery 2001: 51)

Clown (red nose)

For Lecoq, this smallest mask is the ultimate in self-revelation: 'self-humour is the only true alienation effect' (Felner 1985: 166). Here one confronts and confesses by sharing what one normally represses: brings out one's 'shadow', as it were, and lets it dance in the light. As with all mask work, the 'technique' has to do with *not* acting, with letting the mask speak. Here, it speaks for the self, and the actor is most naked, most offered to the audience.

Uses, problems, methods

Dymphna Callery ascribes much of the resurgence in British mask work to the influence of Lecoq-trained John Wright (Callery 2001: 51) as well as to the influx of other Lecoq trainees. Companies like Trestle, Improbable and Geese exemplify the uses to which masks can be put in devising shows.[11] None of these companies can easily or reductively be described; masks and improvisation are creative means rather than ends for all of them, but all are distinguished by the inventiveness with which they use them.

Geese use masks whose form lies between the larval and the expressive for their work with offenders; each signals a single psychosocial 'attitude' ('it's not my fault'; 'don't give a toss') and enables the wearer rapidly to explore its effects on the group. Improbable's work is rooted in Keith Johnstone; they define themselves as 'yes-sayers', leave unscripted gaps in their productions, and are often deliberately cavalier about learning lines in order to maintain the sense of excitement about being on stage (Lamden 2000: 30–1): their work 'blurs the distinction between process and product'. Co-director Phelim McDermott claims that the use of masks was revelatory:

> To play someone from a totally different culture and learn about their story can be a real honour. In San Diego we used Julian [Crouch]'s techniques of building masks on people's faces quickly and we got this guy to play his Great Grandmother who used to tell him stories about the American Civil war when he was a kid. It was spooky . . . like she was there. It is the closest I've come to experiencing some kind of channelling experience, being connected to this point of history generations back.   (Svich 2003)

Masks may take the actor back to the original state of transformation – the shamanic act of self-annihilation. They allow the transformation to happen safely, providing a format within which a new, creative self can appear. Thus they are crucial in improvisation work. But there can be problems. Johnstone in particular uses a kind of 'magical language' when speaking of the power of Masks – implicit in his capitalisation of the initial 'M' (Johnstone 1981: 143–4). It is perfectly possible to put on a mask (small 'm') and pretend to be someone else. But Johnstone is concerned with the induction of trance states in the performer via mask work. For him, it is almost impossible to define the changes wrought in the performer by the assumption of a mask without resorting to terms like 'possession'. For most European and American actors, it is probably more useful to refer to the understanding of John Emigh, who documented masked performances of all kinds throughout Papua New Guinea, India and Indonesia, that the masked state is paradigmatic of the 'relationships between self and other (and self and self) that lie at the heart of the theatrical process' (Emigh 1996: xvii).

It is true that in some non-Western theatre, the mask is still frequently seen as the repository of something not entirely human.

Despite this, and in spite of often lengthy ritual preparation and/or make-up processes designed to induce a trance-like state, performers are often surprisingly matter-of-fact about what they do, freely inhabiting two quite dissimilar worlds simultaneously. Issues about trance and transformation are too complex to explore further here (see, for example, Coldiron 2004 for an extended discussion); but the crucial thing from our point of view is that however you work with a mask – meditatively, as with the neutral or in *Noh*; dynamically, as in *commedia*; or 'shamanistically', as with McDermott's description above or the Balinese performer who searches 'for the meeting place between himself and the life inherent in [the mask's] otherness' (Emigh 1996: 275) – you are targeting a mode of extended being, knowing and acting. So it is appropriate to be matter-of-fact but also precise and disciplined.

To begin it is helpful to let the masks do the talking, as it were. Actors can be asked to encounter the masks as characters, encouraged to find out about them – what they like to do, whom they like to be with and so on – treating them rather like intelligent children, perhaps. The actors could be childlike (never childish) too, and begin simply by putting them on and seeing what the mask suggests to them. Mirrors can stimulate and later 'recharge' the masked actor, but should not be overused. Far more essential is for the actor to work off the *feeling* experienced in the mask and the *feedback* received from the audience. Too much gazing in the mirror tends to trap the wearer into unproductive narcissism.

Too little respect, and the masks will remain lifeless cardboard props; but too *much* respect – treating the masks as if they were truly the repositories of ancient demons – can stifle creativity altogether. Masks begin work by ambushing their wearers. If the atmosphere is good, the work respectful, open, honest and good-humoured to begin with, the mask will animate the actor rather than the reverse. But it is essential that the work be undertaken with care, so as not to stifle the emergence of that new self. A good way is to encourage the actors to make and to decorate their own masks – and from as many materials as possible (paper, papier mâché, leather, wood, plaster bandage, photographs stuck on cardboard). What is important here is the emphasis on working *with* the mask, developing a relationship with it from which the new self can emerge, as a seamless – but never entirely *comfortable* – 'fit' between mask and actor's body.

Eldredge's book presents a training in mask improvisation.[12] The programme includes:

The Learning Objectives
- experiencing release from the tyranny of the analytic, the critical, and the logical in the flow of the improvisation;

- discovering that masks demand total commitment (physical, mental, emotional) to make them come alive;

- discovering how to use the total bodymind economically and appropriately, and therefore effectively, to communicate;

- discovering and utilizing the techniques of playing with and against the mask (text), thereby creating and developing mask and countermask, public face and private face. (Eldredge 1996: 22)

Ground Rules for Mask Improvisation
Many of these are appropriate to all forms of drama training and to improvisation exercises.

1 Have respect for the mask.

2 Work on yourself and for yourself until told to do otherwise.

3 Work in silence.

4 Avoid touching the mask while wearing it.

5 Keep the separation clear between your Self and your mask. (A participant should not speak in her own voice in the mask. The mask does not talk with her voice: it has its own voice.)

6 When you are told to stop and come out of the mask, you will do so.   (Eldredge 1996: 42)

Ultimately, the 'trance' or power to change is not in the *mask*: it derives from the conjunction of mask, actor and audience. The wearer responds to stimuli both from the mask and from teachers and/or audience: what is involved is a dynamic process of co-creation.

In this chapter we have looked at a variety of ways of developing whole-body awareness, opening up the actor's resources and developing his or her performance vocabulary. In the process the imagination is liberated and rechanelled to offer the possibility of new physical and intellectual invention and expression.

Chapter 8

Applied Improvisation Work

Who/where/what

The 'who/where/what' exercises stem primarily from the work of the American teacher of improvisation Viola Spolin (Spolin 1963). Keith Johnstone finds this technique unhelpful (Johnstone 1981: 27), but this is because his aims are different. We have found it most useful in the creation of a consistent piece. It concentrates the attention, and removes distractions, without limiting creativity. It gives the actor something to start with, and to build upon. Given either a 'who', a 'where' or a 'what', the actor can create the other two. Given nothing, the actor can still choose one of these and generate a consistent and coherent piece of improvisation – and a writer faced with a blank page can use the same exercise to initiate a scene or an entire play (*Hamlet* begins with *the* fundamental stage question: 'Who's there?'). For example, the 'who' might be a 'farmer': this suggests the 'where' (in a field), and the 'what' follows quite naturally (planting potatoes). But the 'who' might as easily be 'yourself', in the same field doing the same thing – or some other 'where' doing something else – 'drawing the short straw', for instance (see Callery 2001: 166). Or the 'who' might be the character that one is developing in a formal, scripted play (or an action or a location) – which can then be examined carefully in another context. The exercise asks that the imagination remain constant to the 'set' chosen or specified. If the 'who' is a king, the actor has a constant imaginative focus to return to: he must behave consistently like a king (which implicitly involves status work too) or consciously choose to alter the imaginative set.

The 'who/where/what' exercise can overcome the automatic tendency of any group of inexperienced improvisers to 'play for laughs' at inappropriate moments – to make the scene as absurd and laughable as possible. The reasons for doing this are fourfold. First, the actor hasn't entered fully into the piece, either through not concentrating or not listening to what the other actors have created. Second, it's a subtle but very aggressive form of 'blocking', which rejects the creativity of the other performers (effectively saying 'no' by ironising their work). Third, it's an easy way out, avoiding the responsibility of having to remain consistent and 'true' to the situation. Fourth, it evinces a deep insecurity about this type of work felt by the actor.

This fourth type of response is very common. In a scripted play, the actor has a set of reassurances to rely on: the rehearsal process, the learned moves and gestures, the other actors doing preordained things. Above all, the actor *knows where she's going*; she knows what the outcome should be like, and works towards that.

In improvisation the actor doesn't know where she's going, and isn't always comfortable going there. She isn't sure that she doesn't look very foolish. Her defence against this can be to make the scene funny. It disarms criticism and, at the same time, gives the actor the reassurance that those watching accept that what she's doing works (they laugh). Del Close warns: 'The most direct path to disaster in improvisation is trying to make jokes', and stipulates: 'Don't try to make jokes in improv! ... the most effective, satisfying laughs usually come from an actor making a connection to something that has gone before' (Halpern et al. 1994, 26).

The 'who/where/what' discipline helps to remove actors' anxieties and blocks. It gives the performer a reassuring and familiar structure within which to operate, and insists that the creativity keep within the bounds of the initial idea. It's another way of taking pressure off, without losing genuine spontaneity.

Spolin's 'disciplined' approach doesn't preclude the fantastic: action, characters and setting can be as absurd or outlandish as the imagination can make them, and the exercise is always a useful generator of narrative capacity, zany physical humour and enjoyable group process. Dymphna Callery documents a number of instances where devising groups have implicitly worked in this way, tracing its heritage to the *commedia* starting point of given characters (Callery 2001: 165). Make one of the constituents odd or frame-breaking, and there are invitations to stretch imaginative response in other ways (examples we have used in urban and rural environments in the UK and India include: patients, pineapple, waiting room; fisherfolk, dinosaur, river). But Spolin's formal method is less purely generative, less likely to overcome internal censorship, than Keith Johnstone's freer 'impro' work; it is perhaps best applied, therefore, to specific exercises on plays, to play writing, and to the improvised creation of sustained and 'true-to-life' scenes.

Objectives and resistances

Improvisation workshops and rehearsal situations are great ways of teaching fundamental principles of acting *and* dramatic theory. A group of students will 'discover' many of the major theories of acting for themselves, among them the Stanislavskian idea of the 'want' or 'intention' and how to play it against the conflicting wants of other characters. This playing of 'objectives and resistances' can work in some very strange ways, and not only ways connected with Stanislavskian theatre.

For example, an actor wants to pass through a doorway. What might happen if the doorway (played by another actor) chose to resist him – or if he imagined that it did? He would have to talk or fight his way through, or invent a way round or over the obstacle. Almost any set of circumstances can be dramatised by the idea of resistance.

Exercises to discover this may start with an individual actor walking in different imaginary physical circumstances (through waist-deep water, through treacle, on ice, over hot sand, through a shrinking space, etc.), which problematise the simple act of walking. Lecoq's guided exercise through the elements extends this into a developmental sequence of physical actions. This may proceed to simple physical group improvisations with one member attempting to achieve a simple task while the rest find ways to baulk him or make the task difficult. The resistance serves to make the stakes clear: how important is it to achieve this task, action or sequence, to articulate this idea or make this request? Spoken improvised scenes can explore performance modes (melodramatic, absurdist, political, naturalistic) in which a series of basic interactions are similarly problematised. Melodramatic: hero wants girl, but villain abducts her; absurdist: hero wants girl, girl loves an aardvark; political: girl and boy want each other, but the world is out of joint; naturalistic: they want each other but each thinks the other is gay.

The principle of resistance can be utilised in the generation of improvised speech, and in the process of writing. It's implicit in the idea articulated by Halpern and Close that 'finding the action' of a developing improvisation is dependent on recognising the *event*: 'the situation that makes this day different from all the rest' (Halpern et al. 1994: 81–2), which they relate to Keith Johnstone's idea of the interrupted routine. Red Riding Hood's encounter with the wolf, in Johnstone's terms, is an interruption of the routine of taking goodies to Grandma, which the audience responds to as eagerly as she does. Johnstone sees resistance functioning to disrupt routinised narrative and avoid what he calls 'cancelling': the unfortunate gravitational tendency of actors – and writers – towards closure in scenes, cancelling out the energies they have liberated and failing to move the narrative forward. Scenes (improvised or written) which go nowhere can be transformed by the simple discovery that there is a routine at their root which needs to be disrupted, made difficult, looked at afresh (Johnstone 1981: 138–40).

Whenever a scene is flagging, or lacking in impact, it helps to devise or strengthen a resistance, and make the actors overcome it. This invariably produces new improvisations. The Stanislavskian terminology is very useful, keeping the 'want' active by shaping the idea (always using the most active verb possible) and getting the actor to concentrate on physical objectives.

Point of concentration (focus)

Viola Spolin uses the term 'points of concentration' (abbreviated to POC) as the focal point of her system. She regards it as the 'ball' with which the game is played. It relates to concentration of attention as already discussed, but disciplines the work and enables each exercise – and moment of performance – to be worked on in isolation. Most of her exercises have a specific POC to which the performer can attach herself, enabling the aspects of acting to be separated out and put together afresh (she also provides for evaluation of each exercise and gives the session leader a 'point of observation'. For example, describing an 'orientation session' in which a single performer becomes involved with a large, entangling object, she writes:

POINT OF CONCENTRATION: on the selected object.

EXAMPLES: spider web, boa constrictor, tree branches in forest or jungle, octopus, parachute, man-eating plant.

POINT OF OBSERVATION: Watch the wording when stating the POC to be certain that the player's concentration is on the object and not on disentangling himself from the object. This is an important difference and one which comes up continuously throughout the work. (Spolin 1963: 77)

Many of Spolin's exercises evoke and liberate the emotionality inherent within a situation, Her *'theme-scene'* exercises exemplify this. 'Theme' she describes as 'the moving thread (life) that weaves itself into every beat of the play and unifies all the elements of the production' (p. 394) in terms clearly reminiscent of Stanislavsky's 'through-line of action'. 'Scene' is defined as 'an event that grows out of the POC' (p. 390). A scene is

[t]he results of playing; a fragment; a moment in the lives of people needing no beginning, middle, or end . . . The scene is the game coming out of the rules; playing is the process out of which the scene evolves by involvement with an object (the POC) and relationship with fellow players. (p. 390)

The theme-scene exercise takes as its starting points a given theme (an 'activating phrase' often randomly selected or distributed to acting groups) and a place (a 'where' or setting). The group's point of concentration is the 'constant repetition of the theme'. She gives an example theme, 'The World Owes Me a Living', and sets the scene on a city rooftop.

Two sweethearts on a New York tenement roof during a hot summer night. They are tense over the problem of her pregnancy, for he is not willing to take the responsibility of marriage and parenthood. He feels himself to be an artist, and nothing will make him take a drudging nine-to-five job. He is 'special' and feels indeed that 'the world owes me a living'. The girl commits suicide by jumping off the roof. (p. 219)

By no means all Spolin's improvisations are as emotionally fraught (or as melodramatic) as this, and she clearly recommends that the theme-scene exercise be introduced only after several months of preparatory work. She is also concerned that the theme-scene implicitly privileges narrative and can 'lapse into group play-writing'. But, at its best, the theme preoccupies and moves the players (as object), rather than them manipulating it (p. 219). The totality of *structure* (Where-Who-What), *object* (POC) and the imaginative essential of group *agreement* (a consensually established reality between players, and between players and audience, 'our guests') Spolin defines collectively as 'The Rules of the Game' (p. 390).

Spolin's work is highly systematised and at first may hardly seem to relate to Johnstone's pure spontaneity of response. But she is concerned with focusing the individual performer – child, student or professional – very tightly onto the work at all moments during training in order not only to liberate, but also to *channel* that spontaneity.

Memory

Andrea Perrucci wrote in 1699 about the internal consistency of improvised comedy:

> The actors must, above all, be careful not to make a mistake with regard to the country where the action is going to take place; they should realise whence they come, and for what purpose; the proper names must be kept well in mind . . . actors must pay attention to the distribution of the houses, so that each player may know his own house, for it would be too ridiculous for anyone to knock at or enter into somebody else's house instead of his own: one would regard such a person as a booby or a drunkard. (quoted in Nagler 1952: 258)

In any kind of consistent piece, memory plays a large part. It stores the 'rules of the game' and allows the player to improvise within them. Memory games are, therefore, very useful as 'mental warm-ups'. The most basic examples are the numerous name-games found in all handbooks and manuals, which rely on a combination of movement, rhythm, sound, attention and recall. Slightly more demanding but still simple games of mental concatenation can be great fun. Player 1 announces that she's going to a party and taking 'some yellow jelly'. Player 2 announces that he, too, is off to a party and is taking 'some yellow jelly and a trilby hat'. Player 3 (by a great coincidence) also has an invitation to a party and plans to take 'some yellow jelly, a trilby hat, and a dustbin full of red knickers'. The game passes to Player 4 and so on around the circle until it arrives back at Player 1 who has to reel off the whole string of unlikely objects. It's good, too, if the players can relax into this, and have an attitude to what they are taking (maybe 'yellow jelly' is yummy!) If anyone breaks down, or goes wrong, the game starts all over again from the beginning with new objects. After a few breakdowns, the relationship between concentration, memory and the body is quickly learned. The mnemonic tricks for learning which we all possess are sharpened in an enjoyable way.[1]

'Set'

A paper by the Georgian psychologist R. Natadze poses the following question:

> When, with a spontaneity convincing to the spectators, the actors acts in conformity not with a real, but with an *imagined* situation imposed upon him by the play, embodying thus in his stage performance experiences and conduct not his own – what is the psychological mechanism of such behaviour?   (Natadze 1962: 421)

Natadze implicitly recalls Diderot's *Paradoxe sur l'Acteur*, and the controversy between the ideas of 'real feeling' versus 'cold virtuosity'. His hypothesis is that it is

> *fixated set* evolved on the basis of picturing to oneself the particular imaginary situation imposed by the play that constitutes the foundation on which stage impersonation rests.   (p. 421)

His experiments with gifted actors and promising students of the Tbilisi Theatrical Institute, as well as with non-actors and a comic performer, strongly suggested 'a high correlation between the ability to evolve a set on the basis of imagination and the capacity for stage impersonation' (ibid., p. 421).

'Set' means a mental construct, a set of rules which apply to the world of the play, which then becomes 'fixated' through rehearsal. The actor has the ability to behave in conformity to that 'set', even though it isn't real. The non-actor finds it difficult (and the comedian finds it downright impossible!).

Natadze's work implies that actors have a combination of a powerful imagination allied to strong concentration (which enables them to hold on to the construct and to shut out perceived contradictions). His work rewrites Stanislavsky in psychological terms. But that is in itself important.

The improviser makes use of Stanislavsky's 'magic If' all the time. And he does so without the benefit of rehearsal to fixate the evolved set. He plays the set *as it evolves*. So the improviser must be trained in the evolution of set, of imaginary and self-consistent worlds. His training must encourage him to accept and act upon them – to go with the products of his imagination as if they were real, to accept their rules and statements as if they were not fantasies – which bleeds out into the key rule for acting in farce, which is for the performers to behave as though everything taking place is entirely normal.

Character

Although in *pure* improvisation ('impro'), character is not key, in *applied* improvisation, rehearsal 'improvs', character is the dominant concern. Actors undertake improvised explorations about 'previous circumstances'; for example, meetings between characters that have happened before the action of the play begins.

This exercise puts the *actor* in a situation where he has to respond 'as if' he were the person he portrays. It allows the actor to develop what Natadze calls 'set', and practise being within it, with other actors, exploring its rules and its boundaries. And as Stanislavsky (in the person of 'Tortsov' guiding the student 'Kostya') wrote:

> Now I hope you realise the difference between approaching and judging a role in your own person and in that of another, between looking at a role with your own eyes instead of those of the author, or director, or drama critic.
>
> In your own person you live your role, in the person of someone else you simply toy with it, play-act it. In your own person you grasp the role with your mind, your feelings, your desires, and all the elements of your inner being, while in the person of another, in most cases, you do it only with your mind. Purely reasoned analysis and understanding in a part is not what we need.
>
> We must take hold of the imagined character with all our being, spiritual and physical. That is the only approach I am willing to accept. (Stanislavsky 1963: 182)

The improvisation is not about the *character's* inner life, but about the *actor's*. It awakens responses in the performer which are primal, and personal. Afterwards, they can be analysed and adapted and assimilated into the actor's conception of the role. As they are happening, though, they force the actor to respond directly and imaginatively to the situation, to see her fellow actors as the characters they are portraying and to respond to them within the agreed rules of the 'set' they are jointly constructing. They tighten concentration on the role, since distractions will destroy the edifice the actors are building, and the greatest distractions arise from her own intrusive thoughts. The actor is given no time to think, to stand back and judge, to split herself into simultaneous performer and critic. And it makes the acting company into a genuinely creative ensemble, involved in the 'writing' of their own play, bonding them and tuning them into their own group wavelength.

In approaching this situation, structure and clarity are important. Clive Barker says:

> I rarely use free improvisation, preferring to use some games activity as a structure within which the actors can improvise.
>
> The principal use of improvisation, as far as I am concerned, is to overcome the actors' failure to penetrate the text to the actions which underlie it. The words make sense, but have no real meaning. (Barker 1977: 167)

Improvisation work before textual rehearsal begins bonds the group and establishes a common language and way of working. It may also, in group creative enterprises, begin to evolve any aspect of the piece, whether for Mike Leigh or Improbable or Boal. But working on a pre-existing text at an early stage, and avoiding mere verbalisations, with actors standing, talking and *explaining* at each other, rather than discovering action, it often helps to ask actors to 'translate' the scene into another form: perhaps 'taking away' the text and replacing it with improvised mime or *Grammelot* or 'inarticulate' sounds or singing or dance. The actors have to communicate – perhaps non-verbally at first, through touch and movement, or through sounds other than words – rather than simply translate their ideas into words which will only block interaction. If this can be achieved, then the two primary goals of applied improvisation will succeed: the inner actions will be explored, and the inner life will be felt. Scenes in which actors have difficulties with the apparently cloistering implications of the text can also be freed up in this way, perhaps to the accompaniment of music or rhythm, which help to engage the visceral and affective body.

The character to concentrate on is not always one's own. In a solo improvisation piece the actor feels the burden of having to create everything on his own. This can be overcome by sharing the responsibility for initiation (just as in a group piece) with one's own partners – except that, in this case, the 'partners' are the imaginary characters in the scene. Create the other characters in the scene and take *time* to stand back and 'hear' what they have to say. For example, the chosen 'who' might be 'an auctioneer', the 'what' and 'where' conducting an auction in a posh saleroom. Having accepted the 'set', and decided the rhythm and physical shape of the central figure of the auctioneer (the only character the audience will actually see portrayed) the actor needs also to create selectively the other participants in the scene: by imaginatively characterising them, visualising them in the acting space, they can be made to do much of the work.

The little old lady in the grey pullover wonders if she can afford a few pounds more, and the auctioneer has to cajole a bid from her. The red-faced farmer in the pork-pie hat can easily afford it; the auctioneer need only appeal to his greed. Is the housewife continually gesticulating to her friend in the red coat making a bid or not? The invisible other characters become a series of *prompts* for the solo actor's imagination. Without these external foci, the scene will quickly lose shape and rhythm; and the actor will probably lose his grip on his own character, and descend rapidly into cliché. With them, even a solo performer can develop the simple action (Spolin's 'what') into a consistent and coherent narrative.

Narrative as generative structure

At all points in the process of improvising drama, the actor is involved in creating narrative. This does not mean simply 'telling a story'. That might be the result; but the process is concerned with other activities. All good improvised scenes have content and meaning, though the improviser need not strain to impose them on the work. Handled properly, they arise organically, often created as much by the audience as by the actors.

Keith Johnstone stresses two narrative skills, *free association* and *reincorporation*. These two processes sum up many of the techniques we have already discussed, and turn them to account in the creation of a piece to be shared with an audience.

Free association means spontaneous response, 'going with' whatever has been offered, by oneself or by one's collaborators. It means letting one idea generate the next without trying to force it into shape, without trying to *make* it mean something (it undoubtedly *will* mean something). It means accepting, too, that part of the meaning (the true 'content' of the story) will be the performer's revelation of himself. Free association exercises (like Johnstone's 'Automatic Writing', 'Lists', 'Dreams') if used properly can encourage the actor to bypass the 'censor' in himself. It takes a lot of trust. That is why it shouldn't be concerned with interpretation; if the actor realises too soon that the underlying content of the story is sexual, for example, he may not wish to continue it, or may try to force the story to change direction.

Johnstone abandons the notion of content, and concentrates instead on structure – the key to which is reincorporation. When telling a tale, either singly or with others, reincorporation means making use of what has already been introduced. It means coming back to ideas previously established, and then using them in ways that both bind the story together and take it forwards. Free association takes care of invention and development; reincorporation takes care of structure.

> The improviser has to be like a man walking backwards. He sees where he has been, but he pays no attention to the future. His story can take him anywhere, but he must still 'balance' it, and give it shape, by remembering incidents that have been shelved and reincorporating them. Very often an audience will applaud when earlier material is brought back into the story. They couldn't tell you why they applaud, but the reincorporation does give them pleasure. (Johnstone 1981: 116)

The audience, in fact, is enjoying structuring the story in its mind. They are looking for meaning, and making meaning out of what is being offered. Apparent randomness is given sudden illumination by reincorporation. So the applause, laughter or cheering that sometimes greets this reincorporated material is often the audience congratulating *itself* as much as the actor. They are saying 'Got it! Now it makes sense!' – and it's also an affirmation, a way of saying 'Go on! What will happen now?'

The technique of reincorporation is central to the structuring of Chicago long-form impro. Del Close refers to it as 'delayed justification' in that, when an idea mentioned earlier recurs (is reincorporated), it appears to be the justification for the whole scene. 'Nothing is ignored. Nothing is forgotten. And nothing is a mistake.' Whatever is said is heard, picked up, filed away, and later brought back into the scene (Halpern et al. 1994: 74).

The English comedian Al Murray (whose irascible, politically very incorrect 'Pub Landlord' character won the Edinburgh Fringe's Perrier Award in 1999) exemplifies the *ad hominem* form of reincorporation in his stage act, as many stand-up comics do. At the start of the act Murray talks to the audience, and learns the names and occupations of a number of people. After some initial improvised reactions to their jobs (God help any students – the Landlord *hates* students – who of course form the bulk of his audiences) Murray moves into the show proper, only to unexpectedly weave in these names and jobs as part of the performance. Audiences sometimes respond by lying to him; coming up with imaginary, 'funny' jobs. As Close and Halpern argue, in *Truth in Comedy* (Halpern et al. 1994: 15, 24), the audiences here are unskilled improvisers, trying to catch Murray out and play for a single laugh – in the suicidal way that hecklers always think they can be funnier than the comedian. Murray usually comically demolishes these lies. And their actual jobs, no matter how mundane, are always funnier, and a source of much richer comedy. Sometimes, the real jobs are more gloriously bizarre than anything anyone could invent: he once had a man whose job was to scientifically measure dog dirt for Newham Council (the jingoistic Landlord was incensed that he measured the turds in metric rather than imperial units!).

Mike Alfreds, the founder of Shared Experience, works on 'trampoline' words within the known text of the story. These are the transition points from narrative to dialogue. The exercise was developed during rehearsals for Shared Experience's early show, *The First Arabian Night*. In this piece the actor operates both as narrator of learned text and as improviser of action; he has first to find a personal way of narrating (creating his own text so that it bears the performer's personality). A way then has to be found of moving from narration into action.

> Say the actor has text such as: 'When the prince heard this much from his royal sire, he was moved by youthful folly to reply, "Thou art great in age but small in wit".' (Alfreds 1979–80: 15)

Here the 'trampoline' word is *reply*. At that point he is going to change from narrator to actor. He has to be able to pitch right in to the scene at the correct energy level, that of the prince's youthful indignation,

> so he uses the previous sentence of the narration as a sort of run up, knowing that when he gets to the word 'reply' he has to gather all his forces to take off into the action; he literally has to bounce himself on that word and it gives him the time to change his focus from the audience to his partner in the scene. (p. 15)

Once the transition has been made, improvisation takes over. The partner will respond as the prince's father and a scene will develop (in much the same way as a *commedia* scenario is fleshed out). The sections of learned narrative link the improvised passages together.

The audience's delight in the virtuosity of the actor becomes allied with its pleasure in the developing tale. The third-person narrative 'bounces' into the first-person improvisation, and whenever a scene is complete another narrator will take the thread. Then, as it perceives the complex structure of tale-within-tale, the audience responds with 'this wonderful reaction of "Oh, there it is!!" ' (p. 10).

Finally, there are other ways of using improvisation in the creation of a play. Group improvisation has been used by a number of professional playmakers for a long time. It can take the form of collaboration between writers and actors in the generation of an ultimately scripted play. It can lead to a play put together through improvisation in rehearsal – a play created entirely by the acting ensemble. Or it can be totally free, self-generating: the 'play' is entirely created in front of its audience.

We discuss these variants further under the section entitled 'Improvisation and writing' in Chapter 10. We finish this chapter with a couple of examples of the kinds of *journeys* which can be constructed from the work we have been looking at in Part II.

Sample sequences

Boal's structure for games and exercises appears in Chapter 3; Babbage's sequence for working with Boal's examples is:

- Preparing the body
- Games (energy, focus, power)

Table 8.1 Exercises and Activities

Preparation		Working together		Towards performance		Applied improvisation	
Activities	Examples	Activities	Examples	Activities	Examples	Activities	Examples
Relaxation and balance	Tag T'ai chi Yoga Feidenkrais Suzuki	Trust and respect	Trust circle Fish dives Blindfold Making contact Relay race Machine Laughing snake	Senses	Blindfold Warm-up Massage Flowing Trust games Journey	Who/where/what? Objectives and resistances	Farmer, field, potatoes Intention Journey Interrupted routine
Games and body/think	With ball Fight in the Dark Grandma's Footsteps 'What are you doing?' Bears	Group games Making a machine	Body sculptures Finding by sound	Tenses Dramatic modes	Presence Restoration Melodrama	Point of concentration Memory	Theme-scene The party
Space and movement	Laban Winearls Lecoq	Showing and telling	Mime-stick	Objects	Naming Telling story	'Set'	Magic 'if' Auctioneer
Circles of concentration and attention	Attention Listening Observation M. Chekov	Entrances and exits Meetings and greetings	Entering door Group walk	Observation Status	Rhythms Gestures Walks Party Games Allocate nos./cards Master/servant	Character Narrative	Previous circumstances Stories Free association Lists Dreams Reincorporation
Impulses and directions	Starfish Change directions Eclosion Walk, clap, freeze 'Song and dance'	'Blocking'	Use video Yes/yes but Gibberish	Masks	Neutral Expressive/counter mask Larval Commedia		Trampoline words Collective writing

OBJECTIVES

	Individual	Group		
	Relax	Interactions	Confront inadequacies	Extend in time/space
	Tune-up	Trust/support partners	Extend body awareness	Incorporate/play/want
	Balance	Encounter as dramatic structure	Sharpen awareness of interaction	Develop structures
	Feel good	Sensitize to others	Play with possibilities	Link imagination and organisation
	Enjoy			Explore inner action
				Feel inner life
	Begin individual 'unblocking'	Recognise mutual dependence	Discover performance dynamics	Develop organisational skills
	Explore resistances	Extend sese of 'self'	Extend performance vocabulary	Work with complex structures
	Find mental/physical centredness	Establish confidence in group	Develop focus and commitment	Generate text
	Develop 'presence'			
	Establish self-confidence			
	Socialise	Overcome taboos	Liberate imagination	Build sequential performance

ACTIVE MEANINGS

Psychodynamics (individual)	Psychodynamics (group)	Text as performance	Process of thinking
Play	Meaning as interchange	Signs and meanings	Hierarchies
Readiness/disponibilité	Co-creativity	Multiplicity of possibility	Intervention and realignment
Mind–body relationship	Negotiation	Group creativity	Complex imaginative acts
Creativity	Form as process	Organic understanding	New combinations

- Images (dynamisation, transformation)
- Themes

(and in practice this may lead to 'desires' – 'Rainbow' work).

Preparation examples are things like mirroring, games like 'The Bears are Coming' Johnston 1998: 249), or the 'Slowmo' Race. A key juncture is the 'Complete the Image' exercise (Babbage 2004: 117–18): one partner offers, the other completes, first steps out and returns to complete a second image and so on; it is frequently used to lead to group images, scenarios and issue-oriented work.

Simon Murray gives a sequence of exercises – a kind of 'distillation' compiled with recent Lecoq teacher Thomas Prattki – based around pushing and pulling and leading to the three dramatic modes of melodrama, tragedy and *commedia*. They are valuable in emphasising the indispensability of working through basic vectors of bodily movement and of engaging in a committed and sequential manner with the work. Even so they remain somewhat condensed, and it is worth underlining that some of them (for example improvisations on journeys, divorce, reconciliation, etc.) could well both require a very lengthy time-frame to explore all possible nuances and also generate material which could deflect from the goal.

Example: Melodrama:

(*a*) physical preparation: (i) pairs face same way, one close behind holds the other round pelvis, each attempts to move in different direction; ii) bamboo stick joins partners at palm of hand, they push/pull each other round space;

(*b*) into dramatic territory: pair exercises with imagined link (string or stick) which is used to alter body position, to move around space, and finally to experiment with moving towards or away from each other – subsequently adding single words to this last phase.

Both (*a*) and (*b*) are followed by an improvisation exercise: (*a*) to continue physical exploration by imagining being giants, (*b*) by a 'departure' scenario involving family members, to be played without words. The aim of the sequence is to get students to focus on the space between characters, to see how any movement in that space charges it ('pushes' or 'pulls' it) emotionally. (Based on Murray 2003: 136–40)

Whereas for melodrama the dynamic is 'I push . . . I pull', for tragedy it is 'I am pushed/pulled' and for *commedia*, 'I push myself . . . pull myself'; preparation for tragedy moves through aspects of the work on elements (see p. 147) and leads into an exercise producing the sense of being spoken by a choric text, whereas for *commedia* a neutral mask exercise is used to generate the energy to overcome obstacles. No improvisation is given for tragedy, whilst a pair of scenarios ('divorce' and 'reconciliation') are used for *commedia* (Murray 2003: 140–50).

There is in the charting of these exercises no particular confirmation of Lecoq's assertion that 'tragedy is always vertical' and the sentimental – thus melodrama – is diagonal (Lecoq 1997/2000: 83), so they might be a good way to test whether these directions are in fact the most dominant in a spontaneous sense.

The skills and activities we have dealt with in this section promote qualities of focus, consistency and structure in both individual and communal improvised performance, and these qualities allow the performance to present character and narrative. At the same time it becomes clear that these are based on and emerge from the personal and group work outlined earlier, and can often profitably return to it. There is no fixed hierarchy in improvisation work, except in the sense that everything has to do with the enriching of *performance*: whether this is seen as individual realisation of action, expression and response; as a communal act of composition; as something shared with an audience; or as a celebration of the full resources of individual being and the ways they can be combined to create new patterns of significance.

Part III

Why? The Meaning(s) of Improvisation: Towards a Poetics

Introduction

We have looked at *who* improvises and at *what* they do. We need to understand the meaning of these acts for individuals, for performers and for society. Improvisation, like any physical or spoken act, necessarily produces meaning: indeed it may be said to be primarily a way of generating a plurality of meanings through performance. It can tell us a good deal about how we create meaning.

The practice of improvisation works initially to *free* the producer of meanings, both as an individual and in the network of relationships in which he or she operates, and to enable him or her to develop a larger 'vocabulary'. There are two main issues here: physical and psychological unblocking, which has both theatrical and paratheatrical implications for the quality of self, creativity, imagination and of relational acts between individuals and groups; and the acquisition of an enlarged range of communicative skills, which produce an extension of being, knowing and interacting. These processes impact upon the personal, cultural and political spheres of life.

Both these issues have important psychological, social and aesthetic implications for the nature of performative acts, the creation of form and the concept of 'play'.

Since meaning in improvisation is performative, we also need to consider the kinds of impact improvisation has upon the status of performance, its effects in terms of the relationship between performers, text and audience, and the possibility that it represents an alternative theatrical tradition.

The sections which follow therefore examine how meanings are created, shifted, enriched or relocated through improvisation, and also reflect on the meaning of this process itself. They both implicitly and explicitly refer back to the examples of practitioners and practices presented in the preceding two parts.

Chapter 9

Enriching the Communication of Meaning

Communication involves a sender, a receiver and a message. If the message is to be as meaningful as possible, sender and receiver need to be as intelligent, sensitive, skilful and so on as possible. This is particularly the case with impro and, by extension, performance generally. It isn't simply a static mechanical model in which the sender takes priority and emits 'top-down' and unchangeable data, but an essentially mobile, organic one in which all elements are dynamic and intercommunicative. The basic requirement then is to unblock resistances, develop all kinds of responses and skills upon which personal and interpersonal behaviour depend. Many of the practices we have considered work to this effect. Their full implication can, however, be most usefully perceived in the light of paratheatrical and psychodramatic approaches. Developing the sender positively affects the quality of the message, and gives him or her more practical resources (verbal and physical imagination) in order to construct it. The vocabulary (sign potential) of the communicative process is thus extended, as is its capacity to generate meaning.

Implications of psychodramatic and paratheatrical approaches

Improvisation activities help to discover, unblock, or tune up the psyche and the body, which evidently has implications for performance of any kind. Theatre can be a moral/political thermometer, or perhaps a tonic or an emetic: it is related to the health of a society, to the sense society makes of itself as an entity. The improvisatory act focuses on the gathering of energies, the freeing of possibilities of articulation, an alertness of giving and receiving, the establishment of connection. It has to do with developing wholeness through developing the sense of self.

In psychotherapy, the 'protagonist' enacts his life-drama with or without the help of others, and may in the course of so doing reveal or give shape to fundamental situations, attitudes, complexes of which he or she may have been only dimly aware, or which taboos may have made it impossible to speak about directly. This kind of activity can of course also be valuable in other, not specifically psychotherapeutic, contexts (for example, the use of role-play and simulation exercises in personal and professional development).

'Psychodrama' is related to a whole range of psychotherapeutic techniques which have as their aim the discovery, acknowledging and valuing of 'the whole person', of all aspects of the human being both individually and in all forms of relationship. There are generic similarities between psychodrama, mainly developed by J. L. Moreno, and, for instance, Jung's concept of 'integration', Maslow's 'self-actualisation' and Rogers's emphasis on 'client-centred' therapy. Therapy in general has become more eclectic, using techniques from a number of complementary approaches as appropriate, and one finds references to the same kinds of activity under different headings. Many approaches make considerable use of theatre games and impro exercises (for example, trust exercises, role-plays, mirroring) in addition to using active work with scenarios which involve the protagonist, and often the therapist as well, in 'improvising' his or others' roles in life-situations.[1] We discuss aspects of Moreno's 'Psychodrama', Augusto Boal's 'Theatre of the Oppressed' and Jonathan Fox's 'Playback Theatre' elsewhere, but it is worth noting here the example of Boal's recognition of the need to address internal oppressions ('The Cop in the Head') and the structure of desire ('The Rainbow of Desires') as evidence of this spectrum of work; practitioners using theatre process in social contexts – work in prisons, with marginalised or disadvantaged groups, to address particular community issues and so on – have increasingly found that the initial group or community-centred political focus requires means of negotiating the personal, often traumatic, circumstances of participants. Impro and psychodrama are both about transforming what seems closed off, taboo, frightening, inaccessible, impossible, inexpressible, or even just plain boring: disclosing it, not running away from it, releasing its negative or damming energy. The situations through which Grotowski or Johnstone or Lecoq take their 'players' are akin to the psychological (and maybe, in our increasingly complex, globalized or multicultural world, psychosocial) situation of not knowing who one is or how to go on. The aim is not necessarily the discovery of a single or stable self in the conventional sense; it may be more the activation of a range of possible roles and modes, the discovery of the ability to play with one's own life. Improvisation, as it extends into the 'paratheatrical', may be a spearhead of methods of changing the environment from within, from the individual outwards.

But as well as the internal, psychological forms, the blockages or resistances have their external and political manifestations, as we shall see.

The censor's nightmare

The chief opponent of the improviser is not the writer of scripted drama; it is the censor. The antonym of 'improvisation' is 'censorship', because while improvisation represents the permission (and self-permission) for artistic expression, and the acceptance of one's own as well as others' creativity, censorship self-evidently stands for denial and refusal. This is true both literally and figuratively; and equally true whether the term refers to an external, political, public manifestation or to an internal, private and psychological process.

Impro has always been the censor's nightmare. The censor functions best when dealing with a precomposed, literary artefact – ideally a manuscript. The censored manuscript of a poem or a novel can be delivered to the printer and the finished artwork disseminated in a controlled manner. Or it can be suppressed utterly, expunged from official culture (though it may appear in unofficial culture as *samizdat*, the underground, secretly circulated, self-published literature of resistance).

But theatre has always been a problem area for censors because of its immediacy and its dependence upon 'texts' other than the purely literary. In fact, the 'text' of a play is rightly understood by the censor to include every word *and* every bit of business.[2] The censor's nightmare is that, having licensed a play for performance, and thus given it official sanction, the performers will alter it in performance by improvising. They will make their own substitutions, deletions, insertions and restorations. Or they will introduce non-verbal elements which contradict the censor's intentions.

Joan Littlewood's Theatre Workshop, pioneer of improvisation, was singled out for prosecution in 1958 for the 'very wide divergence' between the text authorised by the Lord Chamberlain and that actually experienced in the theatre. The censor particularly objected to a new scene in which a mock opening ceremony was performed in a public lavatory, by an actor who vocally imitated Sir Winston Churchill while appearing to urinate.

Technically, improvisation has only been possible *on stage* in Britain since 1968 (though, of course, no such restrictions applied to rehearsals). The act of improvisation was seen by many as subversive in itself, and allied to subversive politics, or, in the British postwar climate, protest.[3] Littlewood's work at Stratford East is exemplary. And the battle against censorship, which reached its climax at the Royal Court in the mid-1960s, was also the battle for the freedom to create appropriate artistic as well as political forms.

Keith Johnstone's Theatre Machine was born in that climate: *Clowning* had to be presented officially as a lecture-demonstration for the Royal Court Studio. Under the censor, improvisation was condemned to remain a rehearsal device: as a performance tool, or even style, it was forced to remain an academic exercise – a lecture-demonstration, not a play. To commit oneself to a vision of a theatre based on improvisation was a remarkable act of faith.

At the other extreme, the experiences of Teatr Ósmego Dnia (The Theatre of the Eighth Day) in Poland demonstrate that improvisation may be the best way for a company of artists to function in a repressive situation. Ósmego Dnia began in Poznan in 1964, and at first modelled themselves on Grotowski's Laboratory work before finding their own distinctive style which, although still concerned with the exploration of theatre language, was more consciously political. Tadeusz Janiszewski, one of the actors, explains:

> After 1976 we had more and more trouble from the security services. It was the year of the founding of KOR – the Committee for the Defence of the Workers [punished for the riots in Radom and Warsaw] – and we never tried to hide our sympathies. (Howard 1986: 296)

The theatre group was not allowed to disseminate information about itself, to perform in some cities (especially Warsaw) or to travel abroad. They were actively harassed by the security services, and dragged for five years through the courts on trumped-up fraud charges. Two members were imprisoned briefly. Their 1984 production *Absinthe* was based on the farcical but sinister events of that period. By the end of the 1970s (and before the upsurge of Solidarity in 1980), most other radical Polish groups had either retreated into naturalism or abstracted themselves from the political situation by doing laboratory research work. Ósmego Dnia were virtually the only company still involved in activist theatre. Their relation to the censoring authorities is described by Janiszewski:

> You have a special performance for one person, the censor. A scenario has to be submitted too . . . . But it is possible to outmanoeuvre the censor, particularly when there's considerable improvisation. We've been developing our own creative method since 1973, based on improvisation. (Howard 1986: 297)

The condition of working against censorship is not an uncommon occurrence, whether in the form of explicit state oppression, or internalised ideological self-repression. Louis Althusser saw ideology as materially operative in society via what he termed 'ideological state apparatuses' (to distinguish them from the more mechanical and punitive forms of oppressive 'state apparatus' such as the government, police, army, prisons etc.). Among the ideological forms, which operate diffusely in the private realm of life, he lists religious structures, family norms, legal systems, the political party and trades union systems, communications media (press, radio and TV) and culture which includes literature, the arts, and even sport (Althusser 1971: 127–86). It is as much against this internalised ideological framework as against formalised state oppression that improvised theatre struggles to liberate itself.

Ideological censorship is reflected in Eugenio Barba's early accounts of working in Poland with Grotowski (Turner 2004: 3–4), no less than in the struggles of Judith Malina and Julian Beck to find a haven for the Living Theatre at the same time in America. It is evident in the responses to the establishment of the politically engaged Indian People's Theatre Association (IPTA) in the 1940s; in the struggle of female Indian artists like Gul Bardhan to emerge from this male-dominated cultural field in the 1950s, and, as extreme counterexample, the tragic 'street-theatre' murder of the playwright and activist Safdar Hashmi by Congressman Mukul Sharma and his followers in 1989 (Yarrow 2001: 178ff., 182–3). It is visible in Augusto Boal's observations in Brazil in the 1960s which led to the emergence of his Theatre of and for the Oppressed (Boal 1992: 1–3), and to his resistance to the inner censor, 'the Cop in the Head'. An interface between politics and group therapy is represented by Boal's Image and Forum theatre work which aims directly to empower and give voice to the oppressed, marginalized and silenced, and this empowering is understood as both a therapeutic and developmental process.

Lecoq claims a pivotal status for the rediscovery of the improvisatory at certain moments in history; this could be seen as opening up a space for aesthetic renewal, but at the same time as a psychological and political intervention. The kinds of physical and mental openness and flexibility involved could be seen to produce an (artistic) reconstruction of the 'identity' of the performer and of the form s/he works in; and to operate across a dis- and re-articulation of body and language (and of body as language), as a challenge to the closed, the received and the repressive and protective mind-sets which legitimate that repression. If in poststructuralist thought 'performance' mounts a challenge to the hegemony of 'text', then improvised performance represents the epitome of that capacity. In its process, as well as often in its product, it *is* a politics, an operational mode of generating structural and attitudinal change.

There is however a question about how far improvisation has now (in the early twenty-first century) become a norm in itself, and the last few decades have repeated, rather even than recycled, the practice of Lecoq, Grotowski and others. To some extent, the virtues of games and improvisation are now a part of mainstream training, and to a lesser but still significant extent, public performance: where for instance *Whose Line Is It Anyway* was a fairly rare marker, there have since been many TV shows which draw on the model. Even Complicité, who in the intervening years moved away from the largely improvised play to inventive engagement with – often collaborative or adapted – scripted work (*The House of Lucie Cabrol*, *Street of Crocodiles*, *The Elephant Vanishes*), offered a fairly identical repeat of their early piece *A Minute Too Late* at the National in 2005. Many companies are still using a formula which certainly includes engaging physical work and sometimes uses it to illuminate places language is slower to go; but equally, there is not infrequently an overreliance on the physical to mask the inadequacy of script. Does improvisation need to unmake and remake *itself*? If so, where can it look for models?

Julian Hilton speculated whether the increasing presence of multimedia and the kinds of parallel processing it required would set a new model for performance (Hilton 1993: 156ff.). The increase of the techno-heavy, however, even in so-called interactive mode or site-specific work, has not always liberated and activated its audience. There are instances of brilliant inventiveness, in the work of Mike Pearson (particularly with the Welsh company Brith Gof and latterly with Mike Brookes as Pearson–Brookes) in the UK, and the Dutch/South African Odd Enginears, where combinations of the human and the industrial/mechanical have offered potent insights into history and human action and generated stimulating and multi-perspectival encounters. Founded by former electrical-engineer-turned-sculptor Mark O'Donovan and Dutch percussionist Geert Jonkers, Odd Enginears define themselves as 'an African laboratory for unusual site-specific theatre', whose work forms 'a collage of artistic disciplines, objects, materials, sound and movement as well as interaction with both their surroundings and the audience', where 'strange and evocative sound machines and visuals replace the spoken word' (http://www.artthrob.co.za/04feb/listings_cape.html, accessed 6 June 2006). Here, however (for example, in the group's 2003 *Donker Gat* installation project in Cape Town), there is also a need for particularly meticulous planning in order to ensure the safety of performers and audience when working with industrial machinery or sites; the improvisation comes more in the daring process of conception than in the final realisation, though it may give rise to new ways of seeing as all good theatre can do. And in many other cases, technology – itself another kind of ideological state apparatus, exemplifying consumerism – has deadened rather than stimulated the creative input and response.

Other possibilities might be found in the South African model of intercutting languages – both performative and verbal. Several impro games, from Keith Johnstone onwards, start with linguistic improvisation as a path to de-inhibition and spontaneity; and various forms of mixed or garbled *Grammelot* are found within the history of improvisatory forms. South African theatre however – and to a lesser extent this is also true of much postcolonial work around the world – uses a variety of languages in parallel. Historically (under apartheid), this was frequently a strategy to confuse the censor and, along with the incorporation of physically, rhythmically and musically resonant techniques based on indigenous forms like praise-singing and the adoption of multiple roles in storytelling, to celebrate the officially exiled or eradicated linguistic and corporeal bodies of the performers and their (numerically superior but politically disempowered) communities; more recently it has in part served as evidence of political correctness towards the ideal of the 'Rainbow Nation'. In spite of these limitations, it has at the same time tended to result in scripts whose focus and scope of reference can shift rapidly, and in the production of actors who can negotiate different linguistic and cultural positions with ease.

La disponibilité

Availability – openness – readiness – acceptance: the precondition of creativity. It implies not resisting, but flowing *with* the world and the self. It implies (to us) nakedness, but not (strangely) defencelessness. The performer is without *armour*, but not without *weapons*: such as wit, agility, mobility and inventiveness. He or she is resource-full. *Disponibilité* is the state of 'armed neutrality' from which all movements are equally possible.

For Lecoq it is a state of calmness, of balance, in which the readiness is all. The performer (most pointedly in improvisation) is always ready, always aware and always able to respond: he or she is 'rendered open to what is happening in a situation, a gesture, a word . . . the imagination provoked to the invention of languages' (Lecoq 1987).

By 'open to what is happening' (*'disponible à l'événement'*) we believe Lecoq infers open to all the processes which compose the situation, on all levels. It is a state in which the truth is revealed, not covered up by tricks. By 'the invention of languages' (*'provoquant son imagination à inventer des langages'*) we understand him to mean that the actor is stimulated to create as many types of response to the truth of that situation, gesture or word as are appropriate. The 'languages' may be gestural, verbal or purely tactile, but they give truthful expression to the moment and whatever it holds.

Disponibilité sums up in a single term the condition improvisers aspire to. It offers a way of describing an almost intangible and nearly undefinable state of being: having at (or in) one's fingertips, and any other part of the body, the capacity to do and say what is appropriate, and to have the confidence to make the choice. It's a kind of total awareness, a sense of being at one with the context: script, if such there be, actors, audience, theatre space, oneself and one's body.

For Grotowski, technique is not abstract or external: it is how the body accedes to its own resources; how it discovers that it can be, say, do, understand and transmit – with and to anything and anyone. The bodily condition in which that capacity is touched is a tensed and balanced orderliness which – like an act of love, Grotowski says – is not closed off from anything.

Disponibilité is an appropriate word for this condition, for several reasons. It is an alien word, which means it is totally without misleading connotations in English. Just as, for example, Roger Caillois used Greek nouns to define the various types of play activity (Caillois 1962), we feel we can usefully borrow this French word to suggest the *condition* the improviser seeks to discover and maintain.

Disponibilité suggests not just a theory but an experiential condition; a way of being which can be sought and found. It is a condition of being *centred* (in oneself) and balanced, ready to go in any appropriate direction. We might translate it as *neutrality*, but in English this has unfortunate connotations of asensuality and of being disengaged (like a car idling, without purpose). *Disponibilité* suggests a charged and sensual state: Gide relates it to a process of coming-to-be-aware of the body. In this state the actor is fully inhabiting the world outside and the world within his body. He is 'neutral' only in the sense that he is *poised* between all possibilities. *Openness* might be a better English equivalent, but openness may also suggest passivity. *Disponibilité* doesn't suggest a passive, purely receptive state. It is armed, pregnant with possibilities. It carries the sense of becoming aware of oneself and one's possibilities; aware of having *choice*. It represents the power to *dispose* of oneself and one's activity. As such, it pre-eminently *embodies* the condition of existentialism.

Disponible suggests, then, that the performer can dispose, can choose, can act. It suggests sensory alertness, even sensual alertness. The whole being is opened to the moment. And the moment of performance includes the audience. Stanislavsky enjoins the actor to keep his intentions 'this side of the footlights', and Grotowski, following Osterwa, warns against 'publicotropism'. But we are not talking of exhibitionism. The improviser accepts (and shares creativity with) the audience. As *art* it may be chancy, less certain of success than other methods, but it is close to the condition sought for by Rilke, a kind of tuning in to organic form. As such, it may be the only way to arrive at genuinely new insights: it is less likely to leave anything out; it doesn't force the pace or the pattern; it has more chance of avoiding the trap of cliché.

It is a condition of relaxed awareness where one does not need to *impose* order on the external world or on the imagination: order is found *in* the world and in the imaginative response to others. One does not need to deny the ordering intelligence, the analytical self. Rather, that self takes its proper place. One does not need to subjugate the mind: the mind knows when not to dominate, and the body knows when to be still as well as when to move. For Lecoq (the body learning to think), *disponibilité* is a natural condition, harmoniously accepted; for Grotowski (the analytical brain learning to move) it is a condition sought through pain and denial. They are moving towards the same point; but they are coming from different worlds. In yet others, it may be called *hana* (the flower of Japanese *Noh* theatre) or *rasa* (the taste of Sanskrit aesthetics). When the flower blooms or the taste is savoured, the full symbolic and aesthetic resonance of the performer's creation is awakened in the audience: it can only ever be as a now-moment in which the sharing is sudden, always new and unexpected, and certain (see George 1999). In neither of these highly technically circumscribed traditions would one initially expect anything called 'improvisation': but in both it is – only – acknowledged as a crowning phase, a sign of mastery, of grasping and being able to deliver the key experience of art, that of being in the moment of the genesis of form.

Disponibilité is a condition of responsiveness, but it implies *giving* as much as receiving. Reciprocal giving between two or more *disponible* creators (like the North American Indian custom of *potlatch* in which individuals and whole communities compete in giving) opens up a truly new form of artistic creativity. We have seen how, for example, the clown gives to his partner on stage, or how the improviser passes *élan* to his fellow actor in order to make things possible for both of them, or how the failure to do this destroys the possibility of creation. When the blocks are removed, and when the giving is reciprocal, the result is a creativity shared by both the performers and the audience. Murray suggests that '*Disponibilité* is a precondition for play, while *complicité* is an outcome of successful play' (Murray 2002: 70); the latter could also be described as a 'collusion between celebrants' (Complicité programme for *Lucie Cabrol*).

Transformation and the plural self

Among her 'triggers of transformative experiences', Marilyn Ferguson includes 'improvisational theater, with its requirement of both total attention and spontaneity, [and] Psychodrama, because it forces an awareness of roles and role-playing' (Ferguson 1980: 90). This appears in a list of 'psychotechnologies' which includes mental (meditative) and physical (t'ai chi ch'uan, Alexander) techniques, therapies, self-help and mutual-help networks and programmes, and various 'shamanic and magical techniques'. The function of all these is to shift awareness beyond Watts's 'skin-encapsulated ego' (Watts 1972) to open up new possibilities of being. Many of the methods she mentions figure in drama school activities.

Improvisation frequently has to do with breaking down barriers. Our conscious, rationalising ego operates within boundaries which afford security of behaviour and identity, and are useful in many contexts. But boundaries also inhibit, and the kind of lateral thinking which arrives at new insights is precisely an example of the value of bypassing them and discovering a new shape to knowledge and experience. Improvisation in one sense is about 'lateral being', if you like; about allowing and encouraging this productive 'digression' with as much of the organism as possible. One result is to permit subliminal or subconscious material to surface, to make use of the sudden crazy idea, to allow a sequence of action or speech to develop from a sensation or bodily position. This can be both frighteningly insecure (the comfortable limits of 'who/what/why' are left behind) and frighteningly chaotic. But used profitably it is both a discipline in itself and a means of exploring extra possibilities of synthesis. Jung and others suggest that the use and incorporation of subconscious psychic activity (dreams, fantasies and so on) is not irrelevant or narcissistic, but a way of drawing on a different and perhaps more extensive kind of knowing. Improvisation may also frequently work by sudden symbolic associations, or make logical leaps; and it often (like some kinds of comedy) appeals to an audience precisely because it stimulates the ability to function likewise. It becomes an exciting game, and in so doing it *makes sense* in another, not merely logico-rational way.

Grotowski, too, sensed that what is occurring in the intense work on the authenticity of self – which in his process has of necessity to be unscripted and non-externally directed – is an encounter with these at first dim, often uncomfortable and confusing forms of knowing and being. But the belief is that pursuing them can result in a more total and organic awareness and a freer capacity for action. Awakening these may require a passage through confusion and unknowing, and through a loss of identity as commonly conceived (as with masks). It is no accident that theoretical and textual theatrical visions of recent decades (Artaud, Beckett) have aimed at a parallel exploration or explosion of the limits of language, self and their accepted configuration. Modernist and postmodernist art of all genres, plus associated theory, has often featured 'difficulty': paradox, lack of conventional plots and characters, frequent digressions. 'Reading' and understanding has become a challenging and perhaps dangerous business, precisely because the act of arriving at a new framework or symbolic nexus is – like reading metaphysical poetry and like the creating of works of art – one which involves a splitting apart and reconstituting of the self in its articulation as word and image. Learning to accept a feeling of loss is an essential part of the process.

This requires a different, and difficult, kind of discipline. Grotowski and his actors have not drawn back from the demands, but the same assumption underlies the work of Chekhov, Copeau, Johnstone, Lecoq and others. That is why Grotowski rejected the label 'improvisation' where it might be thought to equate with a lapse into a vague notion of spontaneity or the imitation of 'primitive' behaviour. He preferred to call his preparatory work 'studies' or 'sketches', and emphasised that they involved intense discipline and a concern for conscious realisation of structure; aiming at a blend, or *conjunctio oppositorum*, of spontaneity and discipline which to him seemed to fuse the best from the Stanislavskian and the Brechtian/Meyerholdian approaches. Similarly, the use of 'neutrality' by Lecoq and others we have discussed has nothing to do with lamenting or attempting to regain some kind of prelapsarian 'innocence' as a form of cultural nostalgia. It identifies a precise psychophysiological condition which is, as with all genuine experiential research, achievable and repeatable by anyone here and now. This condition is 'prior' to language, form and ideas not in an idealist, but in a strictly – though subtly – physical sense. It is not a permanent, or even in most cases a very extended, situation, but a relatively momentary pause, gap or stillness which, like the shaking of a kaleidoscope, allows mental or physical material to begin to form new patterns and impulses. It does not seek any kind of retreat into paradisial vacuity or irresponsibility, but its quest is undertaken with the clear goal of enabling precisely these kinds of re-formation to occur: its focus is towards freer and more extensive action generated by the 'motors' of thought, movement and form.

Lecoq himself does not use emotive language to discuss this

work. He does occasionally make use of paradox, as Murray notes (2003: 153). Paradox and juxtaposition – which is frequently found in work which interrogates the problematic nature of what we call 'reality' – is sometimes referred to in a similar vein as 'mystical'. The term is frequently misused and confused – perhaps deliberately – with 'mystery', suggesting fuzziness and lack of clarity. The thinking (very often a more inclusive kind of operation than much of what we normally do during the day, and one involving extreme degrees of attentiveness to mental and physical events) of people seriously engaged in trying to see how life works at its most subtle levels is however rarely fuzzy, and where it engages with paradox – as in the case of Beckett, for example – it does so with the greatest precision, because at the levels where things begin to take shape, simple dualistic opposition is less prevalent. Things are not yet black or white, they may be perceived in a condition where a tendency to both criteria is still present. 'Neutrality' is precisely a tactic to open up access to this kind of substratum from which it is possible to 'reinvent' the languages of performance and thus of meaning. If you can (occasionally) work from here, there's a chance you may not get too clogged up by the dead hand of habit and convention. This is, ultimately, also a *political* choice, as is the choice to dismiss the possibility of this kind of operation by resorting to academic clichés.

In any consideration of the psychodynamics of performance, the boundaries of self, others and otherness begin to come into play. For instance, R. D. Laing's gloss on Sartre's use of role, image and authenticity picks up the sense in which recognition of *another* is also acknowledgement of repressed (Freud) or 'shadow' (Jung) aspects of the self.

The 'recognition scene' is one of drama's stocks-in-trade – sometimes profound (as in the moments of *anagnorisis* in Greek tragedy), often comic, but always involving a shock and relativisation of the notion of self. The shock is something like that in an 'Aha' experience: sudden conscious appreciation of something you 'knew' at a more intuitive level. It's an articulation of organic knowledge – another possible definition of theatre – which is experienced as a gasp, a gape or a gap: a momentary burst of just awareness, without as yet a clearly defined content to give it specific shape. The recognition process, therefore, involves a *stopping* or unseating, a prising loose from former bounds of identity which is uncomfortable, or puzzling or exciting, or all three. It is essentially a challenge and a proposal: a challenge to find the context, the mental and physical resources, to cope with the new situation; a proposal that the very gasp of recognition implies that those resources are available, if as yet undefined.

Sartre's characters are often like reluctant improvisers who spend all their time denying the possibility that they might be different, preferring to hide behind a familiar and usually flattering (or at least not too damaging) image which they try to project. This image is always carefully preserved and yet less consciously chosen than they like to think: it functions as a protective screen for things they don't want others to reveal to them, for *les autres* always serve as mirrors, although by no means mirrors that don't lie, since they have reasons of their own for what they reflect. This kind of hide-and-seek proposes a whole web of inauthenticity, and its perpetrators are castigated by Sartre as *salauds* – both cowardly and devious. Others are a threat precisely because they represent this potential offer of knowledge which one is desperate to barricade oneself against. They are shunned or attacked because characters are unwilling to take up the challenge to confront more of themselves. Excluding the other or defining oneself against him/her is therefore a way of denying the full possibility of self: role becomes a refuge for the insecure (actor or person).

Improvisation, then, requires a courage which enables you to get *out* of role – although you may then be able to get back *into* it later – and discover other resources which you didn't 'know' you had. That is never an easy option. One of the most difficult improvisatory tasks for any actor is the basis of Lecoq-style red-nose clowning: coming on stage as yourself, with no other resources available, is intensely vulnerable, especially as any 'acting' is immediately 'drummed off'. I Gelati's work with masks similarly transfixes any inauthenticity (masks readily reveal discrepancies between body and gesture or speech) by insisting on maintaining *presence* and input of energy. Maude-Roxby's work, too, is about being fully present, working off whatever is there, being prepared to respond and go with whatever comes up. There's nowhere to hide in the face of this scrutiny of presence. Any slip into a familiar – learned or practised – response is a give-away.

Absence of strict form is here only apparent: it is a way of escaping from the fixed, the *a priori*, the already done, the dead and the repetitive. Accepting and *staying with* the state of not knowing 'who' or 'what' is a quite precise step towards activating a degree of present awareness, which is ready to sense and respond to a more coherent and extensive range of sensation, intuition and expression.

This is an authenticity of being which acknowledges that I am what I am in the present moment, and is prepared to keep that open for scrutiny rather than cloaked in a role. It acknowledges too that the present includes the full range of the 'past'; both in the historical/genealogical sense and in terms of 'buried' psychic material (for Grotowski this material is overtly that of the levels of collective consciousness of a community, nation or generation). I cannot be fully present unless I own that range of experience as fully as possible in my body.

To be authentic is to be in touch with oneself in this extended sense, which is an opening to one's own life and to levels where it may touch on or merge with the life of others. That is why a great deal of creative energy can be liberated in this kind of work: energy which derives not from 'inspiration' in the clichéd sense of external aid, but from a breathing in, a being in tune with one's own powers as a human being.

The openness of this condition is risky: risky to achieve, and risky in that it is always improvising, always performative, never static. Form is dynamic, the self in its articulation is always in the flow of change and needs to adjust to it. Stasis is death and stultification, in self-satisfaction at the 'right' action, word or image; what is crystallised soon becomes brittle. In Tom Stoppard's *Rosencrantz and Guildenstern are Dead* the Player says:

> Why, we grow rusty and you catch us at the very point of decadence. By this time tomorrow night we might have forgotten everything we ever knew. That's a thought, isn't it. We'd be back where we started – improvising.   (Stoppard 1967: 16)

Perhaps then, historically and essentially, improvisation is the basis of all theatre, and of the creation of a role or a life. 'Forgetting' at that 'point of decadence' may also be the very mechanics by which we gain access to 'everything we ever knew'.[4]

What these perspectives have enabled us to discover is therefore a vital shift in the sense of self and in its function. They start with work which allows a freer sense of (*meaning for*) *self*; offer ways of 'unblocking', both in the personal and psychological sense, and in the social, political sense; move towards an awareness that *self is a capacity for generating a* plurality of *meaning*; and establish this as a directable *voluntary* operation through which self ceases to be merely the passive receptacle of deterministic influences and opinions and becomes a *productive agent*. By passing through the condition which Lecoq and Copeau identify as neutrality, Grotowski as disarmament, the self is prised free of its encrustation in habitual role, and becomes an active producer of its own meaning.

Under the influence of the improvisatory, self may thus begin to redefine itself: it is liberated both psychologically and semiotically. As it participates more effectively in the making of meaning, it is no longer so limited and closed off in solipsistic regard. It begins to operate as a generator of relationships; that is to say it becomes active in the context (environment), a vital part of processes of exchange. All of this can be seen as important for individual behaviour and for what happens in a theatre between actors and each other and actors and audience. This relocation of the self within the 'community' illustrates an important set of meanings for the 'wholeness' referred to earlier.

An extension of relating and communicating occurs through the medium of a sign system. The acquisition of extra sign potential parallels the freeing of physical and mental capacities and is the means by which they are realised or actualised. In an important way, improvisatory practice enhances the languages available to the performer. Lecoq calls this 'provoking the imagination to invent languages'. If you can do things you couldn't (or daren't) do before, you can now *say* things thereby which you formerly could not articulate.

Since improvisation has to do with the extension of knowledge of the self, and with the deploying of its resources in action, it is not surprising that it has found a place in education. Not merely in drama schools and on drama courses, where it can (though not always) play a vital role, but also in 'Theatre in Education' (the use of drama, sometimes partly or wholly improvised, to bring to life any appropriate classroom study), in language learning and as a means of facilitating communicative skills. Its uses here have been dealt with by others, but it is worth pointing out that in these contexts, improvisation is not seen as something sloppy. It has a clearly understood contribution to make within certain parameters.

We have already indicated the kind of disciplined attention which Grotowski, Lecoq, Johnstone and others require. Improvisations can degenerate into loose and purposeless meandering or self-indulgence. But not if the participants are enabled to experience for themselves that what they are acquiring is the ability to use and direct the emergence of form. That means having a clear understanding and purpose to activity and maintaining critical alertness throughout. If the *process* is clearly understood (by teacher and/or participant, depending on the kind of activity and the stage it has reached), there will be a framework which enables one to decide when to let things develop and when to intervene. Used in this way, improvisation can become a means of experiencing crucial processes of choice in the construction of any creative work.

Jon Nixon, in an article in *New Theatre Quarterly* (Nixon 1987), suggests that drama in education can be seen as *social interaction* (developing ways of exploring feelings, of imaginative insight into situations), as *discourse* (opening up ways of using language) and as *cognition* (emphasising the *process* of knowing as a move through experiencing towards understanding). Lecoq's teaching results in what Murray terms 'a politics of the imagination' (Murray 2003: 110). Much of what he does acquaints students with the places and forms from which 'languages' arise, and as such it requires the ability to function in between de- and re-construction, to be prepared to accept the condition of not knowing as a prerequisite to creativity. A 'creative pedagogy' (p. 108) is one which encourages quite the opposite of what passes for knowledge in many subjects and institutions, as Dickens knew very well when he wrote the opening scene of *Hard Times*. You learn only where (and what) you do not know, and you learn most where you have to formulate your knowing as you go.

In an account of a University of East Anglia student project with Polish theatre, which attempted to create a physical and textual collage of the kinds of work central to *Street of Crocodiles* (though drawing on a range of other nineteenth- and twentieth-century texts), one of us asked to what extent this could be seen as 'a radical model of learning, which constantly foregrounds the moment of break-up and reformation at both the individual and the collective level'. What are its processes and practices, its dangers, its potentials and its implications both for 'student-centred learning' and for models of knowledge? If work like this proposes new attitudes and configurations, and a belief that learning occurs principally in the body in motion, it does so in conscious evocation of a pedagogy which understands that to locate that work at the nodal point of form and praxis is a political choice. For Murray, Lecoq represents 'an ethical preoccupation with the power of theatre to break down barriers' (Murray 2003: 109). When you ask people to make the 'theatre to be created', you imply a radicalisation of both form and function: neither the business of teaching nor the business of acquainting students with the processes of deconstruction (as opposed to academic theory about it) are value-neutral undertakings.

All the functions of improvisation which have emerged from this discussion indicate that it has to do with the extension of being, knowing and communicating. In one sense, you can't train people to improvise. But you can train them to set up the conditions in which improvisation can begin; you can assist them to recognise what inhibits it and to have the courage to face up to those blocks; you can get them to play, to enjoy, to let go and to learn to work with focused but not cramped attentiveness from that state. Such a form of training is most demanding and least coercive, because it leaves the responsibility for how far the process goes and for what emerges from it with the performer.

Chapter 10

Meaning and Performance

Improvisation promotes the capacity for creating meanings. Those meanings are created in performance, as a process occurring in the present moment. We now turn to some ways in which improvisation illuminates the nature of performative acts: how it amends, revises or interferes with the meanings they appear to offer, how it may interact with texts of various kinds, including the process of writing or constructing them, and how it may suggest alternative models or roles for performance (particularly of theatre) in the context of society.

Meaning as performance (or vice versa): the place of the improvisatory

Improvisation underlies and underlines the fact that meaning is created in performance as the collision or negotiation of different sets of meaning: that, for instance, which appears to reside in the 'text' and that which individual performers perceive and/or mediate; that which the audience expects and that which they receive. Julian Hilton notes that performance involves (*a*) incarnation and transmutation, and (*b*) execution and origination (Hilton 1988: 4–5). All of these features are *processes*, that is to say, they are ongoing and open-ended. They involve a change of state and the creation of something new. Improvisation contains all of them, but is particularly strong in terms of the second element of each pair. However, that element depends for its realisation upon the first, as for example Lecoq would stress that forms of play must be enacted physically (per-formed). The integrative ('body/think') function of improvisation links the two terms in each pair; it articulates changes of statement through changes of the state of the performer. Since, as we note with reference to the 'message' content of communication, the quality and significance of the communicative act depends on the condition of the actor/communicator (and on that of the responder/receiver), the ability of improvisation work to produce a charged-up condition makes the communicative and performative act much more potentially resonant; it carries an increased capacity for meaning, which means that additional levels or possibilities of significance are opened up.

The integrative condition sought by impro work is an organic balance, an ease of performance ('free play' in both the mechanical and the aesthetic sense) which may indeed be 'natural', but is not at all 'everyday'. It represents a highly tuned level of activity which invites or stimulates the further integration of performer and audience.

Improvisation also points up another feature of performative acts, namely that each is quite *different* from every other. No two appearances wearing the red nose are the same, nor do they develop the same sequence of events in time and space. Each occurs now, and only now, enacting a new configuration.

Thus all improvised acts can be defined as *integrative*, yet each is also both *specific*, defining itself by its own parameters (for example, its own who/what/why?) and *polysemantic*. This curious and powerful combination may indicate why the experience of performance created in the present can have such wide-ranging effects.

The development of multiple significance is responsible for much of the richness which emerges from performance. One major way in which improvisation can affect this is through *interfering* with what appears to be the established sequence and expectation of meaning: not merely as occasional serendipity or brilliant ad-lib, but as a constant readiness to challenge 'the rules of the game'. This refraction has political as well as aesthetic implications, as we indicate below in our discussion of improvisation and writing. And as Peggy Phelan says of performance, it is 'the art form which most fully understands the generative possibilities of disappearance' (Phelan 1993: 27).

This ephemeral quality, much interrogated by writing on performance in recent decades, has always been the core of the improvisatory. Indian and Buddhist aesthetics pre-empt Plato and Shakespeare in recognising that theatre above all arts exemplifies the play (*lila*) of transience (*maya*). It thus manifests both the risk and the revelation of all our assumptions about value, status and significance. Improvisation is a way of living in and out of that moment. We think that 'theatre', in its fullest sense, has always recognised this. What the improvisatory in theatre can highlight, in distinction to a generalised approach to 'performance', is a precise and focused methodology of working towards a particular quality of 'acts' and action. The plethora of writing on performance tends to suggest that it is everything from cultural signifier to anarchic intervention, which is intellectually interesting and practically useless. As Parts I and II have shown, improvisation hones specific skills, mental and physical processes, in marked and identifiable stages, in order to cultivate the ability to reprogramme and regenerate corporeal, linguistic, imaginative, receptive and collaborative abilities. These qualities are essential to makers of theatre and performance alike. It's not surprising that they have surfaced in the range of domains and geographies that we have located.

Texts, signs and meaning

The changing nature of 'text' is an important issue in the kind of meaning-production implied by the improvisatory style. Many of the theatrical events which give us pleasure and stimulation begin as a written text, the personal creation of an individual mind. On this basis actors, technicians and directors come together to work. After the completion of a production the published text can, of course, be used to generate new performances. The script of the play does not however always precede the performance. Nor can it convey half the complexity of the finished production: the multiplicity of signs which communicate (though they need the active decoding of alert receivers).[1] These include set, make-up, masks, movement, gesture, spatial relationships, vocal inflexion and so on.

The process of reading theatrical or *performance* text, however, is central to our understanding of how improvisation works. Semiotic analysis reminds us of two things: (1) that the improvising performer is continuously and spontaneously generating information on many levels (much of it unconscious); (2) that the process does not only involve a 'sender' and a 'receiver' (an 'active' performer and a 'passive' spectator); the spectator is active, too – more than usually so when watching something improvised. Decoding information implies the creation of new, often unsuspected or unintended, meanings from the signals received. The audience does not only 'read' the performance – in a very real sense it 'writes' it, too: performances, as David George says, are 'exercises in restless semiosis' (George 1999: 17).

The shamanic performer's mask, for example, activates what Peirce calls the 'triadic' system of signs. By being *there*, physically present amongst the audience, and by feeding the audience with simultaneous *iconic*, *indexical* and *symbolic* information, the mask makes the dissolution of the boundary between the actual and the virtual possible.[2] The audience understands, or at least operates on all three levels simultaneously. So the shamanic mask enables the spectator to apprehend the intended meaning, and also to create that meaning. The performer has to do very little but to be there.[3] The spectator is the active partner: the one generating the meaning, the one 'writing' the play as it happens; and the meaning that is 'read' and 'written' in this way is of vital importance, for it concerns the belief system which underpins the whole community. But all performances put in play belief systems, 'grand narratives', social and cultural assumptions which are thus, ideally (from a deconstructionist viewpoint) revealed as such, as versions or fictions among others, up for grabs and for renegotiation.

The information set supplied (the totality of words, sounds, movements, colours, textures and proxemics) depends for its transmission upon a parallel set within the mind of the spectator. This second set is a matrix of language, associations, memories and images which enables the received information to be simultaneously contextualised and recontextualised. It is the interaction of these two complementary sets – their collision, or fusion perhaps, sometimes called by semioticians 'intertextuality' (Arthur Koestler refers to it as creative 'bisociation' generating '*collision* ending in laughter, or . . . *fusion* in a new intellectual synthesis, or . . . *confrontation* in an aesthetic experience: Koestler 1964: 45) – that creates both purpose and meaning, charging the event with significance.

This indicates the complexity of a 'text', and of the processes by which it is 'read'. In a deconstructive understanding, 'text' principally signifies a network of propositions or provisional narratives, not a definitive statement; playing with meanings, or the play of meaning itself. Thus text itself approaches the *ambiguity* or *hesitation*[4] which is found at the heart of all performance and is the key to improvisation, in the sense that 'anything can happen'.

Improvisation doesn't work entirely without a pre-existent 'text', any more than language or creativity do: but what it does is to operate with the ever present possibility of reorganisation – of shaking the kaleidoscope again – which can keep you on your toes, on the edge of your seat or on the limits of your mental and physical world. It turns text into texturing, into the art of weaving new patterns. We have indicated in Part I the range of 'texts' and kinds of retexturing that occur.

Improvisation and writing

Michael Chekhov, in *To the Director and Playwright*, makes the point, familiar to anyone who has written a play, that the playwright is as much an improviser as the actor: consciously or unconsciously, the playwright is 'an actor on paper'.

> [T]here is not a single instant of the playwright's creations that is not preceded by improvisation, even though . . . maybe all of it, is done mentally. (Leonard 1963: 35)

How much of what has been discussed in this book, therefore, is applicable to the (usually) solitary practice of writing as opposed to the communal activity of playing; how much is transferable from studio to study?

It is easy to accept that 'just as the actor must be his own playwright when he is improvising without a script, so the playwright must be his own actors when he is devising their dialogue' (p. 35), for, as every writer will admit, the construction of each line, and the inner listening to its imagined responses, is a kind of intellectual improvisation. There are passages in any play which playwrights will say 'wrote themselves'; where the writer's critical consciousness dissolves temporarily and they seem to 'channel' the voices and actions of imaginary beings. This inspired, Pirandellian, state is quite common and expresses the organisation at a state just below consciousness of the play's materials. Frequently (generally when there is no one around to think them deluded), writers vocalise lines aloud, as if acting out the parts they have written. They do this to test the *muscularity* of a phrase (its potential for action), as much as its sonority, or its ability to catch the imagined rhythm of a character.

So writers naturally improvise (whatever they consciously think of the process). Chekhov suggests that the process is akin to mask-wearing, too, with the 'mask' the playwright wears while creating characters consisting of six elements in simultaneous interplay.

These are: (1) surface dialogue (by no means the most important element); (2) the underlying feelings and emotions of the characters; (3) their objectives; (4) their tactics to disguise their wants and feelings; (5) the 'individual, subjective atmosphere' of the character and, finally, (6) the Steinerian 'higher ego' of the playwright, the artistic perception which governs the choices they make. This subjective mental penetration into the diegetic world of the play certainly occurs, whether or not one accepts Chekhov's post-Stanislavskian categories, and differs in kind from the more cerebral processes of research, planning and conscious scripting that are also necessary. (Leonard 1963: 165–6)

Improvisation, too, is a tool much used in the *teaching* of creative writing. Keith Johnstone ran the Royal Court Writers' Group under George Devine, from 1958, where playwrights like Wesker, Bond, Jellicoe and Soyinka learned their craft at weekly sessions, and 'anyone suffering from writer's block could bring material into the group where it formed a starting point for improvisation' (Wardle 1978: 199).

Improvisation remains both a personal technique for averting blockages, and an explicitly communal technique for a different kind of writing which resituates the writer as a member of a creative ensemble. The plays of Anthony Neilson, among many other contemporaries, are sometimes deliberately 'unfinished' as they go into rehearsal, because material will be generated in the rehearsal process to complete them. Devising is an increasingly common and acceptable means of play creation, particularly with young people and groups, and clearly overlaps with improvisation, using many of its techniques to generate and develop a performance text.[5]

In the creative writing classroom, improvisation exercises and games abound, because they serve many of the same needs as in the acting studio. They help young writers overcome the internal censor or 'Cop in the Head'; generate starting points for personal creativity and liberate subconscious ideas; stimulate and stretch the imagination; encourage creative listening and group co-operation; discover alternative possibilities for scenes and characters; suggest lines of plot development; explore subtle shifts in status within scenes; provoke new material for rewrites; and actively 'performance test' the written word. Many of the same exercises are easily adapted by more experienced writers, too, as a way of shaking loose stubborn ideas, or revitalizing a project that is in danger of becoming stale.

Some are useful starters. Del Close's 'Ad Game' (Halpern et al.

1994: 52–5) generates energy and teaches writers that everything is usable; everything can be justified and woven into a developing story. Spolin's 'Where–Who–What?' exercise works just as well for a writing improvisation as an acting one. In the writing class, suggestions are solicited from, and elaborated upon by, the whole group. It rapidly becomes clear to them that whichever factor (character, action, location) is chosen first, the other two are easily generated; if one has two of these factors, the third is always implicit in them. A Spolin derivative that works well is to ask for a location, two characters and a random line of dialogue, and then tease out the story they contain. Something like 'finding the game' in Del Close's terminology occurs. The pattern-making mind instantly tries to connect the snippets and from them is able to propagate narrative – and ultimately dialogue. The group may come to conclusions about what's going on: individual writers may then write the material up in a personal rather than a collective vein. Keith Johnstone's 'Status' exercises are invaluable, as are his storytelling impros. Writers (like actors) have to learn to see status as a verb rather than a noun, and to interpret subtle shades and shifts of status, in both language and action. The playing cards liberate the writers from the stress of having to *invent* by simply telling them that the next line (or character, or action) is higher or lower status than the preceding one. Close's 'Three-line Scenes' encourage rapidity and economy; but also challenge writers to *listen* closely to lines one and two, and to search for the story, scene or 'game' implicit in them, which line three will materialise (Halpern et al. 1994: 67–9).[6]

Chris Johnston elaborates on a Keith Johnstone *Newsletter* which lists twelve 'mistakes' to be avoided in impro or impro training, which are eminently redeployable in training writers. They include: *Cancelling* (avoiding or negating the project); *Sidetracking* (getting away from the main action and substituting another), or its variant, *Being Original*; *Instant Trouble* (rushing straight to the central conflict rather than working up to it); *Gossip* (chat rather than action, conversation rather than dialogue) and *Gagging* (playing gags rather than scenes); *Blocking* (discussed elsewhere: refusing the offer, saying 'no' rather than 'yes, and ...') (Johnston 1998: 190–2). Whatever the terminology, the faults are instantly recognizable to all writers.

Fay Lecoq, in her Afterword to the posthumous, 2002 edition of her husband's book *The Moving Body*, notes an extension rather than a diminution of the Ecole's activities with the addition of an *atelier d'écriture* run by playwright Michel Azama (Lecoq 1997: 186). It seems an important and timely inclusion in the Lecoq curriculum. We have seen many breathtaking performance moments by improvisation-trained graduates, yet frequently regretted the lack of a dramaturgical structure to unite them, a coherent narrative to be shared with an audience, or a literate verbal text commensurate with the physical lyricism of the actors' bodies. Like Copeau's injunction to Saint-Denis and the Copiaus, at the end of the Burgundian phase of their experiments, to return to working with the playwright André Obey, the establishment of the *atelier d'écriture* signals that improvisation can resume its place as a crucial, but not the only, component in the production of the drama.

Improvisation, which includes the devising of pattern, of movements or words, may also take the form of spatial collective writing or creative participation: a group working on an idea, or individuals contributing different (sometimes thoroughly researched) parts to a communal effort. As such it can form part of a working method for groups in education or in creative writing courses.

Incorporating the actors' research – both academic/investigative (going out and taking notes) and physical (finding out what it feels like to walk or talk like that kind of person) – into the performance means on one level involving them in the choices from which the play evolves, and on another level making them both discover and generate the 'subtext' or underlying motivation for each character or event. They are involved in an *existential* (how to find the resources in their own experience), *psychological* (how to motivate) and *semiological* (how to present in words and actions) commitment to the development of character and incident.

Emanating largely from the 1980s activist/socialist/feminist spectrum is a considerable body of 'collectivist' work – Caryl Churchill and Joint Stock, John McGrath and 7/84, co-operative theatre companies like Red Ladder, Split Breeches, Gay Sweatshop. Similar kinds of input from company members is involved (for example, historical research by cast members for Churchill's *Light Shining in Buckinghamshire*); the process is quite largely collective though there is usually only one name on the final playtext, in contrast to some well-known anti-apartheid work in South Africa at the same time (Fugard, Kani and Ntshona's *Sizwe Banzi Is Dead* and Simon, Mtwa and Ngema's *Woza Albert*).

The argument that collaborative or collective writing or devising of this kind may be a form of *écriture feminine* also suggests links with Ariane Mnouchkine (see above, pp. 93–5), both in the early co-operative phase of Théâtre du Soleil's work and in her later collaboration with Hélène Cixous. Although not all the companies mentioned have particularly gender-related policies, *écriture feminine* is not only about women writers or solely about a focus on gender issues It can refer to an increased sensitivity towards the processes of production and a freer, less ratiocentric compositional and structural method. As such it may also be applicable to group devising and creation of all kinds, for example to workshopping with creative writers. The connection with our focus here is in terms of how working like this can:

1 free up inhibition through interactive debate, dialogue, sharing;
2 suspend mainly 'right hemisphere' logocentric process in favour of more spontaneous, imagistic, metaphoric or metonymic activity;
3 supplement a singular ego-driven dynamic with a more communal, perhaps 'collective' consciousness.

If such a group includes a writer/director, he or she can supply the basic information (or organise its collation); ask the actors to translate it into scenes via improvisation, which they will then take away and write up; or take on the status of a recording mechanism, transcribing the improvised actions and polishing the (probably) clumsy dialogue that emerges.

In the second case, working on an agreed subject, the whole company is the 'writer'. The director is the editor of a fully collaborative process; until, that is, the point is reached at which the work is to be scripted. Here the democratic process may become again, by default, an autocratic one. The editorial voice becomes an authorial voice. It may be that the group wants this to happen. If it doesn't, then the only way to proceed is for the entire company to be involved in assembling the final script – a clumsy way of working sometimes, but often surprisingly fertile. Some writers are afraid of collaboration. It diminishes their sense of their own inviolably unique creativity. But theatre is a collaborative art.

The ultimate form of this is a third case, where the play is the result of a collaboration not just between the members of the acting ensemble before the public is admitted, but between the ensemble and the audience during performance (for examples see Part I). The audience may be involved in shaping the play that it sees, offering suggestions, even taking roles. Or it may be left implicit, the collaboration one of mind and feelings as the actors shape their play in front of the audience, going along one pathway and abandoning others as they sense the mood of the spectators.

Dymphna Callery recalls Zeami's classic principle of *Jo–Ha–Kyu* – and Meyerhold's *otkaz–posil'–tochka* – as ways of rhythmically controlling material, and offers the 'circus' or 'variety' show (bound together by spectacle, each act having its own internal rhythm and dynamic) as alternative structuring models which both eschew the causal structure of traditional narrative and avoid involvement in any character's interior journey.

She reminds us that Odin Teatret under Barba's direction have developed 'a distinctive way of using montage to structure improvisation work so that an audience has an active and individual response rather than a collective empathy for a central protagonist' (Callery 2001: 193).

> Barba will suggest a theme to actors; they create improvisations from their personal response to the material, which he then reworks. He does not enter into any dialogue about the actor's motivations, but orchestrates their solo improvisations into 'actions', sequences of action, and scenes, re-ordering and structuring according to his own intuitive sense of tempo and rhythm. (Callery 2001: 193)

In responding to an Odin production the straightforward pleasure of narrative clarity is frequently denied. Likewise, interpretation is deliberately made difficult. 'Meaning is virtually shunned. It is the experience of the spectators that counts' (p. 193). There is not always a single visual focus (*Andersen's Dream* is set in a relatively small, specially constructed, encircling and containing theatre 'capsule'; even here, events happen above, around, behind the spectator), or a single character upon whom we can map a developing narrative. There is deliberate discontinuity and discontiguity.

Jane Turner applies Patrice Pavis's narratalogical terminology – the 'condensation' and 'displacement' of narrative readability, via 'accumulators', 'connectors', 'secators' and 'shifters' – to Barba's complex intercultural performance scores (Turner 2004: 86ff.). 'In other words, what we as spectators see and experience, we displace or substitute with a series of our own associations and connections' (p. 89). Callery summarises:

This is closer to the idea of circus spectacle than narrative unity, yet Barba's work is much more than variety acts. What unifies the work are deep philosophical concerns rather than simply entertainment, plus a desire to affect the spectator on a primal level. (Callery 2001: 193).

The process here is prising open the tendency to narrative predictability or closure (see above regarding writing), in favour of 'accident' (Fo on the Molière troupe) or 'refraction'. Performers and/or spectators are offered the space to play (irreverently): as Philippe Gaulier says, '*Amusez-vous Merde!*' The 'deep philosophical concerns' are enacted as the identification of key moments in which to *intervene in your own story*, not to let it be told only by others.

On a more conscious – though by no means superficial – level, this links directly with what Frances Babbage notes of Boalian Forum work as a 'space for dissection and debate', because 'as each intervention takes place ... the narrative is unmade and remade before our eyes' (Babbage 2004: 45), thus offering the possibility of imaginative engagement in the production of a new story of the world. The collision of improvisation and writing opens up this operation, in which metaphysics and politics are not disjunctive realms.

Co-creativity

An act of theatre has many sets of meaning. There are those which are created in the act of performance *jointly* by actors and audience members; and those other kinds of 'performance' which arise *privately* in the mind of either after the event is concluded and the partners in the original act have separated.

The meaning of a theatre event (unlike, say, the meaning of a novel) is not only experienced singly, but communally. This type of meaning derives not so much from the intention, but from the 'flavour' of the experience. Obvious examples might be the communal laughter shared during the performance of a successful farce, or the hushed stillness, when the communal heartbeat of the audience seems to race, during the performance of some terrifying stunt in the circus.

Meaning is never solipsistic, in spite of the illusion generated by private reading (whose text? whose language?). Where we mean, we bleed: across our boundaries, out of our skins, into each other. In improvising meanings, we always depend on others to acknowledge or accept them, and on 'others' in ourselves sometimes to generate them against the grain of habit or taboo. On the others we can invoke or conjure or parody or exorcise too, linguistically or attitudinally or empathetically. I am more than I seem, if I can learn to seem effectively, as Hamlet and others imply. To make music together is a politics, an act and praxis of negotiation, as well as a buzz or a vibe.

Improvisers need proximity. They cannot be isolated from their co-creators. Practically, during improvised performances a lot of *small* things happen. Being spontaneously created, there isn't time for the actor to rehearse and selectively enlarge them. They happen briefly and are then extinguished. The audience has to be close enough to notice them, and to nudge itself in the ribs to call attention to them.

After the claims for decorum laid down by the nineteenth-century theatre space, we can observe a kind of Freudian volcanic upsurge of cabaret-type activity at crucial points in the twentieth century – in the 1920s and 1930s in Germany, for instance, or in the 1960s in Britain. Much of this work used the methods of improvisation in its development (especially a direct, creative response to the immediate social and political context) and relied upon acute audience participation. Athol Fugard recalls how, in apartheid South Africa, the audience for *Sizwe Banzi is Dead* – a play constructed from workshop improvisation with actors John Kani and Winston Ntshona – in a township meeting hall in 1973 not only swamped the auditorium and spilled over onto the stage, but viewed the event more as a political meeting than a play, resulting in 'the most amazing and spontaneous debate I have ever heard' *during* the performance (Kruger 1999: 160).

The relationship between theatre – both as institution and as event – and society is a complex and reciprocal one, but it can be argued that forms of social change are at the least reflected, and possibly instigated or supported, in the form and content of drama. The problem at the beginning of the twenty-first century may be that improvisation has become so accepted – embedded in school programmes at many levels in the West, and through applications such as Boal's, as a form of theatre training in many parts of the world – that it reflects a social tendency to render anodyne through familiarity. The resolution will at least in part depend not only on sociopolitical context, but on the inherent resilience of the kinds of processes instigated by improvisatory method. Those kinds of questions are being asked in situations where the context is government corruption,

HIV/AIDS, female foeticide, land exploitation and the economics of global capitalism.

The improviser marks this possibility and the challenge of operating in these zones too, of defining as it were the extreme limit of play, the edge of the road before it drops over the precipice. If you dare, you can go right up to the edge. And once you know that, it affects the use you subsequently make of the road. We may view our life-scripts in a different way afterwards. The improvisatory mode, as Jacques Lecoq and others have suggested, has frequently posed this challenge to orthodoxy. Its origins seem linked to a cultural matrix which the last few centuries have marginalised and reduced to 'alternative' status: the shamanistic, the clown, the carnival. Though its beginnings may be the beginning of theatre itself (Dionysiac rites, integrating community and environment, and centred on a state of being 'enthused', operating in a kind of psychic overdrive), many social orders have seen the need either to repress or to marginalise (by licensing in a strictly limited way) anything to do with the spirit of creative play. Individual creativity, from the point of view of order, is a dangerous and disruptive thing (as Keith Johnstone and Teatr Ósmego Dnia strikingly record), and even more dangerous if it issues in communal ceremony and performance. The 'double' of society, anything to do with the liberation of instinct and feeling, has frequently been subjected to this kind of treatment. Fo and Rame provide a contemporary example which the figure of the (sometimes 'divine') Fool extends through history in many cultures.

New combinations; saying Yes, hearing No

The practice of the *via negativa* and *via negationis* ('the negative way', 'the way of negation') may seem at odds with Keith Johnstone's primary injunction to say 'yes' (or, with Del Close, to say 'yes, and . . .'), but the contradiction is, really, only apparent. The terms have their origin in Neoplatonic thought; in the Plotinian practice of *apophasis*. Plotinus argued that, since the deity is not an object in creation, no words, no language, can approach its description: all one can say is what God is *not*. The idea is hardly unique to Western theology (the concepts of *neti neti* – god is 'not this, not that'; 'neither this, nor that' – in Hinduism, *ein-sof* in Cabbalistic Judaism and *bila faifa* in Islam address the same impossibility).

Grotowski, along with Barba, Lecoq, Prattki, Gaulier, Pagneux and many others, has a shared understanding that the object of the tuition is, ultimately, indescribable. Hence, they naturally (and no doubt temperamentally) gravitate towards the apophatic in their teaching style. It is frequently only possible to say what is not working, rather than specify what is required (Murray 2003: 143).[7]

A similar apophasis underpins Samuel Beckett's spiritual autobiographies: it is not possible to say what is sought, there is only the constant experience of seeking, and failing, and seeking again. However, this, as with the practitioners referred to above, is not just a question of saying that you can't say it: it is actually about *inhabiting* the area of the unsayable, because that's the only place you haven't been before and therefore the only place worth being now. So to be such a writer, or an actor in such a theatre, means an endless commitment to the search: to saying 'yes' all the time – even as the tutor, director, *metteur en scène*, *auteur*, audience is bound (most of the time) to say 'no' – or, less bluntly but just as frustratingly, 'yes, that's not it either!'

Eugenio Barba's pursuit of 'Disorder' enters the same inexpressible territory of verbal regress. With a lower-case initial, the word signifies 'the absence of logic and rigour characterising nonsensical and chaotic works'. With a capital D, however, it signifies for him 'the logic and rigour which provoke the *experience of bewilderment* in the spectator'. Orthography serves to distinguish what ought to be distinguished in vocabulary, between 'disorder as a loss of energy, [and] Disorder as the irruption of an energy that confronts us with the unknown' (Barba 2005: 50).

As he approached his seventieth birthday, Barba recalled not only forty years of work with Odin Teatret but certain theatrical moments (Brecht's *Die Mutter*, *Kathakali* in Kerala, Grotowski's *The Constant Prince*) indelibly imprinted on his memory which typified for him that strange encounter with the ineffable:

> Similarly, in an unexpected and involuntary way I have experienced and still experience Disorder while working with my actors. From the very beginning, certain designs of their physical or vocal actions, continuously repeated and refined, leap into another reality of being.
>
> I have personally witnessed it: a denser, brighter and more incandescent body than the bodies we possess emerges in the theatrical space from an *elsewhere* which I cannot place. This body-in-life irrupts, regardless of good or bad taste, by a combination of chance and craft or because of an unforeseen event in a highly structured calculation.

Today it is clear to me: theatre has represented a precious tool to make *incursions* into zones of the world that seemed out of my reach. (Barba 2005: 60)

What has the training of my actors been if not a bridge between these two extremes: the incursion into the machine of the body, and an opening for the irruption of an energy that shatters the limits of the body? ... Disorder that rocks my familiar ways of living the space and time around me and, through bewilderment, compels me to discover another part of myself. (p. 61)

Improvisation continually nibbles at meaning and nudges towards meanings. It highlights the way performance can be creative as well as normative, implying a dynamic model for the role of theatre and performance both for individuals and within society. It can assist in shifting the parameters by which we live. In bending the rules it proposes new forms: Lecoq's focus on 'the spirit of the play', found in many forms in improvisation work, picks up Schiller's sense that man is fully human only when he plays (Hilton 1988: 45–6): it is the 'will to play' (*Spieltrieb*) which produces new combinations of matter and form.

Notes

Introduction

1 Here we mean what Durkheim calls the 'taboo sacred'; that which acts as a social or political boundary policed by religious authority. In another sense – closer to the shamanic and the improvisational – the mark of sacred *experience* (as opposed to doctrine) may be said to be precisely that it escapes all such boundaries. See Yarrow et al., *Sacred Theatre* (forthcoming 2007).

2 'He that schal pleye Belyal loke that he have gunne-powder brennynge In pypys in his handis & in his eris & in his ars whanne he gothe to battel' (from the fifteenth-century *The Castell of Perseverance* (see Southern 1957: 19). Not recommended for improvisers of a nervous or combustible constitution.

3 The account given by Bakhtin of the grotesque accords not only with ancient representations of the *mimi*, but also with Jacques Lecoq's *bouffonerie* (although Lecoq may be thought to shade out of the true grotesque into the fantastical).

1 Improvisation in Traditional Drama

1 See also Martin (2002).

2 'Improvisation was Vakhtangov's basic experimental technique. Vakhtangov allowed the form of his plays to develop through a series of improvisations by his actors from which he would select the interpretation he considered most appropriate. Then with a more dictatorial attitude, he carried out the final honing. But the discovery through improvisation was a collaborative endeavor' (Hull 1985: 230).

3 Carnicke provides a detailed account of Stanislavsky's ideas,

their language, publication and reception. The book, centred on a reinterpretation of Stanislavsky's Russian, includes an excellent glossary (1998: 169–82).

4 'Doctor Dappertutto' is to be found in E. T. A. Hoffman's *Fantasiestücke in Callot's Manier*, part II.

5 See Doisy 1954: 105; Donahue 2001: 61–72, esp. p. 69; also Copeau's *Journal, Deuxième partie: 1916–1948*, Vol. 2 (1991: 87) for an account of Bing's work with the Vieux-Colombier actors and children at Morristown. See also Hodge 2000: 69–75; and Kurkinen 2000: *passim*, for a discussion of her mime teaching.

6 See Copeau 1974: 17; images of his original *affiche* appear on the Comédie Française website at http://www.comedie-francaise.fr/aujourdhui/hiervc.php; and, at a more useful scale, can also be seen at http://gallica.bnf.fr/anthologie/notices/01549.htm. Copeau's aim was 'to scour the sclerosis of routine from the drama and liberate the expressive spontaneity of the actor' (Doisy 1954: 79; our translation).

7 The second phase of this development was designed by Louis Jouvet, who was stage manager, leading man and part-time architect.

8 Meyerhold's view of the *cabotin* differs from Copeau's; for him 'The cabotin is a strolling player . . . a kinsman to the mime, the histrion, and the juggler . . . [who] keeps alive the tradition of the true art of acting' (Braun 1969: 122). There was no disagreement between them as to the qualities required for the new acting: what Copeau opposed was a style of acting made up of the conglomerated tricks of the *cabotin* – the shortcuts of the 'old pro' and 'ham-ateurism'.

9 There is a fascinating reverse parallel here with the puppet alteregos ('bio-objects') of the Polish director Tadeusz Kantor. These outgrowths, carried on characters' backs in his *Dead Class*, signal the self which has been lost or suppressed by adulthood's subservience to social or political violence. The Copiaus's Masks, on the other hand, embody a celebration or liberation of the inner or 'other' life.

10 Similar difficulties would undermine the Second City troupe in their attempt to find American comic archetypes (see pp. 53–7).

11 Since we wrote the first edition of this book, le Théâtre du Vieux-Colombier has been reopened. Purchased by the state in 1986, Copeau's original building was renovated in 1993 by

architect Bernard Kohn as a second house for the Comédie Française.

12 It is worth noting that Lecoq, in our interview with him in Paris in April 1987, made a strong distinction between Copeau and the 'Copiaus': for him, it was the work of the latter during this period that laid the foundations of modern impro work. Léon Chancerel's 1935 Théâtre de l'Oncle Sebastien specialised in improvised work for children. Dasté and, of course, Saint-Denis expanded performance and training skills.

13 One candidate might be the Lyric, Hammersmith, which supported much of the developmental work of The Improbables (see p. 233, n. 11), and staged shows by them which included large elements improvised afresh each performance. Michael Boyd, as incoming Director of the RSC, announced plans for a devised play, *Pontius Pilate*, created via improvisation as part of a project, political rather than necessarily dramaturgical, 'to reinvent the collective theatre-making process at the RSC' which he felt had declined during Adrian Noble's tenure. It is interesting that group devising emerges again as the expression of dramaturgical democracy, in the RSC's first attempt at devised work for its main stages (five performances as part of New Works festival 'in and around' The Other Place in Stratford in 2004).

14 Mike Leigh's works to date fall into four main periods:

(1) **1965–74**: mostly stage plays (two out of sixteen were filmed);
(2) **1975–85**: mostly TV (three out of fourteen also staged including *Abigail's Party*);
(3) **1987–2004**: mostly film, including *Secrets and Lies* and *Vera Drake* (three out of thirteen stage only);
(4) **2006**: marks the start of a fourth period (stage: *Two Thousand Years*).

For full details up to *Naked* see Coveney 1996: 237–43; and for the rest see Watson 2004: vii.

15 Main offshoots of the original Compass idea were: Second City, Chicago, founded in 1959 by Sills and still going; The Premise, founded in New York by Theodore J. Flicker, 1960–4; The Committee, founded in San Francisco by Alan Myerson, 1963–73.

16 Lenny Bruce (1925–66): legendary stand-up comic, writer and satirist. Mort Sahl (born 1927 in Montreal): comedian and screenwriter, and at the time of writing still doing stand-up, e.g. Child: 'What did you do in the War, Daddy?' Parent (George W. Bush voice): 'I started it.'

17 See obituary and biography by fellow Harold player Kim 'Howard' Johnson at http://www.geocities.com/SouthBeach/Pointe/2765/ KimHowardJohnson/khjdelcl.html (accessed 28 June 2006). Johnson recounts that Del's last joke was to bequeath his own skull to the Goodman Theatre, so he could get acting credits in any future productions of *Hamlet*.

18 The story (Halpern et al. 1994: 7) is that Bill Mathieu of The Committee christened the new form facetiously ('What shall we call it?' 'Harold. 'OK.') and the name stuck: the analogy is made with Beatle George Harrison's moment in the 1964 film *A Hard Day's Night* ('What do you call that haircut?' 'Arthur.'). Close always rather regretted the silly name for a serious invention. For details of other long-form styles, see Lynn 2004: 100ff. and Kozlowski 2002: *passim*.

19 LARP theory centres on the Scandinavian countries, and much of it is web-based: see particularly Montola and Stenros 2004; Gade et al. 2003; Bøckman and Hutchison 2005 (all contain combative, spiky essays in English); and Geir Tor Brenne's 2005 graduate thesis, 'Making and Maintaining Frames: A Study of Metacommunication in Laiv Play', University of Oslo. The *Amor Fati* website has an extensive electronic library (at http://fate.laiv.org/in_arti.htm) and includes articles on dramaturgy and improvisation in relation to LARPing.

20 Reviews can be seen at http://www.musicalthemusical.com/reviews.htm.

21 Holmes was hitherto best known for writing *Escape: The Piña Colada Song* and for his compositions for Barbra Streisand, Barry Manilow, Dolly Parton and others. Although a fully trained clarinettist and composer, he was principally a pop song writer and arranger, with no Broadway track record. Britain's Josie Lawrence has a remarkable facility for improvising meaningful lyrics in almost any style, which she has demonstrated on *Whose Line is it Anyway?* The playwright, singer, actress and comedienne Victoria Wood also excels at improvised songwriting. *Calypso* improvises lyrics to well-known and well-loved music, the interest being often in the sexual challenge conveyed

in the lyrics; and '*Freestyle*' rap aims to create meaningful lyrics spontaneously, instinctively, rhythmically and at high speed: the rap artist – or performance poet – is 'raising his voice to be heard'.

22   Richard Christiansen wrote of the Broadway version that it 'catches the customers in an embrace of agreeable partnership' (*The Chicago Tribune*, 17 December 1985). In the Induction scene to Ben Jonson's 1614 *Bartholomew Fair*, the 'covenant' between spectator and playwright and company is ironically drawn up by a Scrivener.

2   Improvisation in Non-Western Drama

1   Zarrilli et al. (2006), although claiming to 'relate the histories of performance and theatre throughout the world to the key developments in modes of human communication' (p. xvii), makes only five references to improvisation – and only one to Jacques Lecoq, whose name is misspelled.

2   Literally, 'the place that receives the light' (Watson 2001: 91). See also Coldiron 2004: 92–9; she indicates that *taksu*, like the *Noh hana*, is a 'performance state' comparable to Czikszentimihalyi's 'flow' – 'merging of action and awareness' (Coldiron 2004: 45).

3   There may be parallels here may with the Dutch colonialist character in some *Topeng* performance and the figure of the English sahib in Indian folk forms. Both tend to be used as comic relief.

4   In other contexts the term has more profound and theological connotations: the root meaning is 'imitation'. The cognate Turkish term is *taklit*.

5   *Orta* = middle and *oyun* = play: hence 'play in the middle'; *meidan oyunu* means 'play in the open air' or 'play in the round'.

6   In the late nineteenth and twentieth centuries occasional indoor performances were given in large coffee houses or even in Western-style theatres, with audiences segregated by sex. There was a single stage entrance, and (until Kemal Atatürk's social reforms of the 1920s) women in the audience sat opposite it, physically segregated from the men, obscured from the male gaze and from the stage behind a large veil. These women's areas were called *kefes*, or 'cages'.

7 This probably relates to the Anatolian narrative tradition where the *meddah* ('praisegiver', 'panegyrist') or storyteller's solo performance peoples the audience's imaginary stage; and to the shadow play, where the *haialdji*'s mimicry conjures forth a host of characters from behind the screen. Much African story-telling adopts a similar mode.

8 Usually he is shorter and squatter than Pişekiar, though both of them are typically middle-aged or elderly characters in tradi-tional Turkish dress and form an eternal dyad identical to that of Karagöz and Hadjeivat in the shadow play. Tosun Effendi carries a cudgel as Karagöz sometimes does (both deriving perhaps from an earlier phallophoric comedy) and often lays about him with it.

9 Barber and her collaborators all had the experience of partici-pating in the forms they describe as well as recording them anthropologically. Collins played as a bandsman in the Ghanaian 'Jaguar Jokers' concert party; Ricard made a film about concert party in Lomé; Barber herself acted in small roles with the Oyin Adéjobi Yorùbá popular theatre company.

10 For example, under apartheid, in the work of Athol Fugard with John Kani and Winston Ntshona (*Sizwe Bansi is Dead, The Island*); Barney Simon with Percy Mtwa and Mbongemi Ngema (*Woza Albert*); Workshop 71 and later Junction Avenue (*Sophiatown, Randlords and Rotgut* – Malcolm Purkey with the improvisations of the late Ramolao Makhene and others); Handspring Puppet Co. (*Ubu and the Truth Commission, Woyzeck on the Highveld*).

3 Improvisation in Alternative Drama

1 'Impro-Olympics' (and 'Theatre Sports' generally) are booming, one example being the radio and television improvisation game *Whose Line is it Anyway?* Games (which also make useful exer-cises) include 'Authors' (impro on an audience-suggested subject in a given literary style), 'Every Other Line' (one partner reads from a classic play, the other improvises an unrelated scene) and 'Improvising a Rap' (improvising rhyme and rhythm).

2 Also, to Grotowski, 'the actor' means 'an individual in action, who aims not at acting, but at acting less than in daily life and who draws others to the simplest, the most human, the most direct actions' (cited in J. Kumiega 1985: 236).

3   Most quotations by Lecoq in this section are derived from brochures published by the Ecole Jacques Lecoq, 57 rue du Faubourg Saint-Denis, Paris (unless otherwise attributed). These are supplemented by information provided by M. and Mme Lecoq themselves during an interview with the authors in Paris in April 1987. All translations are ours.

4   The systematisation of space in Lecoq's analytical work parallels that of Laban, at least in its recognition that 'There's a link, a reverberation between inner and outer space. If I make a physical action – pulling or pushing – it's analogous to internal emotion, love or hate. An oblique gesture can be sentimental, melodramatic. A vertical gesture is tragic. I indicate passions in space' (Hiley 1988).

5   Lecoq's students are often surprised, at least initially, to discover how much time is taken up by the *auto-cours* – and about how much they are expected to teach themselves. But many of the groups stemming from Lecoq first worked together and first discovered common interests in the *auto-cours* sessions.

6   Lecoq calls it 'a state of unknowing, a state of openness and availability for the rediscovery of the elemental' (1972: 41).

7   We are indebted here to Clive Mendus, who has worked with the Mediaeval Players and Théâtre de Complicité, both for his account of training at Lecoq's school and for excellent workshops on improvisation and clowning based on Lecoq's method. Much of Lecoq's clowning work has been developed by some of his early graduates who returned to teach at the school, in particular Philippe Gaulier.

8   There is an English translation of *Mistero buffo* by Ed Emery (1988).

9   'In my show, because I've worked on it, and especially because I've worked on it with audiences, I get a thousand or so laughs. Here it's a couple of hundred, because they've cut the translation, chucked out what they don't understand, and distorted the overtly political aspects' (Rame 1983: 115).

10 Fo's *Grammelot* is generically related to Saint-Denis's *Grummelotage*. In 'Dario Fo from One Language to Another', Valéria Tasca (1996) defines *grammelot*, a term deriving from Venetian *commedia*, as 'the semantization of free phonemes'. Ron Jenkins describes Fo, at the site of the Oracle at Delphi, translating 'classical Greek poetry into an onomatopoeic simulation of ancient Greek so convincing that classics scholars

claim to understand what he is saying' (Jenkins 2001: 13). He even incorporated *grammelot* into his Swedish Nobel acceptance speech.

11 In a conversation on French TV shortly before Lecoq's death, Fo and Lecoq reminisced about their early work together. Lecoq says: 'We just did it; we just made it up, but we had no idea.' And Fo replies: 'We had to throw away everything and construct a world. The world had to be made all over again' (Murray 2003: 14).

12 'Franca Rame belongs to a family of travelling players which even under fascism performed in the small towns and villages of Italy. It was in this hard school that she learnt the art of improvisation (at which she excels), of working with a minimum of sets and props, and of making a major contribution to a company in which everyone shares in the organisation of a performance' (Hood 1981: iv). She herself says: 'I was born into a family of actors who also were born into a family of actors and puppeteers going back to the seventeenth century, so my relationship to the commedia dell'arte is in my DNA' (Rame, cited in Jenkins 2001: 79).

13 Perhaps related to Lecoq's fascination with the grotesque figure of the *bouffon* (less well known in the UK than in Europe), who comments ironically and satirically on the supposedly normal world around him.

14 Fo's attitude towards the unexpected is equally crucial: the 'accident' is the moment at which radical shifts of perspective become available. Fo quotes an exchange between the Italian *commedia* actors and Molière's troupe, in which the *commedia* players asked the French actors how they would react if the roof of their theatre began to fall in. The Parisian actors replied that they would stop the show immediately (no doubt citing seventeenth-century health and safety regulations). Fo then gives the Italian actors' response:

> That's the difference between our theater of improvisation and a theater that relies entirely on a written script . . . You drop the curtains and close down in the face of the unexpected . . . For you an accident is problematic. For us it is an advantage. We perform the accident. The collapse of the theater frightens you. For us it would be a stimulus to create something new. (Jenkins 2001: 11)

The French reaction is, interestingly, the exact opposite of what Artaud later recommends, but the ability to benefit from the abnormal and 'perform the accident' is a crucial characteristic of the politics and aesthetics of improvisation.

4 Beyond Drama – 'Paratheatre'

1 One of the most profound influences on Grotowski's work was Polish director Juliusz Osterwa (1887–1949) who founded the Reduta theatre studio in 1919. This was one of the first theatre *communities*: theatre, acting workshop and school, based on the idea of communal sharing. Similar experiments included that of Copeau at Pernand-Vergelesses; Michel Saint-Denis and Charles Dullin's attempts to set up theatrical communities; Stanislavsky's Studio experiments at Eupatoria (on the Black Sea, where each of the actors built his own house and lived in it, sharing all communal tasks); the Group Theatre in the USA tried it in the 1930s, and the Becks' Living Theatre and Peter Schumann's Bread and Puppet Theatre in the 1960s. All these are precedents and examples for Grotowski's later work at Brzezinka.

2 Grotowski was not alone here: it was typical Polish practice of the time. Artist, writer and director Tadeusz Kantor 'minced' texts – both his own and Polish classics – and his performers interacted and exchanged continuously on stage with objects and art works; playwrights Witold Gombrowicz and Tadeusz Różewicz ironised, exploded and fragmented conventional theatrical form. The historical context was the political and linguistic oppression of Poland by the Nazis and the USSR, in which the naked and sacrificial (or, for Różewicz, ironically passive) body and the transgression of imposed form became statements of humanitarian and political resistance.

3 In *Faustus* the audience was seated at refectory tables, partaking in Faust's last supper, while the actors used the table tops as their stages; in *Kordian* the spectators sat on the beds of the asylum in which Grotowski set the play; in *The Constant Prince* the audience surrounded the action and looked down on the martyrdom below with the detachment/involvement of observers at a medical operation; and in *Akropolis* they sat on platforms in the midst of the concentration camp – by the end of the play they were hemmed in by metal junk, suggesting oppression and, ultimately, the crematorium.

4   The phases of this work are:

> 1969–73: 'paratheatre', working from Polish Laboratory
> Theatre
> 1976–82: Theatre of Sources, working in the Polish forest
> 1983–6: 'Objective Drama', based at University of
> California, Irvine
> 1986–99: 'Art as Vehicle', based at the Workcenter of Jerzy
> Grotowski in Pontedera, Italy

5   The reader is referred to Rene Marineau's excellent attempts to decipher what were probably deliberate obfuscations of Moreno's early life (see Gale 1990).
6   See the Vereinigung Bildender Künstlerinnen Österreichs website http://www.vbk.org/jakob_levy_moreno_elisabeth_bergner.html (accessed on 26 June 2006).
7   This is now disputed: Bergner knew him well, but there's little evidence she acted for him at this time. Lorre, on the other hand, certainly got his start in *Das Stegreiftheater*.
8   See   http://www.vbk.org/jakob_levy_moreno_elisabeth_bergner.html.
9   These concepts and associated exercises are discussed in more detail, for example in Gale 1990: chs 2 and 3; many will be familiar to drama students and resemble exercises discussed elsewhere in this book.

5   Preparation

1   Stanislavsky was introduced to *prana* yoga by L. A. Sulerzhitsky (1872–1916). François Delsarte (1811–71) was the first to propound a modern *system of movement* (as opposed to a system of teaching dance). He influenced Emil Jaques-Dalcroze (1865–1950) whose work captivated Copeau and Bing, and also powerfully affected Adolphe Appia and Margaret Naumburg. F. Mathias Alexander (1869–1955) remains influential in acting and dance training in Britain and North America especially (thanks initially to Naumburg and John Dewey). The *Méthode naturelle* exercises of Georges Hébert (1875–1957) profoundly affected both Copeau's early work and the young Jacques Lecoq. Continuing to have major influence on dance training throughout Europe, Rudolf Laban (1879–1958) had an

impact also on British theatre practitioners like Joan Littlewood and her Theatre Workshop as well as many leading drama schools and university drama departments.

2 It has been followed by many other books; see Bibliography, and especially Boal (1992), Callery (2001), Johnston (1998) and Poulter (1987).

7 Moving towards Performance

1 Proust calls it 'involuntary memory'; believing that it gives us access to the *moi permanent* (a sense of self as more than transitory, extending across time, as a *capacity for* cognitive and affective experience), he makes it the core of his life's work about the processes of memory, imagination and artistic construction.

2 See also Grotowski: 'I want to advise you never in the performance to seek for spontaneity without a score. In the exercises it is a different thing altogether . . . . Today . . . I will create these details and you can try to find their different variations and justifications. This will give you an authentic improvisation – otherwise you will be building without foundations' (1968: 192).

3 'All that is on the stage is a sign' was the central tenet of the Prague structuralist Jiri Veltrusky. Everything seen, heard or sensed, including all aspects of the actor's present behaviour, has *significance* and becomes available for meaning-making. In the case of improvisation, major signifiers may be the hesitations, breathiness, discomfort of the *actor*, rather than the intended signified of the character or narrative. Improvisers need to be in control of the signs they produce, and to draw selectively upon their inner repertoire (see Veltrusky 1940: 7). We shall make further reference to this idea in Part III.

4 Eldredge interviewed or studied with, *inter alia*, Tom Leabhart (the Decroux mime specialist), Jacques Lecoq, Bari Rolfe, Carlo Mazzone-Clementi, Peter Schumann (of Bread and Puppet Theater), Copeau's daughter Marie-Hélène Dasté and the family of W. T. Benda (whose contribution to the study of masked acting needs further exploration).

5 Eldredge regards them as 'wonderful masks, but . . . increasingly questionable in our multicultural age because their physiognomy immediately signals their European heritage . . . No

one Neutral Mask is appropriate for everyone in our diverse culture. The advantage of the simple paper Neutral Mask is that it is more abstract. It signals "human face" but has less indication of a particular nationality'(1996: 43). We disagree, and suggest that the neutral mask signals its own *theatricality*. The Sartori-derived neutral mask isn't gendered or suggestive of ethnicity: its gaze is not locatable in terms of culture or biology (no one's skin is *that* shade of leather). We simply say, 'One mask is slightly bigger than the other; choose the one that feels most comfortable on your face.'

6 Cf. '*Noh* and *Topeng* masks cover either slightly less than the full face or . . . the upper part of the face only' (Emigh 2004: xvi). Strindberg envisioned the use of similar masks by Ensor for *A Dream Play*.

7 By 'Stanislavsky's psychological model', Eldredge means the 'internal conflict between the character's persona and his "real Self" '; by the Brechtian model, a 'focus on the dialectics of the character', either 'rooted in the external social, economic, and political forces' or 'between the psychophysical life of the mask (the character) and that of the actor playing the part' (Eldredge 1996: 99–100).

8 The Tunisian Lassaâd Saïdi (b.1951), chief exponent of this teaching method, was an associate of Lecoq for ten years His work was taught in Britain by, especially, the I Gelati group (whose name is a pun on the famous *commedia* troupe, I Gelosi) led by director James MacDonald and Malcolm Tulip.

9 Another technique we have found useful is to imagine a scene as a double-act by two cross-talk comedians who have to talk to each other via the audience, standing shoulder to shoulder but looking away from each other, so that the focus is always outwards.

10 The idea of Il Magnifico (Pantalone) as a rooster was first suggested by Pierre Duchartre (1924/1929), and eagerly seized upon by Copeau, who played Pantalone and from whom the modern tradition stems. Amusingly, Lecoq – whose name implies a rooster – also specialised in the Mask of Pantalone!

11 Trestle Theatre Company was founded in 1981 by Toby Willsher and John Wright. Wright is also the co-founder of Told By An Idiot and of the Wright School. His book on comedy (Wright 2006) contains over a hundred games and exercises. Trestle's shows include: *Plastered* (1984); *Top Storey* (1987);

Fool House (1997); *The Barretts of Wimpole Street* (2000); and
Beyond Midnight (2005). Improbable Theatre was founded in
1996 by Phelim McDermott, Julian Crouch and Lee Simpson
with producer Nick Sweeting; their plays which use masking
include *Lifegame* (1996 onwards); *Shockheaded Peter* (1998;
actually a Cultural Industry show); and their collaboration with
AMICI Dance Theatre Company, *Stars are Out Tonight* (2005)
– a piece which simply defies the term 'disability' and demonstrates the psychosocial and political dimensions which increasingly frequently develop from improvisatory work. Geese
Theatre (founded in America by John Bergman – who was
influenced by Clive Barker – in 1980, and now running in both
the USA and UK) have always specialised in work in prisons,
and make considerable use not only of improvised work but of
archetypal masks and Sally Brookes's 'fragment' masks (see
Callery 2001: 51).

12   There are other mask teachers who would offer the same thing,
for example Simon (2003).

8   Applied Improvisation Work

1   See also mnemonic games as learning strategies in Buzan
(1974).

9   Enriching the Communication of Meaning

1   See Blatner 1970, table 4, p. 131; Jennings 1973, 1988, 1993,
1994; Hodgson 1972; Bentley, 1973; Watson 1988; Pörtner
1967; Moreno 1946, 1959; also Yon, 1979–80, 42.

2   The (mild, and often mildly absurd – if exasperating) censorship of British drama before 1968 is full of directives to cut
stage business as well as the spoken part of the text: 'there must
be no scratching of private parts' (*Meals on Wheels*, Charles
Wood); 'The statue of President Johnson must not be naked'
(*Mrs Wilson's Diary*, Richard Ingrams and John Wells); 'It is
understood that, wherever the word "shit" appears, it will be
altered, in every case, to "it" ' (*Spare*, again by Charles Wood)
(Findlater 1967).

3   Protest had a literature, exemplified by writers such as Colin
Wilson and Kingsley Amis, and the borrowed writings of Jack
Kerouac and Allen Ginsberg. John Osborne gave it a dramatic

literature. It found its own proper musical form in affinity with the free, improvised art of jazz.

4 'Theatre-people must always have found their marginalization puzzling. Non-theatre-people kept accusing them of practising deception, not understanding how one can live with the creation of artefacts that have no continuous material base; theatre-people shrug: we live in a world of elusive temporality; isn't that what the world is actually like? They always knew that their worlds were "unreal", the product of their wills, consciousness, perceptions, sensations, desires, that they had no substance, no "self". Paradoxically, it was theatre-people who never made the cognitive mistake which Buddhists spend their lives refuting. No-one needed to tell them about dependency arising, impermanence, temporality, insubstantiality, no-thing-ness' (George 1999: 35).

10 Meaning and Performance

1 Roland Barthes thought of theatre as a paradigm for semiological analysis; so dense and rich are its signs that they offer 'a real informational polyphony' which often daunts the analyst – who retreats into textual study (Barthes 1964, trans. Howard 1972: 262; see also Elam 1980: 19).

2 An 'icon' is a sign that is similar to what it represents (the masked actor looks like the imagined demon or god – colourful, impressive, larger than life, inhuman; the mask purports to be, and is assumed to be, an image, a likeness of the spirit). An 'index' is a sign that points to other realities (the mask points to the godliness of the performer). A 'symbol' is a sign bearing imputed, learned associations (the colour red stands for the demonic, for example, or green for heroism).

3 In the Indian *Ramlila*, the child actor playing Rama is often described (by outsiders) as passive and immobile. To the Western way of thinking, the signs transmitted are mostly those of the actor's 'inadequacies'. Not so the Indian spectator. To the devotee, the child is holy – Shiva incarnated. As such he does not need to *do* anything. He has only to be there. His presence provides the necessary visual focus for the act of devotion. It is the spectator who is active and the actor who is passive: the boy player is the blank slate upon which the spectator 'writes' the real drama of the event.

4   The terms figure in Russian Formalism (*ostranienye* – recycled
    by Brecht as *Verfremdung*) and fantasy theory: markers of the
    cognitive leap from the recognised to the unknown.
5   Devising has its own extensive literature, theory and tech-
    niques: see Oddey 1994, Lamden 2000, Bicât & Baldwin 2002,
    and Heddon & Milling 2006.
6   Close and Halpern's exercises include: 'What makes this day
    different?' (Halpern et al. 1994: 82); 'Start in the middle' (p.
    83), 'Finding the scene' and 'Listening for the game' (pp. 81ff.):
    all enjoyable and extremely useful. John Wright's *Why is That
    So Funny?* (2006) contains many remarkable exercises, includ-
    ing 'Five Steps to Heaven' (pp. 172–3), which uses Lecoq's
    tension cycle to discuss how to 'set-up' comic (and dramatic)
    scenes.
7   John Wright affectionately characterises Lecoq as 'a confronta-
    tional teacher', whose use of the *via negativa* is defined as 'a
    strategy where the teacher restricts comment to the negative,
    namely what is *inappropriate* and unacceptable, thus forcing
    the student to discover what is *appropriate*, whilst avoiding
    being prescriptive . . . (compelling) each individual to find his
    or her own way in the work through watching, listening and
    eventually taking a risk in front of the audience. These are
    invaluable skills for a theatre artist which, in the devising
    process, have to be found under pressure' (in Chamberlain and
    Yarrow 2002: 72). Wright and Murray both regard Lecoq's use
    of the *via negativa* as a way of destabilizing and energising his
    students.

Bibliography

*   practical manual, or work containing exercises

Alfreds, Mike, *A Shared Experience: The Actor as Story Teller* [interview by Peter Hulton, London, June 1979], *Dartington Theatre Papers*, 3rd series, no. 6 (1979–80).

Althusser, Louis, 'Notes towards an Investigation', in *Lenin and Philosophy and Other Essays*, trans. Ben Brewster (New York and London: Monthly Review Press 1971).

Amor Fati website: http://fate.laiv.org/in_arti.htm, an extensive electronic library which includes articles on dramaturgy and improvisation in relation to LARPing, e.g. Brian David Philips, 'Interactive Drama: Deconstructing Theatre' (1996), and Susanne Graslünds, 'Building Dramatics' (n.d., *c*.2001), about storytelling in LARP.

And, Metin, *Karagöz: Turkish Shadow Theatre* (Istanbul: Dost, 1975, rev. edn 1979).

Aristotle, 'The Poetics' [*c*.330 BC], in *Classical Literary Criticism*, trans. T. S. Dorsch (Harmondsworth: Penguin, 1965).

Artaud, Antonin, 'Production and Metaphysics' and 'On the Balinese Theatre', in *Le Théâtre et son Double* (Paris, 1938), trans. Victor Corti as *The Theatre and its Double* (London: Calder & Boyars, 1970).

Babbage, Frances, *Augusto Boal* (London: Routledge, 2004).*

Baim, Clark, Brookes, Sally and Mountford, Alun, *The Geese Theatre Handbook: Drama with Offenders and People at Risk* (Winchester: Waterside Press, 2002).

Bakhtin, Mikhail, *Rabelais and his World* (Moscow, 1965), trans. Hélène Iswolsky (Cambridge, MA: MIT Press, 1968).

Bame, Kwabena N., *Come to Laugh: A Study of African Traditional Theatre in Ghana* (New York: Lilian Barber Press, 1985) cited in Etherton, 1988; and Barber, 2000).

Banham, Martin (ed.), *The Cambridge Guide to World Theatre* (Cambridge: Cambridge University Press, 1988).

Banu, Georges, 'Peter Brook's Six Days', trans. Susan Bassnett, *New Theatre Quarterly*, 3/10 (May 1987).

Barba, Eugenio, *The Floating Islands: Reflections with Odin Teatret*, ed. Ferdinando Taviani (Holstebro, Denmark, 1979).

Barba, Eugenio, *Beyond the Floating Islands* (New York: Performing Arts Journal, 1986).

Barba, Eugenio, *The Paper Canoe: A Guide to Theatre Anthropology* (London: Routledge, 1995).

Barba, Eugenio, *Land of Ashes and Diamonds: My Apprenticeship in Poland*, trans. Judy Barba (Aberystwyth: Black Mountain Press, Centre for Performance Research, 1999).

Barba, Eugenio, 'Children of Silence: Reflections on Forty Years of Odin Teatret', trans. from Italian by Judy Barba, in Odin Teatret, *Andersens Drøm* (Holstebro, Denmark, 2005), pp. 50–61.

Barba, Eugenio, 'Improvisation: Memory, Repetition, Discontinuity', in the Programme of the 14th ISTA, on Improvisation, held at Wrocław and Krzyżowa, April 2005.

Barba, Eugenio and Savarese, Nicola, *A Dictionary of Theatre Anthropology: The Secret Art of the Performer* (London: Routledge, 1991).

Barber, Karin, *The Generation of Plays: Yorùbá Popular Life in Theater* (Bloomington and Indianapolis: Indiana University Press, 2000).

Barber, Karin, Collins, John and Ricard, Alain, *West African Popular Theatre* (Bloomington and Indianapolis: Indiana University Press; Oxford: James Currey, 1997).

Barker, Clive, *Theatre Games: A New Approach to Drama Training* (London: Eyre Methuen, 1977).*

Barthes, Roland, 'Literature and Signification', in *Essais Critiques* (Paris: Seuil, 1964), trans. Richard Howard as *Critical Essays* (Evanston, IL: Northwestern University Press, 1972), pp. 261–7.

Bauer, Roger and Wertheimer Jürgen (eds), *Das Ende des Stegreifspiels – die Geburt des Nationaltheaters: ein Wendepunkt in der Geschichte des europäischen Dramas* (Munich: Wilhelm Fink, 1983).

Beare, W., *The Roman Stage* (London: Methuen, 1950; 3rd edn 1964).

Beckett, Samuel, *'Proust' and 'Three Dialogues with Georges Duthuit'*, originally published in *Transition* (1949) (London: John Calder, 1965).

Beckett, Samuel, *The Beckett Trilogy*, comprising *Molloy, Malone Dies* and *The Unnamable* (first published London: Calder, 1959; London: Picador, 1979).

Beeman, William Orman, 'Middle East', in M. Banham (ed.), *The Cambridge Guide to World Theatre* (Cambridge: Cambridge University Press, 1988; rev. edn 1992), pp. 664–76, esp. pp. 669–70.

Belgrad, Daniel, *The Culture of Spontaneity* (Chicago: University of Chicago Press, 1998); cited in Heddon and Milling (2006), p. 8.

Benda, Władysław Theodor, *Masks* (New York: Watson-Guptill Publications, 1944).

Benda, Władysław Theodor, 'How Benda Revived the Use of Masks', *Boston Transcript*, (17 April 1926); cited in Eldredge (1996), p. 171.

Benedetti, Jean, *Stanislavski and the Actor* (London: Methuen, 1998). [An attempt to reconstruct Stanislavky's actor-training exercises at the Opera-Dramatic Studio.]*

Benedetti, Jean, *The Art of the Actor: The Essential History of Acting from Classical Times to the Present Day* (London: Methuen, 2005).

Bentley, Eric, 'Epilogue: Theatre and Therapy', in *Theatre of War: Modern Drama from Ibsen to Brecht* (originally published 1969 in *New American Review*; New York: Viking Press, 1973), pp. 213–29.

Bezā'í, Bahrām, *Namāyesh Dar Irān* ('Performance in Iran') (Tehran: 1965), p. 55; trans. and cited in Beeman (1992), p. 667.

Bicât, Tina and Baldwin, Chris (eds), *Devised and Collaborative Theatre: A Practical Guide* (Ramsbury: Crowood Press, 2002).*

Blatner, Adam (ed.), *Interactive and Improvisional Drama: Varieties of Applied Theatre and Performance* (New York: iUniverse, 2007).

Blatner, Howard, *Psychodrama, Role-Playing and Action Methods: Theory and Practice* (private publication, 1970). See esp. Table 4.

Boal, Augusto, *Games for Actors and Non-Actors*, trans. Adrian Jackson (London: Routledge, 1992).*

Boal, Augusto, *The Rainbow of Desire*, trans. Adrian Jackson (London: Routledge, 1992).*

Bøckman, Petter and Hutchison, Ragnhild (eds), *Dissecting Larp* (2005); published to accompany the Knutepunkt (2005); available at http://knutepunkt.laiv.org/.

Bogard, Travis, 'American Drama', in *The Revels History of Drama in English*, vol. 8 (London: Methuen, 1977).

Boleslavsky, Richard, *Acting: The First Six Lessons* (New York: Theatre Arts Books, 1934).

Bolton, Gavin, *Drama as Education: An Argument for Placing Drama at the Centre of the Curriculum* (Harlow: Longman, 1984).

Boyd, Neva Leona, *Handbook of Recreational Games* (Chicago, IL: Fitzsimmons, 1945; reprinted New York: Dover, 1975).*

Bradby, David, *Modern French Drama, 1940–1980* (Cambridge: Cambridge University Press, 1984).

Bradby, David and Delgado, Maria M. (eds), *The Paris Jigsaw* (London: Routledge, 2002)

Brakel, Clara and Moreh, Shmuel, 'The Term *Bâba* in Traditional Arab and Javanese Masked Theatre', in Clara Brakel (ed.), *Performing Arts of Asia: The Performer as (Inter)Cultural Transmitter* (Leiden: International Institute for Asian Studies Working Papers, Series 4, 1996), pp. 35–46.

Braun, Edward, *Meyerhold on Theatre* (New York: Hill & Wang, 1969).

Brenne, Geir Tor, 'Making and Maintaining Frames: A Study of

Metacommunication in Laiv Play', MA thesis, University of Oslo (2005), available at http://fate.laiv.org/pub/gtb_opp.htm.

Breton, André, *Manifesto of Surrealism* (Paris, 1924).

Brook, Peter, *The Empty Space* (London: McGibbon & Kee, 1968).

Brook, Peter, *The Shifting Point: Forty Years of Theatrical Exploration, 1946–1987* (London: Methuen, 1988).

Brown, Frederick, *Theatre and Revolution: The Culture of the French Stage* (New York: Viking Press, 1980).

Browne, Maurice, *Too Late to Lament* (Bloomington, Indiana, 1956).

Browne, Terry, *Playwrights' Theatre* (London: Pitman, 1975).

Buber, Martin, *Ich und Du* (1923; 2nd edn, Jerusalem, 1957), trans. Walter Kaufman as *I and Thou* (Edinburgh: T. & T. Clark, 1970).

Burgess, Thomas de Mallet and Skilbeck, Nicholas, *The Singing and Acting Handbook: Games and Exercises for the Performer* (London: Routledge, 2000).*

Burzyński, Tadeusz, 'Away from Theatre', in T. Burzyński and Z. Osiński, *Grotowski's Laboratory* (Warsaw: Interpress, 1979).

Buzan, Tony, *Use Your Head* (London: BBC Publications, 1974).

Caillois, Roger, *Man, Play and Games* (London: Thames & Hudson, 1962).

Callery, Dymphna, *Through the Body: A Practical Guide to Physical Theatre* (London: Nick Hern Books; New York: Routledge, 2001).*

Capra, Fritjof, *The Tao of Physics* (London: Fontana, 1976).

Carlson, Marvin, *Performance: A Critical Introduction* (London and New York: Routledge, 1996).

Carnicke, Sharon Marie, *Stanislavsky in Focus* (London: Harwood Academic, 1998).

Carnicke, Sharon Marie, 'Stanislavsky's System', in Alison Hodge (ed.), *Twentieth-Century Actor Training* (London and New York: Routledge, 2000), pp. 11–36.

Carnicke, Sharon Marie, 'Stanislavsky: Uncensored and Unabridged', in Schneider and Gabrielle Cody (eds), *Re:direction: A Theoretical and Practical Guide* (London and New York,: Routledge, 2002), pp. 28–39.

Casson, John W., 'Living Newspaper: Theatre and Therapy', *The Drama Review*, 44/2 (Summer 2000), 107–22.

Chamberlain, Franc, 'Michael Chekhov on the Technique of Acting', in Alison Hodge (ed.), *Twentieth Century Actor Training* (London and New York: Routledge, 2000), pp. 79–97.

Chamberlain, Franc, 'Theatre Anthropology: Definitions and Doubts', in Anthony Frost (ed.), *Theatre Theories: From Plato to Virtual Reality* (Norwich: Pen & Inc, 2000), pp. 171–94.

Chamberlain, Franc, *Michael Chekhov* (London: Routledge, 2004).*

Chamberlain, Franc and Yarrow, Ralph (eds), *Jacques Lecoq and the British Theatre* (London: Routledge Harwood, 2002).

Chekhov, Michael, *Lessons for the Professional Actor* (New York: PAJ Books, 1985).

Chekhov, Michael, *Lessons for Teachers of his Acting Technique* (Ottawa: Dovehouse, 2000).

Chekhov, Michael, *The Path of the Actor*, ed. Andrei Kirillov and Bella Merlin (London: Routledge, 2005). Combines Chekhov's 1927 autobiography of this title and extensive extracts from his later *Life and Encounters*.

Clements, Paul, *The Improvised Play: The Work of Mike Leigh* (London: Methuen Theatrefile, 1983).

Clurman, Harold, *The Fervent Years: Group Theatre and the Thirties* (New York: Harcourt Brace Jovanovich, 1975; repr. New York: Da Capo, 1988).

Coldiron, Margaret, *Trance and Transformation of the Actor in Japanese Noh and Balinese Masked Dance-Drama* (Lewiston, NY: Edwin Mellen, 2004).

Cole, Toby (ed.), *Actors on Acting: The Theories, Techniques and Practices of the Great Actors of All Times as Told in their Own Words* (New York: Crown, 1949).

Cole, Toby (ed.), *Playwrights on Playwriting: The Meaning and Making of Modern Drama from Ibsen to Ionesco* (New York: Hill & Wang, 1961).

Copeau, Jacques, 'Notes sur l'education de l'acteur', in *Ecrits sur le Théâtre* (Paris: Brient, 1955).

Copeau, Jacques, *Essai de Rénovation Dramatique* (Paris, 1913), trans. and cited in Roose-Evans (1970).

Copeau, Jacques, Registres, *textes recueillis et établis par* Marie-Hélène Dasté *et* Suzanne Maistre Saint-Denis et al., vol. 1 (Paris: Gallimard, 1974).

Copeau, Jacques, *Brochure* [Prospectus] of ideal training school, quoted at length in Rudlin (1986), pp. 43–4.

Copeau, Jacques, *A Notebook* in the Dasté Collection, cited in Rudlin (1986).

Copeau Jacques, *Journal: texte établi*, ed. and annot. Claude Sicard, 2 vols (Paris: Edition Seghers, 1991).

Cossa, Mario, Fleishmann Ember, Sally S., Grover, Lauren and Hazlewood, Jennifer L., *Acting Out: The Workbook* (New York and London: Brunner-Routledge, 1996).*

Counsell, Colin, *Signs of Performance: An Introduction to Twentieth-Century Theatre* (London and New York: Routledge, 1996).

Courtney, Richard, *Play, Drama and Thought: The Intellectual Background to Drama in Education* (London: Cassell/Collier Macmillan, 1968; 3rd rev. and enlarged edn 1974).

Coveney, Michael, *The World according to Mike Leigh* (London: Harper Collins, 1996).

Derrida, Jacques, *L'Ecriture et la Différence* (Paris: Seuil, 1978), trans. A. Bass as *Writing and Difference* (London: Routledge & Kegan Paul, 1979).

Dewey, John, 'Introduction', in F. M. Alexander, *Constructive Conscious Control of the Individual* (London: E. P. Dutton, 1923; repr. London: Gollancz, 1987).

Doisy, Marcel, *Jacques Copeau ou l'Absolu dans l'art* (Paris: Le Cercle du livre, 1954).

Donahue, Thomas J., 'Improvisation and the Mask at the École du Vieux-Colombier: The Case of Suzanne Bing', *Maske und Kothurn* 44 (2001), 61–72.

Drewal, Margaret Thompson, *Yoruba Ritual: Performer, Play, Agency* (Bloomington and Indianapolis: Indiana University Press, 1992), cited in Karin Barber, *The Generation of Plays: Yorùbá Popular Life in Theater* (Bloomington and Indianapolis: Indiana University Press, 2000).

Duchartre, P. L., *La Comédie italienne* (Paris, 1929), trans. R. T. Weaver as *The Italian Comedy: The Improvisation Scenarios, Lives, Attributes, Portraits and Masks of the Illustrious Characters of the Commedia dell'Arte* (1929; New York: Dover, 1966).

Elam, Keir, *The Semiotics of Theatre and Drama* (London: Methuen, 1980).

Eldredge, Sears A., *Mask and Improvisation for Actor Training and Performance: The Compelling Image* (Evanston, IL: Northwestern University Press, 1996).*

Eldredge, Sears A. and Huston, Hollis W., 'Actor Training in the Neutral Mask', *The Drama Review*, 22/4 (December 1978), Workshop Issue, 140–7. Also repr. in Zarrilli (2002).*

Emigh, John, *Masked Performance: The Play of Self and Other in Ritual and Theatre* (Philadelphia: University of Pennsylvania Press, 1996).

Emigh, John, Preface, in Margaret Coldiron, *Trance and Transformation of the Actor in Japanese Noh and Balinese Masked Dance-Drama* (Lewiston, NY: Edwin Mellen, 2004).

Etherton, Michael, 'Ghana', in M. Banham (ed.), *The Cambridge Guide to World Theatre* (Cambridge: Cambridge University Press, 1988; rev. edn 1992), pp. 392–4.

Evans, Mark, *Jacques Copeau* (London: Routledge, 2006).*

Farrell, Joseph, *Dario Fo and Franca Rame: Harlequins of the Revolution* (London: Methuen, 2001).

Feldenkrais, Moshé, 'Image, Movement, and Actor: Restoration of Potentiality' [interview with Richard Schechner], *Tulane Drama Review*, 10/3 (1966), 117ff.

Feldenkrais, Moshé, *Awareness through Movement: Health Exercises for Personal Growth* (New York: Harper & Row, 1972; London: Arkana, Penguin Books, 1990).*

Felner, Mira, *Apostles of Silence* (Toronto and London: Associated University Presses, 1985).

Féral, Josette, 'Building up the Muscle: An Interview with Ariane Mnouchkine', in Schneider and Cody (2002), pp. 258–65.

Ferguson, Marilyn, *The Aquarian Conspiracy* (Los Angeles: J. P. Tarcher, 1980).

Findlater, Richard, *Banned! A Review of Theatrical Censorship in Britain* (London: MacGibbon & Kee, 1967).

Flaszen, Ludwik, *Cyrograf* ('The Bond') (2nd edn, Cracow: 1974); cited in Kumiega (1985).

Fleishman, Mark, interview with Ralph Yarrow, 22 July 2005.

Fo, Dario, *Mistero buffo; Giullarata popolare nuova edizione aggiornata nei testi e nelle note* [1969] (Verona: Bertoni, 1977).

Fo, Dario, interview, *Playboy*, Italian issue (December 1974), cited in Mitchell (1984).

Fo, Dario, *Accidental Death of an Anarchist* programme, Washington Arena Stage production (1984); cited in Mitchell (1984).

Fo, Dario, *Manuale minimo dell'attore* (Milan: Einaudi, 1987), trans. J. Farrell as *The Tricks of the Trade* (London: Methuen, 1991).*

Fo, Dario, *Mistero buffo – Comic Mysteries*, trans. Ed Emery (London: Methuen, 1988).

Fo, Dario and Rame, Franca, *Theatre Workshops at Riverside Studios, London* (London: Red Notes, 1983).*

Fowler, Richard, 'The Four Theatres of Jerzy Grotowski: An Introductory Assessment', *New Theatre Quarterly*, 1/2 (May 1985), 173–8.

Fox, Jonathan, *Acts of Service: Spontaneity, Commitment, Tradition in the Nonscripted Drama* (New Paltz, NY: Tustitala Publishing, 1994, repr. 2003).

Frank, Waldo, *The Art of the Vieux-Colombier* (New York and Paris, Nouvelle Revue Française, 1918).

Frost, Anthony, '*Timor Mortis Conturbuit Nos*: Improvising Tragedy and Epic', in C. McCullough (ed.), *Theatre Praxis* (Basingstoke: Macmillan, 1998), pp. 151–73.

Frost, Anthony, 'The Taking of Faces: Aristotle among the Arabs', in A. Frost (ed.), *Theatre Theories: From Plato to Virtual Reality* (Norwich: Pen & Inc, 2000), pp. 45–68.

Gade, Morton, Thorup, Line and Sander, Mikkel (eds), *As Larp Grows Up*, electronic publication to accompany the Knudepunkt LARP festival in Denmark (2003); available at http://www.laivforum.dk/kp03_book/.

Gale, Derek, *What is Psychodrama? A Personal and Practical Guide* (Loughton: Gale Centre, 1990).*

Ganguly, Sanjoy, 'Theatre – a Space for Empowerment: celebrating Jana Sanksriti's Experience in India', in Richard Boon and Jane Plastow (eds), *Theatre and Empowerment: Community Drama on the World Stage* (Cambridge: Cambridge University Press, 2004), pp. 220–57.

Gelb, Michael, *Body Learning: An Introduction to the Alexander Technique* (London: Aurum Press, 1981).*

George, D. E. R., *Buddhism as/in Performance: Analysis of Meditation and Theatrical Practice* (New Delhi: D. K. Printworld, 1999).

Gide, André, *Les Nourritures Terrestres* (Paris: Gallimard, 1917–36).

Gillison, Gillian, 'Living Theater in New Guinea's Highlands', in *National Geographic*, 164/2 (August 1983). See also the Editorial, 'On Assignment'.

Gillison, Gillian, *Between Culture and Fantasy: A New Guinea Highlands Mythology* (Chicago: University of Chicago Press, 1993).

Goldberg, RoseLee, *Performance Art: From Futurism to the Present* (London: Thames & Hudson, 1979; rev. edn 1988).

Gontard, Denis (ed.), *Le Journal de bord des Copiaus, 1924–1929*, ed. with commentary by Denis Gontard (Paris: Seghers, 1974).

Gooch, Steve, *Writing a Play* (London: A. & C. Black, 3rd edn 2001).*

Gordon, Mel, '*Lazzi:* The Comic Routines of the *Commedia dell'Arte*', in *Performing Arts Resources*, vol. 7, ed. Ginnine Cocuzza and Barbara Naomi Cohen Stratyner (New York: Theatre Library Association, 1981).*

Gordon, Mel, *The Stanislavsky Technique: Russia: A Workbook for Actors* (New York: Applause, 1987).*

Gray, Paul, 'Stanislavsky and America: A Critical Chronology', *Tulane Drama Review*, 9/2 (Winter 1964).

Gregory, R.G., *The World of Instant Theatre: Its Origins, Practice and Implications* (Wimborne: Word and Action Wanda Publications, 1990).

Gregory, R. G., personal website at http://www.rggregory.com. Contains a very personal history of the founding of Word and Action (Dorset).

Grimes, Ron, 'The Theatre of Sources', *The Drama Review*, 25/3 (T-91) (Fall, 1981), Actor/Director issue, 67–74.

Grotowski, Jerzy, 'Aktor ogolocony' ('The actor bared'), *Teatr*, 17 (1965); cited in Burzyński and Osiński (1979).

Grotowski, Jerzy, 'I Said Yes to the Past', interview by Margaret Croyden, *Village Voice* (23 January 1969), 41–2.

Grotowski, Jerzy, 'The Theatre's New Testament' [interview with Eugenio Barba], trans. Jörgen Andersen and Judy Barba, in Grotowski et al. (1969).

Grotowski, Jerzy, 'Holiday', *The Drama Review*, 17/2 (T58) (June 1973), Visual Performance issue.

Grotowski, Jerzy et al., *Towards a Poor Theatre*, ed. Eugenio Barba (Copenhagen: Odin Teatrets Forlag, 1968; English translation, London: Eyre Methuen, 1969).

Halpern, Charna, Close, Del and Johnson, Kim 'Howard', *Truth in Comedy: The Manual of Improvisation* (Colorado Springs, CO: Meriwether, 1994).*

Heddon, Deirdre and Milling, Jane, *Devising Performance: A Critical History* (London: Palgrave Macmillan, 2006).

Heritage, Paul, 'Augusto Boal and the Journey to the Centre of the Theatre of the Oppressed (Paris)', in David Bradby and Maria Delgado (eds), *The Paris Jigsaw* (London: Routledge, 2002), pp. 146–52.

Hethmon, Robert and Strasberg, Lee, *Strasberg at the Actor's Studio* (New York: Viking Press, 1965).*

Hiley, Jim, 'Moving Heaven and Earth' [interview with Jacques Lecoq], *Observer* (20 March 1988), 40.

Hilton, Julian, *Performance* (London: Macmillan, 1988).

Hilton, Julian (ed.), *New Directions in Theatre* (Basingstoke: Macmillan, 1993).

Hilton, Julian, 'Theatricality and Technology: Pygmalion and the Myth of the Intelligent Machine', in J. Hilton (ed.), *New Directions in Theatre* (Basingstoke: Macmillan, 1993).

Hirst, David L., *Dario Fo and Franca Rame* (London: Macmillan, 1989).

Hodge, Alison (ed.), *Twentieth-Century Actor Training* (London: Routledge, 2000).

Hodgson, John (ed.), *The Uses of Drama: Sources Giving a Background to Acting as a Social and Educational Force* (London: Eyre Methuen, 1972).

Hodgson, John, *Mastering Movement: The Life and Work of Rudolf Laban* [1997] (London: Methuen, 2001).

Hodgson, John and Richards, Ernest, *Improvisation* (London: Methuen, 1966; 2nd edn 1974).*

Holmes, Rupert, essay for the Toronto Shaw festival production of *The Mystery of Edwin Drood* (2001); available on http://www.rupertholmes. com/theatre/essdrood.html.

Hood, Stuart, 'Introduction', in Dario Fo and Franca Rame, *Female Parts*, trans. Margaret Kunzle, adapted Olwen Wymark (London: Pluto Press, 1981).

Hood, Stuart, 'Introduction', in Dario Fo, *Mistero buffo*, trans. Ed Emery (London: Methuen, 1988).

Howard, Tony, ' "A Piece of our Life": The Theatre of the Eighth Day', *New Theatre Quarterly*, 2/8 (November 1986).

Huizinga, Johan, *Homo Ludens* (Leiden, trans. by the author; London: Paladin, 1970).

Hull, S. Loraine, *Strasberg's Method: As Taught by Lorrie Hull* (Woodbridge, CT: Ox Bow, 1985).*

Hunt, Albert, *Hopes for Great Happenings: Alternatives in Education and Theatre* (London: Eyre Methuen, 1976).

Hurst, Deirdre, 'The Training Sessions of Michael Chekhov' [interview by Peter Hulton, July 1978], *Dartington Theatre Papers*, 3rd series, no. 9 (1979–80).

Hyde, George, 'Poland: Dead Souls under Western Eyes', in Ralph Yarrow (ed.), *European Theatre, 1960–1990* (London: Routledge, 1992), pp. 182–219.

Jenkins, Ron, *Dario Fo and Franca Rame: Artful Laughter* (New York: Aperture, 2001).

Jenkins, Ron and I Made Catra, 'Invisible Training in Balinese Performance', in Ian Watson (ed.), *Performer Training: Developments across Cultures* (Amsterdam: Harwood Academic, 2001), pp. 85–91.

Jennings, Sue, *Remedial Drama: A Handbook for Teachers and Therapists* (London: Pitman; New York: Theatre Arts, 1973).

Jennings, Sue (ed.), *Dramatherapy: Theory and Practice for Teachers and Clinicians* (London: Routledge, 1988).

Jennings, Sue, *The Handbook of Dramatherapy* (London: Routledge, 1993).

Jennings, Sue, *Dramatherapy with Children and Adolescents* (London: Routledge, 1994).

Johnston, Chris, *House of Games: Making Theatre from Everyday Life* (London: Nick Hern Books, 1998).*

Johnston, Chris, *The Improvisation Game* (London: Nick Herm Books, 2006).

Johnstone, Keith, *Impro: Improvisation and the Theatre* (London: Methuen, 1981).*

Johnstone, Keith, *Theatresports and Lifegame Newsletter*, issue 1 (University of Calgary, 1987); cited in Chris Johnston (1998), pp. 190–2.*

Johnstone, Keith, *Impro for Storytellers: Theatresports and the Art of Making Things Happen* (London: Faber, 1999).*

Kennedy, Scott, *In Search of African Theatre* (New York: Charles Scribner, 1973).

Kiernander, Adrian, 'The Théâtre du Soleil, Part One: A Brief History of the Company', *New Theatre Quarterly*, 2/7 (August 1986).

Kirby, Ernest T., *Ur-Drama: The Origins of Theatre* (New York: New York University Press, 1975).

Kirkland, Christopher D. 'The Golden Age, First Draft', *The Drama Review*, vol. 19, no. 2 (1975).

Koestler, Arthur, *The Act of Creation* (London: Hutchinson, 1964; rev. Danube edn 1969).

Kozlowski, Ron, *The Art of Chicago Improv: Shortcuts to Long-Form Improvisation* (Portsmouth, NJ: Heinemann, 2002).*

Kruger, Loren, *The Drama of South Africa* (London: Routledge 1999).

Kumiega, Jennifer, *The Theatre of Grotowski* (London: Methuen, 1985).

Kurkinen, Marjaana, 'The Spectre of the Orient: Modern French Mime and Traditional Japanese Theatre in the 1930s', unpublished dissertation, University of Helsinki, Finland, December 2000. A PDF version is available at http://ethesis.helsinki.fi/julkaisut/hum/taite/vk/kurkinen/ (ISBN 952-91-2963-7).

Laban, Rudolf, *Choreographie, Erste Heft*, vol. 1: *Choreography* (Jena: Eugene Deiderichs, 1926); discussed in Hodgson (2001), pp. 127–9.

Laban, Rudolf, *Des Kindes Gymnastik und Tanz* (Gymnastics and Dance for the Child) (Oldenburg: Gerhard Stalling, 1926), discussed in Hodgson (2001), pp. 125–7.

Laban, Rudolf, *Choreutics*, vol. 1, ed. Lisa Ullmann [1939] (London: MacDonald & Evans, 1966); discussed in Hodgson (2001), pp. 135–41.

Laban, Rudolf, *The Mastery of Movement*, rev. Lisa Ullmann, 4th edn (Plymouth: MacDonald & Evans, 1980).

Lamden, Gill, *Devising* (London: Hodder & Stoughton, 2000).*

Langer, Susanne, *Feeling and Form* (London: Routledge & Kegan Paul, 1959).

Lavy, Jennifer, 'Theoretical Foundations of Grotowski's *Total Act*, *Via Negativa*, and *Conjunctio Oppositorum*', *Journal of Religion and Theatre*, 4/2 (Fall 2005), published online at http://www.rtjournal.org/vol_4/no_2/lavy.html (accessed 16 June 2006).

Leabhart, Thomas, *Modern and Postmodern Mime* (Basingstoke: Macmillan, 1989).

Leabhart, Thomas (ed.), *Theatre and Sport*, edition of *Mime Journal*, (Claremont, CA: Pomona College Theatre Department, 1996).

Lecoq, Jacques, *Le role de l'improvisation dans l'enseignement de l'art dramatique*, transcript of a lecture-demonstration by Lecoq at the Institut International du Théâtre, Bucharest (1964), p. 136, cited in Felner (1985).

Lecoq, Jacques, 'Le mouvement et le théâtre', *ATAC Informations*, 13 (December 1967).

Lecoq, Jacques, *Stage d'été* (Paris: Brochure, 1971), cited in Felner (1985).

Lecoq, Jacques, 'L'Ecole Jacques Lecoq au Théâtre de la Ville', *Journal du Théâtre de la Ville* (January 1972).

Lecoq, Jacques, 'Mime – Movement – Theater', *Yale Theatre*, 4/1 (Winter 1973), cited in Towsen (1976).

Lecoq, Jacques (ed.), *Le Théâtre du Geste* (Paris: Bordas, 1987).*

Lecoq, Jacques, 'Moving Heaven and Earth' [interview with Jim Hiley], *Observer* (20 March 1988), 40.

Lecoq, Jacques, 'Theatre of Gesture and Image', in Patrice Pavis (ed.), *The Intercultural Performance Reader* (London and New York: Routledge, 1996), pp. 140–7.

Lecoq, Jacques, Carasso, Jean-Gabriel and Lallias, Jean-Claude, *Le Corps poétique* (Paris: Actes Sud-Papiers, 1997), trans. David Bradby as *The Moving Body* (London: Methuen, 2000, rev. edn 2000).*

Lecoq, Jacques, n.d., *Brochure* of L'Ecole Jacques Lecoq, 57 rue du Faubourg Saint-Denis, Paris. [All translations by R. Yarrow (1987).]

Leigh, Mike, *Abigail's Party* and *Goose Pimples* [plays devised from scratch through improvisation] (Harmondsworth: Penguin, 1983).

Leigh, Mike, 'An Account of the Development of my Improvised Plays 1965–69: an Application for the George Devine Award, 1969', cited in Clements (1983).

Leigh, Mike, *Abigail's Party* and *Nuts in May* (BBC Video releases, 1988).

Leigh, Mike, *All or Nothing* (London: Faber & Faber, 2002).

Leigh, Mike, *Two Thousand Years* (London: Faber & Faber, 2006).

Leonard, Charles, *Michael Chekhov's 'To the Director and Playwright'*, compiled and written by Charles Leonard (New York: Harper & Row, 1963; New York: Limelight Editions, 1984).

Littlewood, Joan, *Joan's Book: Joan Littlewood's Peculiar History as She Tells It* (London: Minerva, 1995).

Lust, Annette Bercut, *From the Greek Mimes to Marcel Marceau and Beyond: Mimes Actors, Pierrots and Clowns: A Chronicle of the Many Visages of Mime in the Theatre* (Lanham, MD: London: Scarecrow Press, 2000). See esp. chapter on Lecoq, pp. 99–108.

Lynn, Bill, *Improvisation for Actors and Writers: A Guidebook for Improv Lessons in Comedy* (Colorado Springs, CO: Meriwether, 2004).*

Mamet, David, *True and False: Heresy and Common Sense for the Actor* (New York: Random House, 1997).

Marineau, Rene F., *Jacob Levy Moreno, 1889–1974: Father of Psychodrama, Sociometry and Group Psychotherapy* (London: Routledge, 1989); cited in Gale (1990).

Martin, John, 'The Theatre which does not Exist: Neutrality to Interculturalism', in Chamberlain and Yarrow (2002), pp. 57–70.

Martin, John, *The Intercultural Performance Handbook* (London: Routledge, 2004).*

Martinovich, Nicholas N., *The Turkish Theatre* (1933; New York: Benjamin Blom, 1968).

Maslow, Abraham, *Toward a Psychology of Being* (New York: Van Nostrand Reinhold, 1968).

McCullough, Christopher (ed.), *Theatre Praxis* (Basingstoke: Macmillan, 1998).

Mei Lan Fang, 'My Life on the Stage', orig. *Chinese Literature Monthly*, 11 (1961). Originally published just after Mei's death, and before the throes of the Cultural Revolution and Madame Mao's reforms of the Chinese Opera); republished together with Sergei M. Eisenstein's *The Enchanter from the Pear Garden* (1935) (English translators not credited) (Holstebro: ISTA Publications, 1986).

Merlin, Bella, *Beyond Stanislavsky: The Psycho-Physical Approach to Acting* (London: Nick Hern Books, 2001).*

Merlin, Bella, *Konstantin Stanislavsky* (London: Routledge, 2003).*

Meyer-Dinkgräfe, Daniel, *Theatre and Consciousness: Explanatory Scope and Future Potential* (London: Intellect Books, 2005).

Meyerhold, Vsevolod, 'The Fairground Booth', in Braun (1969), pp. 119–28.

Millar, Mervyn, *Journey of the Tall Horse: A Story of African Theatre* (London: Oberon, 2005).

Milling, Jane and Ley, Graham, *Modern Theories of Performance* (Basingstoke: Palgrave Macmillan, 2001).

Mitchell, Tony, *Dario Fo: People's Court Jester* (London: Methuen, 1984; 2nd rev. edn 1986).

Montola, Markus and Stenros, Jaakko (eds), *Beyond Role and Play: Tools, Toys and Theory for Harnessing the Imagination* (Helsinki, Ropecon, 2004); published for Solmukohta 2004, the Nordic role-playing convention: now only available electronically at http://www.ropecon.fi/brap/.

Moore, Sonia, *The Stanislavski System: The Professional Training of an Actor* (New York: Viking Penguin, 1960 as *The Stanislavski Method*; 2nd rev. edn 1984).*

Moreh, Shmuel, *Live Theatre and Dramatic Literature in the Medieval Arabic World* (Edinburgh: Edinburgh University Press, 1992).

Moreno, Jacob Levy, *Psychodrama, I* (New York: Beacon House, 1946).

Moreno, Jacob Levy, *Psychodrama, II* (New York: Beacon House, 1959).

Moreno, Zerka T., *The Quintessential Zerka: Writings by Zerka Toeman Moreno on Psychodrama, Sociometry and Group Psychotherapy*, ed. Toni Horvatin and Edward Schreiber (London: Routledge, 2006).

Moreno, Zerka T., Rützel, Thomas and Blomkvist, Leif Dag, *Psychodrama, Surplus Reality and the Art of Healing* (Routledge, 2000).

Morley, Sheridan, 'Mike Leigh: Anything but Anarchy' [interview], *The Times* (15 July 1977); repr. in Movshovitz (2000), pp. 3–5.

Moseley, Nick, *Acting and Reacting: Tools for the Modern Actor* (London: Routledge/Nick Hern Books, 2005).*

Movshovitz, Howie (ed.), *Mike Leigh: Interviews*, Conversations with Filmmakers (Jackson, MI: University Press of Mississippi, 2000).

Murray, Simon, 'Tout Bouge: Jacques Lecoq, Modern Mime and the Zero Body: A Pedagogy for the Creative Actor', in Chamberlain and Yarrow (2002), pp. 17–44.

Murray, Simon, *Jacques Lecoq* (London: Routledge, 2003).*

Nagler, A. M. (ed.), *Source Book in Theatrical History* (New York: Dover, 1952).

Natadze, R., 'On the Psychological Nature of Stage Impersonation', *British Journal of Psychology*, 53/4 (November 1972), 421.

Naumburg, Margaret, *Child and the World: Dialogues in Modern Education* (New York: Harcourt Brace, 1928).

Newlove, Jean, *Laban for Actors and Dancers: Putting Laban's Movement Theory into Practice: A Step-by-Step Guide* (London: Nick Hern Books, 1993).*

Nicoll, Allardyce, *Masks, Mimes and Miracles: Studies in the Popular Theatre* (London, 1931; New York: Cooper Square, 1963).

Nicoll, Allardyce, *The World of Harlequin: A Critical Study of the Commedia dell'Arte* (Cambridge: Cambridge University Press, 1963).

Nixon, Jon, 'The Dimensions of Drama: The Case for Cross-Curricular Planning', *New Theatre Quarterly*, 3/9 (February 1987), 71–81.

Oddey, Alison, *Devising Theatre: A Practical and Theoretical Handbook* (London: Routledge, 1994).*

Odin Teatret, *Andersens Drøm* [programme of production *of Andersen's Dream* ('*dedicated to Torzov and Doctor Dappertutto*')]. Contributions from, *inter alia*, Eugenio Barba, Judy Barba (translator), Kai Bredholt, Fabio Butera, Roberta Carreri, Jan Ferslev, Tage Larsen, Augusto Omolú, Iben Nagel Rasmussen, Luca Ruzza, Nando Taviani, Julia Varley, Torgeir Wethal, etc. (Holstebro, Denmark: Nordisk Teaterlaboratorium, 2005).

Osiński, Zbigniew, 'In the Theatre', in T. Burzyński and Z. Osiński, *Grotowski's Laboratory* (Warsaw: Interpress, 1979).

Otto, Beatrice K., *Fools are Everywhere: The Court Jester around the World* (Chicago: University of Chicago Press, 2001).

Papadopoulo, Alexandre, *Islam and Muslim Art*, trans. Robert Erich Wolf (Paris: Mezenod, 1976; New York: Harry N. Abrams, 1979). (See esp. 'The Making of a Muslim Aesthetic', pp. 48ff.)

Paterson, Douglas L., 'Theatre of the Oppressed Workshops', at http://www.wwcd.org/action/Boal.html (originally 1997, accessed 17 July 2006).

Perrucci, Andrea, *Dell'arte rappresentativa: premeditata e dall'improvviso* (Naples, 1699), trans. S. J. Castiglione, cited in Nagler, *Source Book in Theatrical History* (New York: Dover, 1952).

Phelan, Peggy, *Unmarked: The Politics of Performance* (London: Routledge, 1993).

Pitches, Jonathan, *Science and the Stanislavsky Tradition of Acting* (London: Routledge, 2006).

Pitches, Jonathan, *Vsevolod Meyerhold* (London: Routledge, 2004).*

Pörtner, Paul, 'Psychodrama: Theater der Spontaneität: Morenos Weg von Wien nach den USA', in *Theater Heute* (Vienna: Bohlau, Sept. 1967, pp. 10–15).

Poulter, Christine, *Playing the Game* (Basingstoke: Macmillan, 1987).*

Preston-Dunlop, Valerie, *Rudolf Laban: An Extraordinary Life* (London: Dance Books, 1998).

Rame, Franca, [interview], *Sipario* [Italian theatre magazine] (September 1983); cited in Mitchell (1984).

Rame, Franca and Fo, Dario, *Female Parts*, trans. Margaret Kunzle, adapted Olwen Wymark (London: Pluto Press, 1981).

Rame, Franca and Fo, Dario, *Theatre Workshops at Riverside Studios, London* (London: Red Notes, 1983).*

Rath, Eric C., *The Ethos of Noh: Actors on their Art* (Cambridge, MA and London: Harvard University Asia Center, 2004).

Richards, Thomas, *At Work with Grotowski on Physical Actions* (London: Routledge, 1995).

Riley, Jo, *Chinese Theatre and the Actor in Performance* (Cambridge: Cambrige University Press, 1997).

Risum, Janne, 'The Sporting Acrobat: Meyerhold's Biomechanics', in Thomas Leabhart (ed.), *Theatre and Sport*, edition of *Mime Journal* (Claremont, CA: Pomona College Theatre Department, 1996), pp. 67–111.

Risum, Janne, 'A Study in Motley: The Odin Actors', in Watson (2001), pp. 93–115.

Roberts, Philip, *The Royal Court Theatre, 1965–72* (London: Routledge, 1986).

Rolfe, Bari, *Behind the Mask* (Oakland, CA: Persona, 1976).

Roose-Evans, James, *Experimental Theatre: From Stanislavsky to Today* (New York: Avon Books, 1970).

Rudlin, John, *Jacques Copeau* (Cambridge: Cambridge University Press, 1986).

Rudlin, John, 'Play's the Thing', in Leabhart (1996), pp. 17–29.

Rudlin, John and Crick, Ollie, *Commedia dell'Arte: A Handbook for Troupes* (London and New York: Routledge, 2001).*

Rudlin, John and Paul, Norman H. (eds and trans), *Jacques Copeau, Texts on Theatre* (London and New York: Routledge, 1990).

Ryan, Paul Ryder, 'A Ru-howzi Evening', *The Drama Review*, Indigenous Theatre edition, 18/4 (T64) (December 1974), 114–15.

Saint-Denis, Michel, *Training for the Theatre: Premises and Promises*, ed. Suria Saint-Denis (New York: Theatre Arts Books, 1982).

Salas, Jo, *Improvising Real Life: Personal Story in Playback Theatre* (New Paltz, NY: Tustitala Publishing, 1993).

Sawyer, R. Keith, *Improvised Dialogues* (Westport, CT: Ablex, 2003).

Schechner, Richard, *Between Theater and Anthropology* (Philadelphia: Univesity of Pennsylvania Press, 1985).

Schechner, Richard, *Performance Studies: An Introduction* (London and New York: Routledge, 2002).

Schiller, Friedrich, *On the Aesthetic Education of Man, in a Series of Letters*, trans. Elizabeth M. Wilkinson and L. A. Willoughby (Oxford: Clarendon Press, 1967).

Schneider, Rebecca and Cody, Gabrielle, *Re:direction: A Theoretical and Practical Guide* (London & New York: Routledge, 2002).

Seham, Amy E., *Whose Improv is it Anyway? Beyond Second City* (Jackson: University Press of Mississippi, 2001).

Sells, Michael A., *Mystical Languages of Unsaying* (Chicago: University of Chicago Press, 1994).

Shrubsall, Anthony, 'Jos Houben: Understanding the Neutral Mask', in Chamberlain and Yarrow (2002), pp. 99–110.

Sicard, Claude, Copeau's editor, on website, http://www.culture.fr/culture/actualites/celebrations/copeau.htm.

Sills, Paul, 'The Celebratory Occasion' [interview with Charles Mee Jr], *Tulane Drama Review*, 9/2 (Winter 1964).

Simon, Eli, *Masking Unmasked: Four Approaches to Basic Acting* (New York: Palgrave Macmillan, 2003).*

Smith, A. C. H., *Orghast at Persepolis* (London: Methuen 1972).

Southern, Richard, *The Medieval Theatre in the Round* (London: Faber, 1957).

Spolin, Viola, *Improvisation for the Theater* (Evanston, IL: Northwestern University Press, 1963; London: Pitman, 1973).*

Stanislavsky, C., *An Actor Prepares*, trans. Elizabeth Reynolds Hapgood (London: Geoffrey Bles, 1937).*

Stanislavsky, C., *Creating a Role*, trans. Elizabeth Reynolds Hapgood (London: Geoffrey Bles, 1963).*

Stoppard, Tom, *Rosencrantz and Guildenstern are Dead* (London: Faber & Faber, 1967).

Strasberg, Lee, *A Dream of Passion*, ed. Evangeline Morphos (London: Bloomsbury, 1988).

Sutherland, Efua T., 'Theatre in Ghana', in Janice Nesbitt (ed.), *Ghana Welcomes You* (Accra: Orientation to Ghana Committee, 1969); cited in Kennedy (1973).

Sutherland, Efua T., *The Original Bob: The Story of Bob Johnson, Ghana's Ace Comedian* (Accra: Anowa Educational, 1970); cited in Barber et al. (1997) and Etherton (1992).

Suzuki, Tadashi, *The Way of Acting: The Theatre Writings of Tadashi Suzuki*, trans. J. Thomas Rimer (New York: Theatre Communications Group, 1986).

Svich, Caridad, 'Dreaming Out Loud: interview with Phelim McDermott about Improbable Theatre', in Svich, Caridad (ed.), *Trans-Global Readings: Crossing Theatrical Boundaries* (Manchester: Manchester University Press, 2003).

Sweet, Jeffrey, *Something Wonderful Right Away* (New York: Avon Book, 1987).

Tasca, Valéria, 'Dario Fo from One Language to Another', in Patrice Pavis (ed.), *The Intercultural Performance Reader* (London and New York: Routledge, 1996), pp. 114–19.

Taylor, Rogan, *The Death and Resurrection Show: From Shaman to Superstar* (London: Antony Blond, 1985).

Temkine, Raymonde, *Grotowski* (New York: Avon, 1972).

'The Theatre of Dario Fo', *Arena*, BBC TV documentary, Dennis Marks, 28 February 1984.

Towsen, John H., *Clowns* (New York: Hawthorne Books, 1976).

Turner, Jane, *Eugenio Barba* (London: Routledge, 2004).*

Veltrusky, Jiri, 'Man and Object in the Theatre' (Prague, 1940), cited in Elam (1980).

Wardle, Irving, *The Theatres of George Devine* (London: Jonathan Cape, 1978).

Wardle, Irving, 'Introduction', in Johnstone (1981).

Watson, Garry, *The Cinema of Mike Leigh: A Sense of the Real* (London and New York: Wallflower Press, 2004).

Watson, Ian, 'Catharsis and the Actor: The Aristotelian Concept in the Context of Contemporary Performance', *New Theatre Quarterly*, 4/16 (November 1988), 306–14.

Watson, Ian (ed.), *Performer Training: Developments across Cultures* (Amsterdam: Harwood Academic, 2001)

Watts, Alan, *The Book: On the Taboo against Knowing who You Are* (New York: Random House, 1972).

Whelan, Jeremy, *Instant Acting* (Cincinnati, OH: Betterway Books, 1994); cited by Phelim McDermott, in Caridad Svich (ed.), *Trans-Global Readings* (Manchester: Manchester University Press, 2003), and also discussed by him at http://www.nationaltheatre.org.uk/?lid=13041 April during rehearsals for *Theatre of Blood* (April 2005), See http://www.on-cue.org.uk/acting14.html which summarises the 'Whelan Tape Technique' approach.*

Williams, David (ed.), *Collaborative Theory: The Théâtre du Soleil Sourcebook* (London: Routledge, 1999).

Willis, Ronald A., 'The American Lab Theater', *Tulane Drama Review*, 9/1 (Fall 1964).

Winearls, Jane, *Modern Dance: The Jooss-Leeder Method* (London: Adam & Charles Black, 1958; 2nd edn 1968).

Wolford, Lisa, 'Ambivalent Positionings: Grotowski's Art as Vehicle and the Paradox of Categorization' in Watson (2001), pp. 117–32.

Wright, John, 'The Masks of Jacques Lecoq', in Chamberlain and Yarrow (2002), pp. 71–84.

Wright, John, *Why is that Funny? A Practical Exploration of Physical Comedy* (London: Nick Hern Books, 2006).*

Yarrow, Ralph, *Indian Theatre: Theatre of Origin, Theatre of Freedom* (London: Curzon, 2001).

Yarrow, Ralph, 'Theatre as Development', *Seagull Theatre Quarterly*, special edition on the AHRC Vidya Project (Kolkata: forthcoming 2007).

Yarrow, Ralph, Haney, William S. II, Malekin, Peter, Chamberlain, Franc and Lavery, Carl, *Sacred Theatre* (London: Intellect Books, 2007).

Yon, Keith, 'Communication Therapy with Mentally-Handicapped Adults', *Dartington Theatre Papers*, 3rd series, no. 4 (1979–80).

Zaporah, Ruth, *Action Theatre: The Improvisation of Presence* (Berkeley, CA: North Atlantic Books, 1995).*

Zarrilli, Phillip B., *Acting (Re)Considered: A Theoretical and Practical Guide* (London and New York: Routledge, 1995, 2nd edn 2002).

Zarrilli, Phillip B., McConachie, Bruce, Williams, Gary Jay and Sorgenfrei, Carol Fisher, *Theatre Histories: An Introduction* (London: Routledge, 2006).

Index of Selected Games and Exercises

General Index

Barber, Karen 74, 76–7, 227 (n. 9)
Bardhan, Gul 193
Barker, Clive 3, 8, 9, 51, 116, 125,
    127, 142, 143, 149, 150, 151, 154,
    175, 234 (n. 11)
Barkworth, Peter 40
Barrault, Jean-Louis 29
Barthes, Roland 235 (n. 1)
battute 7
Beacon Hill 111, 114
Beck, Julian 193
Beckett, Samuel 18, 40, 91, 92, 200,
    201, 220
Beijing Opera 64
Belushi, John 54, 57
Benda, Wladyslaw Theodor, 232
    (n. 4)
Benin 74
Benison, Ben 80
Bergman, John 234 (n. 11)
Bergner, Elizabeth 110, 231 (n. 6,
    n. 7)
Berkoff, Steven 92
Berman, Shelley 54
bhagavata 76, 144
Bing, Suzanne 25–33, 35, 45, 50,
    103, 124–5, 157, 223 (n. 5), 231
    n. 1)
bio-mechanics 24
bios 63, 135
Blair, Les 43
Bleak Moments 43, 44
blocking 122, 143–5, 168, 183, 213
Boal, Augusto 2–3, 9, 112–8, 134,
    175, 179, 190, 193–4, 218
Boal, Julian 118
body/think 121, 126–7, 129, 151, 207
Boleslavsky, Richard 21, 45, 46, 47
Bond, Edward 81, 212
Boston Toy Theatre 50
Bouffon, bouffonerie 100, 222 (n. 3),
    229 (n. 13)
Boverio, Auguste 32–3
Box Play 41, 44
Boyd, Neva L. 50–1, 55, 125
Bradwell, Mike 44
Bread and Puppet Theater 230 (n. 1),
    232 (n. 4)
breathing 101–2, 147, 159
Brecht, Bertolt 38, 52, 55, 85, 92,

106, 112, 115, 117, 149–50, 159,
    161, 220
Brechtian 40, 52, 102, 106, 200
Brighella 7
Brith Gof 195
Brixham Regatta 80
Brook, Peter 40, 68, 73, 92, 124
Brookes, Mike 195
Browne, Maurice 50, 81
Bruce, Lenny 54, 225 (n. 16)
Buber, Martin 101
Buckland, Andrew 77
Buddhist 64, 148, 208, 235 (n. 4)
Building a Character 20
Burgundy 27, 32, 33

cabaret 52, 218
cabotin 23, 29, 95, 99, 223 (n. 8)
Caillois, Roger 197
Callery, Dymphna... 3, 9, 10, 124,
    139, 163, 167–8, 216–7
calypso 225 (n. 21)
Can't Pay? Won't Pay 95
Canada 36, 55, 81
canovaccio, canovacci 7, 100
Cape Town 78, 195
Cardboard Citizens Theatre Company
    2
Cardinal Sins of Impro 142–3
carnival 6, 100, 112, 219
Cartoucherie, La 94
Cassavetes, John 39
Castell of Perseverance, The 222
    (n. 2)
catharsis 112, 117
'Célestine' 33
censor 6, 53, 177, 191–5, 212
censorship 10, 74, 77, 81, 145, 169,
    191–3
'César' 33
Chamberlain, Franc 24–5, 131, 140,
    148
Chancerel, Léon 32–3, 224 (n. 12)
character 4, 18–9, 21–3, 32–3, 37–9,
    42–4, 46–9, 59, 65, 71, 74–5, 98,
    100, 105–6, 116–7, 122, 135,
    140–1, 144, 149, 150, 155–6,
    158–9, 161, 163, 167, 174, 176,
    178, 181–2, 211–4, 216